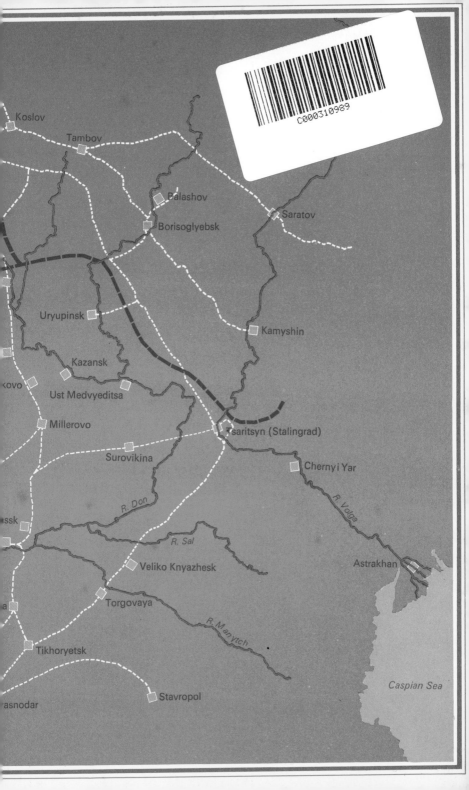

FAREWELL TO THE DON

FAREWELL
TO THE DON

The Journal of Brigadier H. N. H. Williamson

EDITED BY JOHN HARRIS

COLLINS
ST JAMES'S PLACE, LONDON
1970

ISBN 0 00 211164 0

Set in Monotype Garamond

© H. N. H. Williamson and John Harris 1970

Printed in Great Britain
Collins Clear-Type Press
London and Glasgow

LIST OF ILLUSTRATIONS

EDITOR'S NOTE

Hudleston Noel Hedworth Williamson was born on December 27, 1886, the son of Captain Cecil Hedworth Williamson, of Castle Douglas, Kirkcudbrightshire. He was educated at Eton and the Royal Military Academy, Woolwich. He joined the Royal Artillery in 1907 and served in India and in France through the Great War, from 1914 to 1918. He won the M.C. and the Belgian Croix de Guerre, was wounded and three times mentioned in despatches. He went to Russia while the Civil War which followed the Revolution was still taking place.

The story of his stay was written by him originally in diary form and expanded in the years that followed. But, because, as he claims, he was no great literary man and was more used to writing reports, it never saw daylight. When, however, I had occasion to ask him for information about the period for a book of my own which I was writing, he showed me General Sidorin's jewelled sabre, and we began to talk about the diary he kept. Eventually he allowed me to see it, and it seemed to me at once that, since so little has ever been written about the controversial British Military Mission's activities in Russia, his account deserved to be read and I undertook to help.

The British intervention in what was a purely nationalistic quarrel requires some explanation. It began with the Bolshevik revolutionary coup in 1917, that deposed the Tsar and virtually ended Russia's participation in the Great War, and ended with the defeat of the anti-Communist leaders, Admiral Kolchak in Siberia, in 1919, and General Wrangel in the Crimea at the end of 1920, and its causes were largely accidental.

When the Russian army opted out of the War, the Czechs living in Russia, who had offered as early as 1914 to fight for them in an effort to free their own country from the domination of Germany's ally, Austria, decided to set off across Siberia to Vladivostok by railway to join the Allies in France. The regiments of 1914 had grown by this time to an army corps and, though they were supposed to have handed in their weapons, in fact, many retained them, for their personal safety, and fighting broke out between them and the Bolsheviks. By their daring the Czechs seized all the important towns on the Trans-Siberian Railway as far as Irkutsk, and farther east they occupied Vladivostok, and towns on the Amur.

Immediately, seeing their success, various ambitious or wrong-headed people in different areas of Russia began to set up governments in opposition to the Bolsheviks and for a time managed to rule large tracts of the country and make half-hearted attempts to overcome the Red Army, which was by this time being newly organised by a brilliant and blood-thirsty lawyer, Leon Trotsky. Sporadic fighting changed into all-out civil war and before it finished, British, French, American and Japanese troops had landed; there was a near mutiny of French troops at Odessa; British officers were murdered in their beds by their Russian soldiers; and thousands of homeless refugees fled south or into the wilderness of Central Asia to escape the advancing Red Armies or died by the wayside and in mud hovels on the Kirghiz steppes or the barren lands of the Chinese border.

In Siberia and South Russia, awkward young peasants in British khaki fought half-heartedly against their own countrymen, deserting in droves to the Bolsheviks whenever they could, and thousands of refugees lived for months in trains in indescribable filth and misery. It was a story of tragedy, suffering, and futility; with inefficiency, spineless leadership, treachery and cowardice going hand in hand.

Yet in June 1919 everything had seemed poised for victory. From the south, General Denikin had occupied a third of Russia and had advanced almost to Moscow; in the north-west General Youdenitch was in sight of St. Petersburg; and in the east Admiral Kolchak had almost reached the Volga. Yet the anti-Red forces allowed everything to slip through their fingers.

The Allied intervention was severely criticised by both extremes of public opinion. From the militarist point of view, too few troops were sent to be of any help and no concerted action was taken by any of the anti-Bolshevik governments to drive the Soviet leaders from power. The opposite opinion condemned the episode as an unjustifiable adventure which only increased the hardships of the Russian population and had no object but to replace the hated Romanovs in authority.

The Treaty of Brest-Litovsk, which took the Russians out of the war in Spring, 1918, had allowed German troops to pour into Finland, Lithuania, the Don and the Ukraine. Ostensibly they had arrived to assist the weak Soviet Government to maintain order but actually they were there to obtain as much food as possible to combat the Allied blockade which was starving Germany into submission, and to grab at the great stores of war material sent by the Allies to Russia during the war and now lying in railway cars at Archangel, Murmansk and Vladivostok. It was, of course, of vital importance to the Allies to prevent the Germans gaining any advantage from the downfall of Russia, and in March, 1918, a British naval force was landed at Murmansk to guard these stores, though there was no idea at that time of participation in Russian affairs. Encouraged by the success of the Czechs, however, and alarmed at the growing entente between the Germans and the Bolsheviks, the Allies, largely persuaded by Winston Churchill, then Secretary of State for War, landed troops; and the growing disorder, the arrogance of the still undefeated Germans and the atrocities and confiscations of the Bolsheviks, began to give heart to the counter-revolutionary governments that had sprung up. They were further encouraged when the Allied military missions began to arrive – to help in training troops and to restore stable government in a country that was drifting swiftly into anarchy.

British officers like Williamson were soon at work distributing guns, harness, uniforms, et cetera and instructing

Russian volunteers. All these wheels of organisation had been put in motion *before* the Armistice that ended the war with Germany, and when that came it was neither possible nor advisable to stop the machine at once, and after a lot of hesitation and double-talk at the Armistice conference, it was decided to maintain the missions to relieve the distress of the Russian people. The real truth, of course, was that everyone was afraid of the Communist menace and hoped to overthrow the Soviets, and Clemenceau, the French statesman, had actually expressed his belief in the idea of a "cordon sanitaire" as visualised by Winston Churchill, between Russia and the rest of the world. Support in any strength was obviously out of the question, however, in a purely national quarrel and everything that was done was only half done, and the wrong men were backed with monotonous regularity. As a result, in the autumn of 1919, the White or anti-Communist armies began to collapse in a confusion of misery, the railways along which they retreated becoming a *via dolorosa* for decimated regiments and the thousands upon thousands of refugees who accompanied them.

In Spring, 1919, however, when Williamson first became involved, the chances of ending the government of the Soviets and of destroying for ever the threat of Communism which had already begun to spread westwards into defeated Germany and even into France seemed like a great promise to Allied statesmen, and young men like Williamson took themselves to Russia feeling they were doing a wise and honourable thing. They were to be sadly deluded. They had taken on an almost impossible task. The Tsarist empire had been rotten with corruption for far too long and too many of the men with whom they found themselves working were the products of this system. While there were, of course, many brave and honourable men, there were also many more who were lazy, indifferent, bigoted, self-interested and even cowardly. Williamson's diary describes how the high hopes with which he set off for Russia in 1919 ended in 1920 with disillusionment and disaster.

Throughout his story the question of dialogue was always a

very frustrating one, because most of Williamson's dealings
with Russians, whether of high or low rank, were carried out –
when they could not speak French or English – through the
medium of interpreters who were not always his own. From
these men it was often difficult to extract information because
the Russians were often unwilling to give it, often simply
because co-operation with the British might involve them in
the possibility of later criticism or uncalled-for suspicion. To do
them justice, they were often working under appalling difficulties and often personal danger and – later – the very clear
threat of future retribution.

To overcome the problems of a constant three-sided dialogue, I have done away with the interpreters except where
they are important, and have allowed Williamson and his
Russian allies to appear to carry on their conversations as if
there were only two people involved. These conversations
have all been approved by Williamson himself, however, and
wherever possible, they appear as Williamson remembers
them. As for the rest, apart from a little cutting or expanding
where I have found further description necessary, the story is
drawn solely from his own written record.

PROLOGUE

In the autumn of 1915 when I was a captain commanding a field battery, at Croix Barbe in France, I was warned on the telephone to be on the look-out for two distinguished Russian artillery officers who, complete with interpreter, would shortly arrive by car at my gun position. I was to show them round my guns, take them to my observation post and give them a demonstration of the shell power of the 4.5 Howitzers which the British Government was at that time supplying in considerable quantities to the Russian Army.

"See that they enjoy themselves," I was told. "But on no account let them get killed or wounded!"

I had just sufficient time to warn my subalterns and gun crews when the car arrived and out stepped Colonels Vinogradov and Gerkovitch, of the Imperial Russian Artillery, together with their interpreter, Boris Anrep, a well-known London artist.

After an appropriate amount of bowing, smiling and saluting, I discovered that both colonels could speak French, so I was able to join in the conversation and the exchange of personal compliments, snapshots and anecdotes of home and relations.

Meanwhile the gunners stared at the rows of medals, shiny steel sword scabbards and spurs, none of which were in the least suitable for the crawl through the trenches with which their wearers were faced before they could get up to my observation post. But when Vinogradov asked for a tin full of earth from one of the gunpits, which he promised to plant in a Russian gunpit as a token of good will between allies in general and gunners in particular, enthusiasm knew no bounds, and an exhibition of gun drill and gun-laying was put on for his special benefit.

The visit to the O.P. was begun – not without considerable apprehension on my part, as the colonels, their long great-coats down to their heels and in full military panoply, were not in favour of following the duckboards along the inundated communication trench which was our normal line of approach. Starting along the top of the trench, where I was in honour bound to accompany them, we were soon sent jumping into half-filled shell holes by the inevitable sniping German field gun.

After a courtesy call on the battalion commander in the line we eventually achieved the purpose of our visit with a few rounds to register a German strong point, followed by a round or two against some previously registered targets. This was, of course, greeted by a German retaliation on our support trenches – for which we no doubt incurred the abuse of our infantry – and then back to my gun position. More bows, salutes and handshakes, and Colonels Vinogradov and Gerko-vitch passed for ever from my life.

Despite the pleasure they had shown, I wasn't sure how suc-cessful the visit had been. Their comments had not been very illuminating, as they did little more than compare our methods – with great courtesy, of course, but still mildly unfavourably – with those they themselves had employed in the Russo-Japanese War of 1905 and in the early stages of 1914, on neither of which occasions, I remembered, had the Russians achieved any notable military success. Nevertheless, I had enjoyed my guests despite the fact that, as an image of the potential of the much-vaunted Russian steam-roller, they had not been exactly impressive.

Three years later, in December, 1918, I was a very junior major stagnating in a small Belgian town, watching the dis-memberment of army units and the rush for demobilisation. Here, news from the outside world began to resume its normal importance; and more particularly, the news from Russia, our erstwhile ally, became of absorbing interest.

On the Western Front our own war was over, but now it seemed that away in South-East Russia, along the northern coast of the Black Sea, a terrible struggle for survival was being carried on by a few remnants of the Imperial Russian Army which had driven deep into East Prussia in 1914, under Rennenkampf and Sansonov, and, at the price of colossal casualties, relieved the German pressure in the west which was driving the British back on to the Channel ports. Now, so the stories ran, these scattered detachments, loyal to their murdered Tsar, and loyal to the Allies who had entered the war on their behalf and to those of their comrades and their families who might have escaped the preliminary massacres of the Revolution, were in sore distress.

Might it not be that for the moment they were a bulwark against the fast-flowing tide of Communism which was already surging from Eastern Europe into the West, I thought. The fear of it was already widespread because, due to war weariness and dislike of discipline and the subtle Communist propaganda which had its reactions in every country, the threat had become very real.

I thought of those two Russian colonels who had visited my gun position in 1915. Where were they now? Had they been slaughtered by the revolutionaries? I thought of their murdered Tsar, so like in appearance to our own King George. And as the tales of the Communist atrocities came pouring in, I thought of a great army and a great nation in utter dissolution, at the mercy of revolutionary mobs who spared neither women nor children in the frenzied implementation of their so-called liberty.

Out there on the Russian steppes help was sorely needed. And needed now; and when I heard that there was talk of officer volunteers being called for to join a British Mission to provide help to the anti-Bolshevik armies in the administration and use of the equipment and stores which the British Government had decided to supply, the call was irresistible.

I offered myself in a spirit of adventure and of preservation of the traditional ethics of the caste to which I belonged. I had no more time for mutinous soldiers and sailors who ill-treated and massacred their officers than I had for political adventurers from the criminal classes who murdered their Tsar and his helpless family. I came from a group whose privileges in those days were very real, and I saw the Russian revolution not so much as a fight by workers to put right a lot of wrongs as a struggle of evil people to do away with the society to which I belonged. Russian society may well have been wrong-headed and often corrupt and the revolution looked very much like the end for my particular type, but, like a lot of others, I saw myself as committed to a crusade to preserve something which I thought was good. We were not very clever, not very erudite, and possibly very, very wrong, and we attached idealism to certain subjects which may not have deserved it. But that idealism guided our actions and we remained proud of them because they were symptomatic of the generation to which we belonged. This same spirit had sent thousands of young men to the recruiting offices in 1914 and had led them to die on the Somme and at Passchendaele for a cause in which they believed.

Though that feeling no longer exists, it was very genuine in those days and I just could not wait to go.

I was granted a week's leave and went straight to the War Office where I got my name registered for posting to the Mission. Back to Belgium for a couple of days to say goodbye to the last of the disintegrating headquarters of my Division, a week with my mother in Wiltshire, a couple of parties with friends in London – who thought I was quite mad – then on April 12th, 1919, I said goodbye on the quay at Southampton to some of those same friends.

What was this fool's odyssey to which I had committed myself? Was I as mad as my friends insisted? I certainly did not think I was mad then.

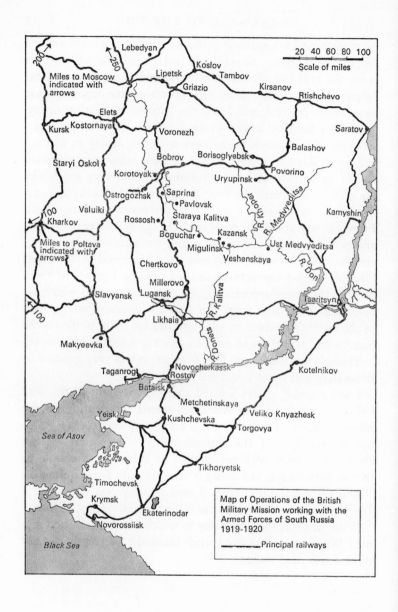

Map of Operations of the British Military Mission working with the Armed Forces of South Russia 1919-1920

————— Principal railways

CHAPTER ONE

Southampton was crammed with tall-funnelled ships and with troops returning from France for demobilisation. They were looking forward to throwing off their uniforms and the discipline of the army, but together with other officers detailed as instructors to the White Russian forces in the Caucasus and the Crimea, I was heading towards another war.

The party included, in addition to myself, Ling, a sturdy, red-faced, red-haired artilleryman; Payne, of the Royal Air Force; and Stanton, of the 7th Dragoon Guards.

We travelled via Le Havre, Modane and Turin, and after three and a half very uncomfortable days in a second-class Italian troop train, arrived at Taranto. We stayed just long enough to get together a few supplies of tinned foods and thin service clothing which we had begun to realise we might require, and to be joined by six sergeants of the Royal Field Artillery, then we embarked on the *Elkantara*. On the second night out, we passed through the Corinth Canal, and the following day we went ashore in Athens. We only had time to look at the Acropolis and the Parthenon, however, before we had to rush back to the ship, but in that short time, we succeeded in getting ourselves mixed up in an enormous street fight involving two tramcars, several policemen and a crowd of at least two hundred of all imaginable nationalities. It had started over the number of passengers allowed on board, but there was only one casualty – the driver of one of the trams – who was stabbed in the neck.

It was in Athens also that we saw the first of the refugees who were already fleeing out of South Russia before the Bolshevik advance.

They were of all classes but were mostly ex-Tsarist officers, members of the nobility and wealthy merchants who had been dispossessed by the Revolution. None of them seemed to lack comfort because they had been able to get away in good time, but they were loud in their complaints. They brought us up to date with what had been happening in Russia since General Kornilov, the first real leader of the White Armies, had taken his stand against the Bolsheviks.

Short and spare, Kornilov was the son of a poor Cossack family and his Mongolian background showed in his small sinewy figure, black goatee and slanting eyes, and the thin legs bowed by years in the saddle. In society he was regarded as crude and abrupt, but the army loved him for his simple manners. Though a rival general described him as having "a lion's heart and a sheep's head", he could still inspire his army by personal example, and he struggled by sheer skill to the highest rank of the Imperial Russian Army at a time when such a thing wasn't easy without birth or influence, and had distinguished himself in both the Russo-Japanese and the European Wars.

Captured by the Austrians, he had disguised himself as an Austrian soldier and escaped, and when the Revolution deposed the Tsar he had been chosen by the new leaders to command the mutinous garrison at Petrograd – the old St. Petersburg. He had disagreed with his political masters, however, over the way they ran the army and resigned to return to the front. Following an abortive attempt to force the government to restore some of the discipline in the army and produce order at home, he had been in danger of being imprisoned. He had once again escaped with his division, however, and, instructing his men to disperse, he had fled across Russia to the Don with a little group of followers. Frost bit into the thinly-clad men, the horses' shoes wore out, and machine gun ambushes waylaid them, and eventually Kornilov arrived alone disguised as a peasant.

He had immediately joined an attempt by General Alexeiev, the former Commander-in-Chief of the Russian army, to form – from escaped officers and Cossacks – a new army to combat the Germans and the Reds, and by February, 1918, he was able to march out of Rostov at the head of 5,000 men, the beginnings of the Volunteer Army which we were to join.

They were accompanied by wives, families, sick and wounded,

and after the loss of Ekaterinodar, had wandered about the steppes
of the Kuban, their uniforms in rags, their medical and surgical
supplies practically nil, their only arms and ammunition what they
had been able to capture from the Bolsheviks. Russian ladies, previously accustomed to the comfort and luxury of the social life of
Moscow and Petrograd, had accompanied the troops as nurses, and
even fought side by side with the men. Capture meant death by
torture for the officers, and the same and worse for the women.
Among the Bolshevik troops were large numbers of the Chinese
Labour Corps, employed on back area work during the war but
now mobilised and armed by Trotsky, and any prisoner requiring
special torture had been handed over to them by the Bolshevik
commissars. The Chinese had lived up to their reputation for
cruelty.

March winds, bitter cold, the fording of icy rivers and forced
marches in snowdrifts or slush decimated Kornilov's men.

"During the remainder of the winter," the story continued,
"typhus raged in all the villages and the Don Cossacks succumbed to the insidious Bolshevik propaganda. But the
Volunteers did not lose heart." Here a sidelong glance was
directed at us. "They were hoping for help from Britain and
France, you see. But no help came." Again, the look – this
time faintly contemptuous. "But the little army held its own
and those Russians you see wearing the decoration of a crown
of thorns pierced by a dagger hung on the old red, blue and
white ribbon of Tsarist Russia, are the men and women who
fought through that bitter Kuban campaign."

Both Alexeiev and Kornilov were now dead, however.

"Alexeiev of typhus," they said. "Kornilov of wounds
received from an exploding shell outside Ekaterinodar in
April, 1918. The command has now fallen on General Anton
Denikin."

But the miracle had happened, and with the Cossacks of the Don,
the Kuban and the Terek rallying on all sides, Denikin's Volunteer
Army had secured a short respite, and the Bolshevik forces had been
cut off from the shores of the Black Sea, the Donets coal basin, the
corn of the Don and the Kuban, and the oil of the Caucasus. Unfortunately, skilful propaganda suggesting that they were only

fighting to restore landlords and a new Tsarist regime had again had its effect on the Don Cossacks and even the French troops in Odessa had become affected, and Odessa had been lost when the French commander there had moved too hastily and ordered evacuation. The civilian population, knowing that the Reds were ready to march in as soon as the French left, had panicked and the evacuation had been a shambles, many of the thousands lining the docks in an attempt to board the French cruisers committing suicide as they waited. It had been a discreditable affair that had affected White morale badly, especially as it was now believed to be only a matter of time before the French got out of Sevastopol as well.

As a result, the Crimea, with the exception of the Kerch peninsula, which was guarded by the guns of the British Black Sea Fleet, had been lost; the whole of the Don north of Novocherkassk was in the hands of the Reds; Tsaritsyn had fallen; and a Bolshevik force had approached Tikhoryetsk Junction which was on the direct line of communication between the Volunteers and the Don Cossacks in the Rostov area, and the headquarters and the remainder of Denikin's army in the Ekaterinodar-Novorossiisk area.

"Every ship which left the Black Sea ports was crowded with refugees – mostly women, sick and wounded officers, and retired generals and statesmen. The Bolsheviks seem to hate *them* most of all."

"What about those who couldn't get away?"

A vast shrug. "Such villages as remained in Denikin's hands are crowded to overflowing with refugees, and as the value of the paper rouble notes has fallen, the problem of finding enough money to purchase even bread's a very acute one for them."

But again the Bolshevik attack had lost its momentum and as they had advanced into the Kuban territory, increasing numbers of the Kuban Cossacks, incensed by the outrages committed by the Red troops to their villages, had rallied to Denikin. A final despairing counter-offensive had been launched in the direction of the River Manytch and Tsaritsyn, and, under the command of General Petr Nicolaievitch Wrangel and led by Generals Skouro and Ulegai, the famous Caucasian cavalry commanders, a force of about 8,000 Kuban Cossacks had driven the Bolshevik cavalry back to the north bank of the Don, surrounded Tsaritsyn, and joined hands with the right flank of the Don Cossacks.

The situation had been saved again and this time there was new hope for the future, because the longed-for help from the British was actually coming. Ship after ship was unloading guns and ammunition, uniforms, and medical stores on the quay at Novorossiisk. Vickers and Lewis guns were already arriving in twos and threes with the regiments at the front, and British officers were arriving with them, explaining their mechanism, firing them at the Bolsheviks and putting heart into the remnants of the Volunteer Army.

We listened to all this with interest. But this was history and we were soldiers and had come to fight a war, and we were concerned with the Red Armies.

"What are they like?" we demanded. "Are they any good?"

"They could be in time," we were told. "Trotsky's a dangerous man and surprisingly efficient."

"And Denikin?"

"An honest soldier and a staunch liberal with a bourgeois background. The son of a humble officer and no friend of the Romanovs. Wrangel comes from a German-Scandinavian family that's produced dozens of soldiers. He always had a brain and graduated as a mining engineer before he entered the army. Skouro's a bit of a brigand."

The refugees seemed to take a White victory for granted and among the British there was a great deal of excited talk about conditions in South Russia.

"Should be interesting," we decided.

"Bags of work by the sound of it," someone said.

It all sounded exciting and we were young enough to hope, as we had in 1914, that the Civil War wouldn't be over before we arrived.

*

Our next port of call was Salonika, where we had to disembark for a week, but we were comfortably ensconced in an excellent rest-house, which had previously been the Turkish Consulate. Here we were joined by Captain Harold Courtenay

Armstrong of the 67th Punjabs who was bound for Constantinople for Intelligence duties. He had been besieged at
Kut with General Townshend and, having passed an examina-
tion as a British-Turkish interpreter, had been used extensively
on Intelligence work. After the capture of Kut, he was interned in Asia Minor but succeeded in making his escape and
rousing the local natives to carry out raids on the enemy's lines
of communications. He had been recaptured through treachery
and interned again, this time in a different camp nearer to the
Black Sea, where he had come up against a prison commandant
who was a notoriously bad character. With his persuasive
manner and his knowledge of the language, however, he had
ingratiated himself to such an extent with the rest of the Turks
with whom he came into contact that when the iniquities of the
Commandant became so pronounced official notice had to be
taken, he had been employed to prosecute him and saw him
sentenced to seven years' imprisonment for brutality. He was
very interested in the Turks, and after the war wrote an authori-
tative biography of Kemal Ataturk.

Armstrong and I met many Turks of all classes in Salonika,
and, although they lived in constant terror of a massacre at the
hands of the Greeks as a reprisal for the times when the
Ottoman Empire had been predominant, they seemed courteous, dignified and well-educated.

In the week which we spent in Salonika we were able to
borrow a car and started up country to visit the Doiran front.
Unfortunately, the only bridge across a very much swollen
stream had been washed away and we had to content ourselves
with a distant view as there was no possibility of getting the
car across.

The heart of the country was at this time infested with
Komitajis, who were Balkan irregulars – little better than
brigands – who turned into partisans or resistance groups in a
national emergency. They had reaped a harvest of stores,
rifles, ammunition and even machine guns after the Bulgarian
retreat at the end of the war and would often take pot-shots at
visitors to their country, although they never undertook

organised action. We had no encounters with them, however, although while we were having our lunch a very picturesque and fierce-looking Macedonian on a white pony came and gazed at us. He looked extremely fierce, but he eventually approached us in the approved manner of the country – with his cap in his hand, begging.

*

Two days later, we received orders to embark on the *Seangbee* which would take us a few stages farther on our journey to Constantinople. Before embarking, some interesting information came into our possession in the Officers' Club. Two men who were speaking were battery commanders in the Field Artillery and were about to hand over the complete equipment of their units. One of them was complaining of the large number of spare parts of which we would be deficient, and was afraid he would be charged heavily on this account.

"Why don't you go to Denikin's dump?" the other officer said, and, on being pressed for an explanation, he pointed out that the park of military stores destined for Denikin was a happy hunting ground for any officer who needed to make up his unit's equipment before handing it over. Apparently there was no guard of any kind, and breech blocks, sights, wheels, anything the heart of a battery commander might desire, could be acquired there for the asking.

Ling looked at me.

"I think we ought to do something about it," he decided. "Otherwise it'll make our work in handing this stuff over to Denikin a lot harder. Let's get along to headquarters and ask for an efficient guard."

Though it didn't make us very popular, I'm sure our action made our job a lot simpler later on.

*

On leaving Salonika one of our party was missing – Captain Stanton, of the 7th Dragoon Guards – who arrived on the quayside when the ship was ten yards away from it and, imperturbable to the point of nonchalance in approved cavalry fashion, remained there. We were, however, joined by a number of officers and other ranks of 47 Squadron, R.A.F., who were to join the Aviation Section of the Mission.

We anchored off Constantinople about 11 o'clock in the morning and were told that we would sail again the same evening. Fortunately, I had correspondence for Major-General Sir Tom Bridges, Chief of the British Mission in Constantinople, and was able to get ashore on the Military Landing Officer's launch. I saw Major-General Onslow, under whom I had served in Ireland in 1910 and tried to prise from him and his staff any information that might be available about Denikin's forces.

"Denikin?" came the reply. "*That* lot!"

"What can you tell me about them?" I asked.

"Not very much. Not quite our line of country."

"Why not?"

"You should see them!"

There was a pronounced indifference, even opposition, to any action that might be taken by the British Mission in South Russia. Nobody knew anything, nobody seemed to want to find out anything, and nobody cared. However, I did arrange to have sent on to me a number of training manuals, handbooks and other literature for which they had no further use, but which I knew I would need when starting an artillery class for Russian officers.

Owing to the number of Turkish mines which still lay round the coast of the Black Sea, it took us two days' slow steaming to reach Varna. It was at Varna in 1854 that the British regiments bound for the battles of the Crimea first caught the cholera which spread into the epidemic that later decimated them, but in 1919 it was a clean and tidy little seaport. French and British troops were in occupation, but the only people carrying arms were the Bulgarians themselves who had been entrusted by the Allies with maintaining order in the town.

From Varna we steamed across the Black Sea to sub-tropical

Batum and arrived in the early hours of the morning, to find the place, as it is often found, shrouded in mist, and with the oil smell from the refineries heavy on the still air. Here we had to find accommodation in the Officers' Rest-house until another ship became available to take us on to Novorossiisk.

In the last week of April, 1919, the situation in Batum was extremely complicated. All the Allies had representative detachments of troops there to guard the port and prevent, as far as possible, the numerous factions in the area from flying at one another's throats. Its great importance was its position at the western extremity of the Baku oil line and its population was dreadfully mixed, the predominant races being Georgians, Tartars and Armenians.

There were also large numbers of Austrian and German officer prisoners of war from the Turkish armies on the Caucasus Front, who filled the two best hotels and seemed to be living in considerable comfort and liberty. The British troops of occupation south of the Caucasus Mountains had their headquarters at Tiflis, the Georgian capital, and their job of policing the town was made easy because, owing to their own family quarrels, the local inhabitants realised they were not capable of keeping order themselves and were extremely grateful to the British for undertaking the work. Nevertheless, after dark, shots were frequently fired in the neighbourhood of the docks and it was not the safest place to walk about in.

The Officers' Rest-house wasn't much to our taste so we arranged to remain in our cabins on the *Seangbee* and to find our food on shore and, as the Russian rouble was standing at 80 to the £ compared to the pre-war value of 10 to the £, we were able to live extremely well. The town had been swept with intermittent epidemics of typhus over the last two years, however, and there was still a considerable amount of it about. Two or three British officers had already succumbed to it, in fact, and the people in the bazaars and lower quarters had suffered terribly; after dark carts appeared, their drivers muffled, and if asked their business would give the hoarse answer "Pour les morts."

It rained a lot and the mist hung about, not improving our tempers as we endeavoured unsuccessfully to find out news of what was happening inside Russia. There were few Russian speakers among us and those who could read the language were in great demand to translate the newspapers.

On our visit to the Rest-house we had met a Turkish war criminal, Nuri Bey, brother of the notorious Enver Pasha, who was charged with the slaughter of thousands of Armenians. He was guarded by a British officer and a few Punjabi infantry, but was allowed considerable liberty. He had a charming personality, speaking English excellently, and had made friends with many British officers, of whom he was very fond of drawing sketches. A year later he escaped while out for a walk, accompanied only by one British officer and two Indian soldiers. He joined Mustapha Kemal – later Kemal Ataturk – who was leading the Turkish national movement in Asia Minor, and amused himself by sending out bombastic messages promising further massacres.

We had just enough time to see as much as we wanted of Batum before H.M. Sloop *Chalcis* arrived from Constantinople with orders to embark all British personnel waiting to proceed to Novorossiisk. On board we found another officer from Constantinople bound for the Military Mission. Captain Lambkirk, holder of the D.S.O. and the M.C., was a British officer of Russian extraction who had served in the Russian Flying Corps and infantry and had twice won the St. George's Cross for gallantry. He came into the British service during the time when General Dunsterville – the original of Kipling's "Stalky" – and General Baratov were co-operating in North-West Persia, and had accompanied an expedition to Krasnovodsk to assist certain Menshevik – or right-wing, anti-Bolshevik – elements in their resistance against the Ural Reds. He was now detailed to the British Military Mission for Intelligence work as he was a brilliant Russian linguist, though his mixed loyalties made him a very doubtful character.

After two days of extremely rough weather, we arrived in Novorossiisk and were disembarked with more speed than comfort, to find ourselves faced with the problem of finding accommodation in a town where apparently none existed. With all the troops that were there, rooms and houses had been let and sub-let, and sub-let again, until no one knew who was in residence and it was virtually impossible to find quarters.

The spring thaw was over but the hot sun and the harsh drying winds of summer hadn't started and it was still very cold and uncomfortable. The town, grey beneath the onion-shaped domes of the churches, seemed to consist entirely of mud. In places in the side roads, it was ankle-deep, dragging at the muscles, and the boards and stones which had been laid down for pedestrians trying to cross were already disappearing from sight. It seemed to be everywhere, on the walls, on the wheels of vehicles, on boots and clothes, hampering the traffic and slowing down the work. The town seemed to wallow in it, particularly as it appeared to possess remarkably few macadamised roads. One or two cobbled avenues built up with shabby public buildings of stone and a few large dwelling houses seemed to make up the centre of the town. All the other streets were filled with the deep mud and carriages sank to the axles in it. Several times we saw the unfortunate fares being carried to the wooden sidewalks. With the Bolsheviks reported not far away, trade seemed to have come to a stop. No one had any thoughts except for the situation in Russia.

The streets were full of penniless refugees and indescribable beggars. The town was a hotbed of crime and, with the White Army's paper roubles practically valueless, a great deal of speculation in foreign currency was going on. There was the same motley collection of races as in Batum – Russians in British khaki, ex-Tsarist officers in grey greatcoats lined with scarlet silk, with epaulettes like great teatrays on their shoulders, foreign businessmen newly arrived after the war in Europe and trying to make the first hesitant steps through the tangle of officialdom, Levantine merchants, Don Cossacks in fur caps, women with dubious reputations, Jews in shabby frock coats, evil-looking Balkan adventurers, long-nosed

Turks, speculators and militia, and finally more German and
Austrian prisoners of war awaiting repatriation.

A great many of the Russians in Novorossiisk and the spas
of the south had fled from cities of the north like Petrograd and
Moscow and formerly wealthy people were living in appalling
conditions, crowding into tiny rooms cluttered with their
belongings and smelling of the creosote they used to try to discourage the wild life. They stood bed and chair legs in little
pans of the stuff in an attempt to keep lice from getting into
their clothing and on to their bodies. It wasn't easy, however.
Everywhere in South Russia seemed to be so crowded at
this time, it wasn't difficult to pick up any disease you
could mention, from smallpox and diphtheria to typhus and
cholera.

Though the Bolsheviks were actually nowhere near at the
time, the people were still in a highly nervous state. Many of
them had lived through the horror of the Revolution and in
their home towns and villages had seen streets crowded from
morning till night with soldiers decked with red ribbons and
gazing defiantly at their officers without attempting to salute
them, insulting the women they had with them, and roving in
noisy gangs which thrust arrogantly through the passers-by.
They had seen endless meetings, held all over the place – in
the riding schools, the barracks, and the schools – and a press
overflowing with slogans. At every cross-roads they had heard
orators haranguing the people against them, and for safety they
had headed for the cities of the Black Sea. But the stations also
had been swarming with drunken, disorderly soldiers parading
under the Red Flag, shouting, laughing and jostling the train
drivers, and they had had to endure them climbing into the
carriages and insulting the women.

When the Red Army, following them south, had reached
Caucasia, they had been persecuted in every conceivable way,
but it was when the Whites had approached that the real terror
had begun. Then the Bolsheviks shot hundreds of them and
almost everyone we met had lost a husband, brother, son or

father, and most of them all their worldly possessions. Great numbers were still terrified the Reds would return.

*

The British officers whom we met were living in the most appalling discomfort with no interpreters, transport or orderlies and no British troops to guard the stores destined for Denikin. These were arriving every day and were being dumped on the quayside just as they came. Officers, helped by a few sergeants who had come to be instructors, were doing the work of storemen, guards and porters, and when discussing the situation at the front gave us the most discouraging reports.

"Everyone who goes up there is sure to get typhus," was one of their comments. "And if you get typhus you're sure to die!"

"Many of the troops with Denikin are not to be relied upon," was another. "And if you find yourself among the Cossacks they might easily turn Bolshevik at any moment and cut your throat."

It sounded a pleasant prospect!

We reported to the Base Commandant and asked to be sent immediately to Ekaterinodar.

"Sorry," we were told. "No orders have been received concerning you. Of course," he added, "you can always stay at Novorossiisk, if you like. There are plenty of jobs you could do."

This was not what we had come for and our complaints became increasingly noisy until our request to be sent north was finally granted and, after a rather scruffy meal at a restaurant called "The Elephant", which however, included plenty of vodka and caviare, we packed ourselves into a train due to start in the evening.

The carriage was comfortless and so old it looked as though it had come from the middle of the previous century. Everything about it – its brasswork, its fittings, its windows – was out-of-date and old-fashioned, and it was as crowded as all Russian carriages always were. Every compartment was packed, luggage and baskets and bundles jammed into every corner, even on the roof and the buffers.

A group of Russian generals who had arrived with us on the *Chalcis* crammed into our compartment with us and we shared a tinned food supper, helped down with indifferent canteen port we had brought from Salonika.

The journey was slow and every time the train stopped at a station to take on fuel and water there was a concerted rush of third-class passengers towards the water tap to collect water for washing or drinking or making tea. The rest of the passengers climbed down to stretch their legs and the British, still caught by the unfamiliarity of everything, pushed through the people buying roast fowls and vegetables from the peasants to the telegraph office to try to post home letters with improbable postmarks on them.

We arrived at Ekaterinodar, name place of Catherine the Great, sometime after midnight. There was a lorry to meet us, and we were driven to the Mission Headquarters, which was in an enormous empty girls' school. Nobody seemed to expect us or to think that it was any use our coming, and it took us some time to find out where we were to sleep. Eventually we divided ourselves among various dormitories with only a wooden bed and an army blanket as aids to comfort. The building had cockroaches, no furniture, no water laid on, and no servants, and the next morning we found ourselves carrying water in buckets to our rooms and cleaning our own boots and buttons and shaving in cold water, surrounded by a chorus of groans and complaints from all the earlier arrivals about the futility of the Mission and everything to do with it.

We hoped for better things after breakfast, but when we saw the meal we were not much cheered. The only food available was prepared in an extremely dirty restaurant about 400 yards from the headquarters building across a waste of mud, and consisted of a cold and gritty omelette. The coffee, which was tipped out of a large chipped pot into any tumbler that happened to be available, quite regardless of who or how many had previously drunk out of it, was cold. The cloth was stained and dirty, and we felt ourselves looked upon with almost complete apathy, if not suspicion by officers who made no effort to show us round or make us at home in our new surroundings.

After breakfast Ling and I reported to the office of the Senior Artillery Officer with the Mission, Lieutenant-Colonel Ross Hudson, hoping to receive orders for immediate employment, but he was absent at the front and we were told we would have to wait until he returned. We were also interviewed by Lieutenant-General Sir Charles Briggs, the Chief of the Mission, who promised to see that other officers should not suffer the delay, discomfort and obstruction we had.

Briggs was a typical old-fashioned cavalry general, and was said to have no liking for his job. We were told, in fact, that he rode everywhere on a long-tailed horse with two greyhounds, laughing at the Russians, and he didn't strike us as being the man for a command we considered important and urgent.

Since we had a few days to spare, we began to look round Ekaterinodar. It was the centre of one of the main agricultural and corn-growing regions of Russia and was surrounded by fields of rich black earth. It was the very hub of anti-Bolshevik resistance and we tried to pick up what news we could and assimilate local habits and customs. At the time, it was the headquarters of Denikin and the attached British Mission and was the capital of the Kuban Province. Like Novorossiisk it was full of uniforms and devoid of lodgings. The country around was inhabited almost entirely by Kuban Cossacks who had supported Denikin very loyally up to that time, because they were opposed to Bolshevism on principle and hoped that in return for their services Denikin would grant them autonomy.

It had been a scene of continuous fighting for the last twelve months and signs of this showed in scarred, bullet-pocked buildings and – in the countryside around – deserted half-burnt villages, their wrecked stations sometimes splashed with dried blood, where occasionally the double-headed eagle of Imperial Russia could still be seen. The houses, smudged by smoke, and roofed with sheet iron or tiles, were decorated with serrated fretwork, marked here and there where flames had touched them. Shutters creaked in the wind and gates rattled untended, showing how the small army of Volunteers composed largely of the Officers' Battalions formed by General Alexeiev in Novocherkassk at the beginning of the revolution had fought desperately for their existence.

Unfortunately, headquarters showed the rankest intolerance to the Cossacks. Denikin's motto – Russia, one and indivisible – was only a vague rhetorical phrase but anyone who held any other view was stigmatised as disloyal. Everyone was called a Separatist and regarded almost as a traitor even, who had served under the Ukrainian flag; and this included many Volunteer officers who didn't give a fig for politics but simply wanted to fight the Bolsheviks.

When we arrived, Denikin, a powerful-looking, handsome man with a grizzled beard and moustache, was grouping and reorganising his troops with a view to carrying the war back into the enemy's country. The Whites were hoping to reach Moscow and Petrograd by a military advance simultaneously from south, east and north-west. On the right flank working from the Caspian Sea was the Caucasian Army, composed mostly of cavalry drawn from the Kuban and Terek Cossacks, and largely officered by ex-Imperial cavalry officers. They were about 10,000 strong, under the command of General Baron Petr Wrangel. On the Don front, about 60 miles west of Tsaritsyn, was the Army of Don Cossacks, drawn entirely from the Don district, but also with many ex-Imperial officers serving in it. The troops were mostly mounted, but owing to the shortage of horses many regiments of Cossacks were on foot under the name of "Plastoune" regiments, from a word which means a Cossack who has lost his horse and is compelled to fight dismounted until he can capture another one. These numbered about 20,000 and were commanded by General Sidorin, a Siberian Cossack and ex-Flying Corps officer.

Next to the Don Army on the west was the Volunteer Army proper, numbering about 10,000, of which a corps based on

General Sidorin in
his pusher plane

Bogaïevski and
Angus Campbell on
the General's
steamer

My Cossack escort
of the III Don Army
Corps

A typical Cossack bridge

The old men of a village near Tsaritsyn

Rostov under General Mai-Maievski, was holding the front to the shore of the Sea of Azov, near Taganrog. Further to the left again was another corps advancing northwards through the Crimea and trying to join hands with Mai-Maievski before carrying out a general advance on Kharkov. Finally, in Siberia, Admiral Kolchak was organising an advance across the Urals and beyond the Volga aimed directly at Moscow, while General Youdenitch was trying to reach Petrograd from the Baltic.

All the southern forces were known as the Armed Forces of South Russia, though the strength of regiments was always doubtful, as recruits could only be obtained from the villages through which the advance was made. They were largely awkward country youths with a tendency to tie wild flowers to their rifle barrels on the march and gape at the unfamiliar brick buildings. Some of them had even been known to shake with fear at the sight of a train. They fought well but, when their villages were freed, they had a habit of leaving the ranks to cultivate the land once more.

Their officers were an extraordinary crowd, dressed in a mixture of uniforms, their badges of rank sometimes marked on their epaulettes with blue pencil. Some of them wore spurs with rowels as big as half crowns that jingled like marbles in a tin, and for the most part they knew nothing at all about what was going on. If they did, they gave only vague answers and, when pressed, took refuge behind the language barrier. Mostly, they were kind-hearted and generous to the point of absurdity but, apart from swearing frightful oaths of revenge on the Bolsheviks, they were not of much use. They were lazy, arrogant, ignorant, and often cowardly, chiefly because they knew their men had no heart for fighting their fellow countrymen and because they had already once seen them desert and mutiny, and were firmly – and rightly – under the impression it could easily happen again.

No one at Mission Headquarters had a very high opinion of them, and no attempts had ever been made to organise any system of supplying reinforcements through depots.

"The only units with 3-inch field guns," we were told, "are those which have been fortunate enough to capture them from the Bolsheviks. What's more, the supply of ammunition's almost exhausted, but as it's made by hand with fuses made by students, it never goes off anyway, and artillery fire's practically negligible."

It sounded as though there might be a great deal to do and, from that time, we saw other more unhappy signs of how the Russians neglected the basic necessities of war, as convoys of wounded passed through the town from the station, the carts pulled by ponies or camels and moving at a snail's pace. The sun beat down on the poor wretches lying in the carts which were devoid of covers or springs, and the axles shrieked for lack of oil. The men moaned in the heat. They hadn't had a drop of water for days and the sight of them didn't help the nervousness of the people of Ekaterinodar, though there was an immediate rise in morale as a result of our appearance on the scene. All possible facilities for travelling were accorded to us, and the hospitality for which the Russians had a world-wide reputation was offered. It was pathetic, in fact, to see people who had suffered so much and lost almost everything vying with one another to do us honour. The wave of bitterness and disappointment which had passed over them as a result of the tardy arrival of Allied supplies and help was forgotten now. "The British have come," was the cry. "Now all will be well!"

CHAPTER TWO

After three days of waiting, Colonel Ross Hudson returned to Ekaterinodar, and explained to us how it was proposed to issue batteries to the Russian units. Two schools were to be formed, one at Armavir for instructing officers of the Caucasian and Volunteer Armies, and one at Novocherkassk for instructing officers of the Don Army. Ling was appointed Commandant to the former, and I was appointed to the latter.

Three British officers, Captains Knight, Linton and Abrahams, had already begun artillery instruction at Novocherkassk with the one partly-equipped battery of 18-pounders which had been sent up to the Don Army, and I was told to report at once to General Gorielov, commanding the Artillery of the Don Army, and to organise classes of instruction on lines similar to those we had employed in our artillery schools in France. Other British officers at Novocherkassk were giving instruction on the Vickers and Lewis guns.

I asked for enlightenment on the political situation and the attitude which the British should adopt.

"Politics!" The languid and disenchanted earlier arrivals I approached looked shocked. "Old boy, on no account should a British officer discuss politics with the Russians. And, for God's sake, avoid being drawn into criticism of the French. Since the Odessa affair they've become rather unpopular with Denikin's supporters."

I was also warned against an individual called Alexis Aladin, who, although speaking English perfectly and behaving in an ostentatiously pro-English fashion, had the reputation of being extremely left-wing. "He had the closest relationship with the Germans when they were at Novocherkassk," I was told. "He's a mischief-maker of the first order."

I wasn't very impressed with all these warnings. Many of my informants, I knew, were men who had volunteered for Russia to avoid being thrown out of the army by the axe that was being applied at home after the war against the Germans. Their attitude was always "Avoid the bloody Russians at all costs!" "Don't do this!" "Don't do that!" "Don't get mixed up in anything, and at all costs keep out of the town! If they haven't got typhus they've got smallpox."

Since, on the whole, many of them drank heavily and didn't hesitate to make use of their position, I regarded their advice as useless. It would, I felt, be quite hopeless, anyway, once my small group had become properly involved with the Cossacks, and it seemed wiser to find out by trial and error.

Before starting up-country, I had to select a British interpreter from among those available at Headquarters. As I had become great friends with Captain Angus Campbell, I chose him. As heir to the Duke of Argyll, he was known as the Captain of Dunstaffnage, and was a Scottish laird. Of C3 physique, he had found in 1914 that all his friends were in France in the Household Cavalry and he had determined to join them. Since he wasn't permitted because of his health to join up, he had bought himself a uniform and, though he had never enlisted, he had been used as a dispatch rider for the Household Cavalry on a quiet "old-pals" basis until, during a dusk action, he had ridden his motor bicycle into a dead horse and been captured by the Germans. Throughout his imprisonment, he had always been with Russians and had learned their language, and now, like many others, felt called upon to help those who were still fighting for the principles which had brought us into the war. Like myself he regarded himself as being involved in a crusade against the Communists. He was a terrific worker and very enthusiastic, though he was so obsessed with his admiration for Russia he sometimes lost his head and was so vocally sympathetic with everything the Russians had ever done that he was regarded with great suspicion by some of the people at headquarters. Nevertheless, he did a great deal of good. He was a friend of Sir George

Buchanan, the last British ambassador to Tsarist Russia, and he later used his influence with Lady Buchanan to have things sent out from England for the refugees. I was very much influenced by his attitudes.

He was only too keen to help me and we set out for Novocherkassk the following night, and arrived, dirty and uncomfortable, at Rostov the following morning. The place was humming with life. It had become the temporary capital of Southern Russia and even the policemen at the station still wore their old Tsarist uniforms.

We bought breakfast in the town and at midday caught another train on to Novocherkassk, which we reached during the afternoon. It was a large country town where the seat of the Don Cossack government had been established. It contained the palace of the Ataman of the Cossacks, the House of Assembly where the Don Kroug – or parliament – met, and a very beautiful cathedral whose five domes could be seen for miles around because of the cathedral's position and the fact that the domes were all gilded and reflected the sun like a mirror. There were also barracks, and opposite the cathedral a bronze statue to Ermak, a famous Don Ataman who had led their armies into battle. The place was packed with Russian officers who by some miracle had escaped death from the Bolsheviks. They had all had to endure imprisonment or other outrages and many had reached the town on foot, hounded all the way like animals.

Placing our kit under the guard of Russian Military Police, we walked up the steep hill into the town to the Hotel Centrale, which was the billet occupied by members of the British Mission. The streets were packed with people and, though there were only three army motor cars and petrol was almost unobtainable, there were a large number of horse-drawn carriages and cabs pulled by jaded hacks. Our strange uniforms were eyed with curiosity as we stopped to stare at the notices – in large red Kyrillic letters – which announced Bolshevik atrocities. Some of them showed pictures and I felt, from the size of the letters, that, instead of encouraging the people to stand firm against the Red invasion, they were more likely to put the wind up them and encourage them to flee.

They made me all the more eager, however, to start work and the following morning I began making the acquaintance of the Russian officers with whom I was to work. In addition to the gunners, Knight, Linton and Abrahams, there were already a few British infantry officers employed on general liaison work and instruction in Vickers and Lewis guns, and classes had already started at the Don Army School. Unfortunately, the work was handicapped by incomplete equipment arriving from Novorossiisk – probably a relic of "Denikinsdump" – and because, so we heard, great piles of the stuff were rotting on the quaysides, untended, uncared for and the target of every pilferer in the town. Some of the clothing even found its way into the market and a British soldier trying to find a souvenir to send home among the inlaid wooden boxes, leather goods, picture frames, metalwork and embroidery, might well find himself staring at some article of British military equipment.

The question of language was a difficult one. None of the instructors spoke Russian, but the town had been searched for English-speaking Russian officers who were attached to us as interpreters, and there was an Englishman – Norman Lack – who, with his wife and family, was living in Novocherkassk after having been hunted out of Petrograd during the Revolution. Lack, who spoke Russian fluently, had been in business with a firm of tea merchants while his wife had been a governess to one of the princely families, and they had joined the southward-bound flood of refugees making for the Don Cossack country where they had been promised safety. I was extremely lucky to have them to help me.

I kept Angus Campbell as my particular assistant, however, and with his knowledge of Russian customs and prejudices, he was able to give me tips on how to do and say the right thing at the right time, and to pay deference to small points of etiquette to which the Russians attached great importance.

Among the Russian officers who were attached to us or worked with us, there was one who immediately stood out as someone out of the ordinary. This was a Count du Chayla who, with an air of authority and bearing greetings from some of the highest generals in the Don Army, called on me during my first afternoon in the town. Though he spoke no English we conversed with ease in French, and I gathered that he was a sort of bear-leader-in-chief, aide-de-camp, political agent and – to my mind – probably also a spy detailed by the Don Army staff to supervise the actions of the British officers in general and myself in particular.

Rather fat, with a smooth red face and close-cropped head, he combined an air of theatrical bonhomie with an energy which, though not remarkable, placed him well in front of the majority of his Russian brother officers. His actual appointment was described as "Chief of the Political Department of the Intelligence Section of the General Staff", but he appeared to be in the confidence of all the local heads of departments, both civil and military, and as his ideas on the system which we should follow in our work seemed at the time to coincide very closely with mine, I put more confidence in him than I should have done, and thereby laid the seed of much trouble in the future. As he seemed to be almost the familiar of General Sidorin, the Commander-in-Chief, and General Khislov, his Quartermaster-General, however, he was obviously a person without whose good offices nothing very much could have been accomplished.

Having inquired what times would be suitable for me to pay my first call on the various personages in the Don capital, I began, accompanied by Campbell, with the Chief of the Artillery, General Gorielov. He struck me as a very pleasant man but he was wholly lacking in energy and was deeply interested in finicky points of detail, but reluctant to discuss or to give any decisions whatsoever on general policy.

"How about a list of Russian batteries under your command?" I asked. "Or a scheme showing which ones are to be re-armed with 18-pounders?"

He shrugged the question aside. He only had one theme. "Short as the Cossacks are of guns," he said, "they are shorter still of ammunition.

"In fact," he went on, "I have only about 200 rounds a day for my whole army and as the British guns have plenty of shells they must, therefore, go to the front at once."

The fact that untrained personnel would ruin them carried no weight at all with him. "My Generals at the front say that the infantry now have to attack without any artillery support at all and they are very reluctant to do it," he said. "Send us the British guns with their shells so that at least our infantry may see them and hear the shells passing over their heads!"

"What about some systematic training of batteries?" I persisted.

None appeared to exist. "Owing to the urgent demand for them at the front," Gorielov said, "they have to carry out their training there."

Finally, he put me in touch with General Greykov, who commanded the schools for infantry, cavalry and artillery officers. At the artillery school, I found Knight, Linton and Abrahams hard at work explaining the mechanism of the guns and how to test sights and measure springs to five or six Russian officers, and about a dozen soldiers. Only eight 18-pounders had arrived, and my hopes of a demonstration section on the lines of our own depot batteries in England were immediately dashed.

"These guns are going to the front in a week with the Partisan Artillery Brigade," I was told. "It is attached to the corps of volunteer students. They form one of the best units of the Don Army."

The fact that the guns were deficient in sights, spanners, and buffer springs, and that the gunners had not yet fired them in action seemed to deter them not at all. The British instructors, however, were assisted by the Russian officer-instructors, who were picking up the mechanism very quickly and were keen and easy to work with. Unfortunately, method was conspicuous by its absence, and any excuse given by a student for his non-appearance on parade was considered good enough to absolve him from censure.

"I had a late night." "My sister arrived." "It was my cousin's birthday." All seemed good enough.

I was beginning to see by this time something of the task we had before us, and, not wishing to interfere with the all-too-brief scheme of instruction which Knight had arranged, I left him to it and returned to the hotel, hoping to arrange for some further interviews in the afternoon. Once again, however, I met trouble.

"Afternoon!" The expressions were horrified. "The working day of the Russian staff doesn't include any time between late afternoon and dinner."

I was politely told, in fact, that the various people I suggested visiting would not even be in their offices that afternoon – which meant, literally, that they would be asleep. Further bitter experience taught me that unless I could actually pin down any Russian officer whom I sought to a certain time in the early afternoon for an appointment, 10 o'clock to midday was the only hope I had of ever seeing him.

However, we seemed to be making *some* progress, because firing practice had been arranged to take place three miles outside the town on the steppes and I was determined to see it. It poured with rain, but we all went out in one of the Don Army's three motor cars, vintage American Packards and Fords – all without spare tyres since there were none in the whole of Russia – and narrowly escaped sticking in the mud which was all the roads consisted of.

The efforts to free the cars were watched by local women washing their clothes or bathing alongside the road in a small stream that widened out into shallow pools. Once he had got inside a car, nothing could ever induce a Russian officer to ease its task over bad going by getting out, and the women stood stark naked in water that reached no higher than their calves, enjoying the spectacle of us trying to force the heavily-loaded cars through the pot-holes; laughing as the wheels spun

in the mud and threw out waves of dirty water on the struggling soldiers pushing behind.

Somehow or other we eventually arrived, escorted on
either side by a couple of Cossacks, who, instructed to look
after us, galloped ahead to warn the battery of our approach.
Quite a show had been put on for our benefit. The guns had
been drawn up in section on good level platforms and targets
representing guns in action and groups of infantry had been
placed on the steppe at about 4,000 to 4,500 yards-range.

The troops were lined up on parade and there was a great
deal of shaking hands as we arrived, either in greeting or on
parting, then a soldier reported to a junior officer, keeping his
hand raised in stiff salute all the time he was speaking. The
junior officer reported to a senior and the senior to an even
more senior and so on. More hands were raised in salute – in
fact there was a veritable flurry of hands in all directions as *all*
officers accompanying a superior officer always acknowledged
all the salutes *he* acknowledged – then the Commanding Officer
began to approach the troops.

They were called to attention as he appeared, and he halted,
stiff, erect, bearded and well-bemedalled.

"Good morning, soldiers," he said cheerfully.

The men answered with a roar. "Good morning, Your
Excellency! We are glad to serve you!"

The general smiled and saluted. The term, "Excellency" was
his right and all those officers who prided themselves on keeping up the customs of the old army insisted on it.

The firing practice was carried out under considerable difficulty as, what with the rain and the numerous spectators who
refused to keep clear either of the battery position or the
Observation Post, the best interpreter in the world could not
have kept us in touch with all that was going on.

Many of the Russians considered themselves quite capable
of carrying on without what they considered interference on
our part. With very few exceptions, the junior officers were
keen to get our opinion and advice, and many of the senior ones
also listened gravely to discussions on experiences gained on

the Western Front, but when it came to introducing innovations or plans of real practical value, the old lack of adaptability, and the conservatism so inherent in the Russian nature, always triumphed. Again and again I was deterred from further suggestions by such remarks as, "Ah, but we found by our experience in the Japanese War . . ." or "If only you had seen the Russian Army in 1914 when we *always* did as you now suggest!" Their incompetence and arrogance were amazing. Once even, when two British officers were instructing them, one of the lounging students gaily remarked, "Isn't it wonderful to see the British doing all the work?"

On leaving Mission headquarters, our orders had been most explicit, "You are not to interfere, or hurt the feelings of the Russians," so it was not easy to overcome the difficulties that arose. And there were plenty!

The Russians seemed to guess the angle of sight rather than calculate it, and their errors were naturally complicated by our different corrector system of fixing the appropriate height of the burst. In addition, their guns had a flatter trajectory than ours, and their system of oil-filled spring buffers was much less complicated, so that they complained constantly that the equipment we used was much too difficult for the hastily-trained men to understand. They also liked firing each end of their ranging bracket at one-second intervals, which to our mind, with efficient laying, was both wasteful of ammunition and increased rather than decreased the difficulties of the ranging officer.

To our intense surprise, they also asked for telescopic sights (long since discarded by the British in France) for laying in the open, and as our guns were much heavier than their own, their horses, which were little more than ponies, had great difficulty in pulling them when the going was heavy. Our harness also was far too large for them and required a great deal of alteration; and, being accustomed to the old-fashioned harness, our modern breast collars were a complete mystery to them so that we had to assemble them all ourselves for a long time.

However, the guns were got into action at last, loaded and

layed somehow, and subsequently fired in the direction of the target. The Russians were all so pleased at having a considerable quantity of ammunition to expend, they insisted on banging away with salvoes of shrapnel with zero and short fuses to show the delighted soldiers how much noise and smoke could now be made with our big 18-pounder shells, compared to the miserable little pip-squeak shells from their own guns, of which around sixty per cent didn't even explode.

The 4.5 howitzer was no difficulty at all, however, principally because it was as near fool-proof as a gun could be, and because we had already in 1916 supplied many batteries of these to the old Russian Army. There were several officers who had used them before, and in fact, in Novocherkassk, there was one of these original pieces, which we used for school work, with an elaborately enamelled design of crossed Russian and British flags on the breech block, which had been manufactured at Coventry in 1916.

This 4.5 battery commander impressed me as most efficient, and, in fact, when the battery arrived at the front, it was rushed immediately into action and covered itself with glory at Millerovo Junction about a fortnight later.

At about 1 o'clock, after a good deal of noise and smoke and periodical small conferences, usually involving brain-racking conundrums for the British instructors, the battery was ordered home. General Gorielov, Knight, Linton and I were asked to lunch at the Brigade mess at Hootenok, a small village running into the outskirts of Novocherkassk. We were given an excellent meal and introduced to the nursing sisters attached to the Brigade, who seemed to be combined mess secretaries, despatch carriers, medical officers, caterers, wives, girl friends, mistresses and comforters-in-chief to the officers and men of the brigade, whom they always followed into action.

I subsequently met many of these sisters attached to all sorts of units at the front, and though occasionally the position was abused, in most cases they set an example which the officers might well have followed in devotion to duty and hard work.

They endured tremendous hardships, were always short of warm clothes and the ordinary comforts of life, and with a few exceptions were there purely for work and to help, and not for the amusement of the officers. Many of them, in fact, were aristocratic women who had to wear rough clothes and possessed none of the things which normally sophisticated women own, so that they were never able to do themselves justice and often looked like peasants.

Whether, however, it was with batteries or regiments, or in hospital trains or little village organisations for evacuating sick and wounded to the few existing hospitals, we were always struck by the stout-hearted way in which the Russian women of all classes did their best to help the anti-Bolshevik forces. The number of them who died of typhus or were captured and murdered by Bolshevik troops will probably never be known. They were always treated with extreme courtesy by the officers, and with a dog-like devotion by the men.

The practice of allowing them to accompany units into the field certainly gave the opportunity for some extremely attractive ladies to accompany their husbands into the war zone, but, from whatever social strata they came, it never interfered with the work they were there to do. It was only in the higher formations and some of the technical services, who spent most of their life in a train on the lines of communication, that comment on them arose.

Many of these staffs had too many women with them and, while they helped with the nursing, when trouble started the generals tended to take their headquarters trains as far from trouble as possible and to keep on going, forgetting their troops.

CHAPTER THREE

Since it seemed I was to work almost entirely with Don Cossacks, I decided I ought to know something about them and I made a point of checking their history.

It was during the Tartar occupation of the Don, I learned, that the Russians first decided to colonise the wild and barbarous tract around the river. The first to arrive were discontented or exiled Russians for whom life in Moscow had become impossible under Ivan the Terrible and the other Tsars of the sixteenth and seventeenth centuries, and when Tsar Alexis Michaelovitch enslaved the peasants towards the end of the seventeenth century, more large numbers emigrated southwards. They were followed by victims of religious persecution and people seeking vengeance on the Tartars or hoping to rescue captives. So arose a heterogeneous collection of people who founded the first military community of the Don.

Called "Cossack" from the Tartar word for saddle, "hozak", they became exclusively light cavalry soldiers when they had to discard their heavy mail for the long journeys of their campaigns against the Asiatics. They formed themselves into camps which they called "stanitzas" and chose their own chief, calling him "Wattman" – from which came the modern title "Ataman". Cultivation of the land was prohibited, and they lived by hunting and fishing and the results of raiding.

They soon divided themselves up into the Cossacks of the upper and the lower Don, and owing to the different conditions under which these two sections lived, their characteristics became quite distinct. Those of the upper Don were essentially Russian, fair, rather lazy and lacking in enterprise and warlike spirit. Those of the lower Don, continually fighting or intermingling with the Tartars and Circassians in the

Caucasus and the district now called the Kuban, developed a dark type with slight figures, black hair and a much more active and pugnacious spirit.

In the sixteenth century, a "Kroug", or Council, elected the Ataman, decided on expeditions and other important questions and laid the foundation of the Diet of the Don Cossacks. The first case of their troops forming part of the Russian Army was in 1550 during the campaign of Ivan the Terrible against Kazan, and from then onwards the role of the Cossacks became that of "Border Guard" of the Empire and they were the principal military community upon whom the sovereign always called, for additional troops in time of national emergency.

Cossack cavalry divisions took part in all the fighting from the seventeenth century up to the Revolution of 1917, in which the Russian Army was engaged. At times they were almost at war with their masters in Moscow over some point of constitutional right, but their position was so strong and their value so great, they were never seriously molested and usually gained their point, thus establishing a national spirit of independence and love of liberty.

In 1801, 41 cavalry regiments were mobilised under Count Orlov and, from 1810 onwards, they were at war with Napoleon under Ataman Platov, their services being recognised by a charter issued to them by Alexander I, guaranteeing the integrity of their institutions. The Crimean War called up numerous regiments of Cossacks, and two of the guns captured from the British at Balaklava were outside the museum at Novocherkassk. When, however, in 1914, the role of cavalry became very much modified by trench fighting, they did not take kindly to the new order of things and, owing to the great wastage both in men and horses in 1916 and 1917, many of them were drafted into units for work on the Turkish frontier and to co-operate with the British in Mesopotamia. The remainder were used as orderlies, lines of communication guards and police.

Following the Revolution, the Cossacks, though demo-

cratically inclined, mistrusted and despised the Soviets and
Leagues of Soldiers and Workmen which were interfering with
military operations, arresting and degrading their officers and
destroying all the discipline of the army, and at the time of
Kornilov's attempt to restore law and order in August, 1917,
they supported him unanimously.

When Kornilov's adventure collapsed, the Cossacks grew
tired of both Provisional Government and Bolshevik ex-
tremists alike and withdrew to their own land, asking nothing
more than to be left alone to work out their own salvation. But
very soon, following the persecutions in the northern cities,
to their country came large numbers of the aristocracy and ex-
Imperial officers hoping to find a refuge from the ever-increasing venom of the Bolsheviks.

In May, 1917, General Kaledin, who had commanded the
8th Army on the South-West Front, was elected Ataman by the
Don Kroug, and in August of that year issued a proclamation
asserting the intention of the Cossacks to carry on the war
alongside the Allies and to re-establish discipline at the front,
and offering a refuge in the Don area for everybody who had
suffered from the spite of the Bolsheviks. "We shall surrender
nobody to the Soviets," he said, and the trickle of people from
the north became a flood. Ex-officers, lawyers, concert artistes,
professors and intelligentsia joined the movement south, and
soon the cities of the Black Sea were full of them. Some were
recruited into the Anti-Bolshevik forces. Some were a mere
liability.

In November, 1917, Moscow declared war against Kaledin
and the Don Cossacks, and risings of workmen broke out
against his Government, especially in Rostov. Novocherkassk
remained loyal, however, and since so many of the Don regiments were still far away and had been unable to return to
their own country, it was necessary to raise volunteer regiments. The students took the lead in this work and a small
force marched against Rostov. It was beaten back but a second
attack, led by Kaledin himself, was successful and Rostov was
captured.

General Sidorin (note his sabre) addressing a parade. The author is standing behind him in a solar topee

My horses and their wagon

Caucasian cavalry

General Bogaievski, the Ataman of the Don Cossacks, is invested
with the K.C.M.G. in a room of the Ataman's palace

During this period, however, the Bolshevik agitation had undermined the discipline of the Cossack troops, and it was possible to rely only on volunteers to carry on the struggle.

In January, 1918, under the supervision of Alexeiev, the Volunteer Army came into existence and soon had among its commanders many of those generals who were now refugees, including Denikin. By the end of January, however, the Volunteer Army detachments, which were still incredibly small, were obliged to leave Rostov to its fate once more and withdraw to the Kuban.

Kaledin could not face the capture of his capital and shot himself in the Ataman's palace on January 29th, 1919. Novocherkassk fell on February 12th, and all that was left of the Don Army – about 2,000 strong – rather than submit, escaped into the steppes under the command of General Popov. The day after they left, a renegade Cossack officer entered the town at the head of the Bolshevik cavalry and murdered the new Ataman, the President of the Kroug and the brother of the present Ataman.

The Cossacks soon began to realise what they had let themselves in for, and by August, 1918, the Reds had again been chased out of Novocherkassk and certain southern districts of the Don. A new Ataman, General Krasnov, a brilliant cavalry general, was elected and under his leadership the Cossacks pushed back the Bolsheviks.

There now appeared on the scene a formidable new influence. The Ukrainians, supported by German occupation troops who had been there since the Treaty of Brest-Litovsk, claimed ownership to certain parts of the Don territory, and the Don Cossacks had to submit because it was only from the Germans that they were able to get the ammunition and guns they so sorely needed for their fight against the Bolsheviks. By August, 1918, an efficient little Cossack regular army was ready to take the field.

The winter set in, however, and again the Cossacks listened to Bolshevik propaganda. Again the Reds drove in the outlying Cossack troops and advanced on Novocherkassk, but the employment of the small but efficient new army saved the situation. After the Armistice on the Western Front, however, the Germans withdrew their troops from the Don and the Ukraine, leaving the coast clear, not only for the Bolsheviks but also for gangs of unscrupulous peasants who had become bandits.

These people, owing allegiance neither to the Whites nor the Bolsheviks, lived in the woods or in trains and fought against Reds, Whites and Ukrainians without differentiation, usually attacking at night, riding in close to trains and sending up coloured flares captured in raids on depots to light up their manoeuvres.

To cope with the situation, a force of the Volunteer Army under General Mai-Maievski was based on Rostov. Another army, under German supervision and backed by German money, advanced from Kiev until it had succeeded in clearing a considerable area round Voronezh of the Reds. Unfortunately it was commanded by the most blatant representatives of the old regime and only replaced the tyranny and mismanagement of the Bolsheviks by the same system under a different name. Very soon local sympathies became so alienated that this army broke up and the remaining fragments drifted into units of the Don Army and the Volunteer Army.

In December, Krasnov, now Ataman of the Don Cossacks, agreed to the unified command of all anti-Bolshevik forces under Denikin, and in February, 1919, General Afrikan Petrovitch Bogaievski, who had fought through the Kuban campaign under Kornilov and was very popular along the Don, was made Ataman with General Sidorin as Commander-in-Chief.

In December, 1918, there was the first sign of interest taken by the Allies in the struggle in South Russia when a Mission arrived under General Poole, and, in April, a British Mission under General Briggs appeared, including among its officers, me.

*

Having found out something about the Cossacks, my first duty in Novocherkassk seemed to be to call upon Bogaievski, the Ataman. With Angus Campbell, I set off to do this the day after my arrival. We were met at the door by a very smart sentry of the Ataman's Guard Regiment, who wore a blue Cossack cap, with the ordinary Russian grey-green rubashka, or shirt-blouse, and blue breeches with a three-inch red stripe. In his hand he held a cavalry sabre, curved like a sickle and quite clearly sharp as a razor. With his sword and bearded face he was quite a terrifying customer.

We were ushered by an A.D.C. into the Chancellor of the Household and he in turn passed us on to the Private Secretary, until eventually we found ourselves entering a small sitting-room in which the Ataman received his guests.

Bogaievski was a round-faced man with a small moustache and a very friendly smile. Having just recovered from an attack of typhus contracted while visiting the front, he was very weak but he greeted us cordially – to my intense delight in French, so I could carry on a conversation without an interpreter.

"We are delighted to have you here," he said. "Our struggle will be made a great deal easier now you've come."

The visit was short and formal but I took a great liking to him on the spot. Despite his high rank, he was conspicuously natural and unassuming.

After Ataman Bogaievski, the next most important persons were Sidorin, the Commander-in-Chief, and Gorielov, his Chief of Artillery, whom I expected would be more important than he seemed to be, but the tightest watertight compartments that ever marred British staff work in France were leaky compared with those of the Russian staff. In addition to Gorielov, Sidorin was accompanied by his Chief of Staff, a Pole, General Keltchevski, and his Quartermaster General, General Khislov. Between them, these four men controlled the whole working of the Don Army. The Ataman was supposed to be kept informed of all moves but I soon came to the conclusion that the forceful and determined Sidorin did practically as he liked, and only consulted the more easy-going Bogaievski when it suited him – which was not often. Not that this was particularly unusual, however, because every town seemed to contain assorted individual commands and what were practically private armies, some run by generals and some by colonels. None of them seemed to be answerable to anybody else.

Sidorin, a Siberian, had been an aviator and a staff officer in the Imperial Russian Army and had not yet reached forty. He was a big man with a close-shaved head, scarred face and coarse features. He spoke little, but when he did it was in a gruff and overbearing voice. In repose his expression was inclined to be cruel and forbidding, but when pleased or amused, it would light up into a curious boyish smile and he would give a strangely pleasant and insinuating chuckle that made him hard to dislike. At my first meeting, he greeted me gravely and began to expound the same theme as all the other Russian commanders.

"The British guns must be sent to the front at once," he said. "There is no time for systematic training."

He wanted more guns as soon as possible and would I ask the Mission to supply them? He was dissatisfied with the proportion of stores that were allotted to his army and wanted me to represent this to Mission Headquarters.

General Keltchevski then gave me a short résumé of the situation at the front and asked me to call again after I had seen the work at the school to give him my ideas on the progress made.

My whole work in Russia was to be closely connected with Sidorin and his staff and, while outwardly our relations were always most cordial, officially I soon found I had the greatest difficulty in obtaining any information from them whatsoever. From beginning to end I do not think that Sidorin would have taken the slightest notice of any British officer except to invite him to dinner and it was only as a last resort that our advice or assistance was sought with regard to the British material which the Cossacks were receiving. It became necessary, therefore, to *force* myself on his notice and at times even to *demand* attention when I saw our equipment ill-used in the hands of his over-confident but unskilled officers.

Nevertheless, it *was* unusual for a junior British major to wish to poke his nose into the complicated machinery of the Cossack Army, and they were probably aware that many at Mission Headquarters thought it by no means necessary that I should interest myself in anything beyond my normal task of instruction.

Indeed, many of the British officers – senior as well as junior – seemed to have little interest outside their own environment and were unashamedly contemptuous of everything the Russians did, ignoring many of the possibilities which arose for giving assistance. They seemed quite convinced already that they were backing a lost cause. Because of this, I could not always act with the confidence of being supported by my superiors, and the situation was not made easier by the fact that Lambkirk, the Russian-speaking officer who had flown with the Russians, was an old friend of Sidorin's and deliberately laid himself out to cause trouble between us.

It was a situation that left a strange void in communication and did not make for good liaison, and I soon realised that things were likely to be more difficult than I had ever imagined when I had volunteered for Russia.

However, having made myself known to the army staff, Campbell then very wisely suggested a visit to the Bishop of Novocherkassk and accordingly, a day or two later, I called on him. He was a venerable-looking man with a tall silk hat, flowing hair and a greasy long black beard. Wearing a beautiful jewelled chain and cross round his neck, he described how the Bolsheviks had desecrated the churches while occupying the city. They had stolen and broken things and used the altars for drunken parties. He himself had been threatened with death and subjected to all sorts of insults. He gave me an Ikon of St. Sergei, a blessing on the work of the Allies, and an invitation to visit the cathedral and attend any service I liked. He finally kissed me. I was horrified but I subsequently heard that the visit was very favourably regarded by the people, who watched and criticised our every action.

My last visit of ceremony was to General Popov, the Prime Minister of the Don Kroug. Popov was a great friend of Colonel Terence Keyes, of the Mission, who was a brother of Admiral Sir Roger Keyes, a Russian scholar and a fine specimen of Indian Army officer transferred to the Political Department.

A brilliant linguist with experience of the most exciting political and military work all over Northern India, Persia, Arabia and Russia – where he had remained throughout the Revolution in some most mysterious capacity – Keyes immediately threw a spell over me so that I gave him the sort of hero worship which one expects to leave behind on leaving school or after the first year of regimental service. Unfortunately, for some reason I never fathomed, he had no love for the Don Cossacks and accused them of Germanism, Separatism and even Bolshevik sympathies and poor fighting qualities. Though once or twice I got into his bad books for my open championship of them, we still remained good friends, though neither of us ever convinced the other and I often felt ashamed to be taking a line that was in direct opposition to the most brilliant and most experienced of all the British officers who served in South Russia. Perhaps he deliberately drew me or perhaps he had inside knowledge which it was not good for me to know, but he certainly continued to think the same way long after he left Russia. He was a tremendous character who was held in very high esteem by the Russians. His sympathetic attitude to them was most unusual, because most Indian Army officers were antagonistic for the simple reason that for generations Russia had been considered to be a menace to the British in the East. Keyes, however, had served in a liaison capacity with the Russian Army in Rumania, and his word was taken by every Russian of rank as "British Law", and he was universally popular. Constantly up at the front, he returned to his headquarters at Rostov only on flying visits.

*

Now that I had laid the foundation of my work, I took the first opportunity of accepting one of the private invitations which I had received. British officers used to go frequently to a family called Abramov, who were well-to-do banking people. Madame Abramov spoke a little French and her husband nothing but Russian, but her two young daughters spoke excellent English. At one of their parties I met Moussia and Alex Smaguin.

Alex, a minor aristocrat whose father had been a famous general, had been a colonel in the Empress's Lancers. He was a good-natured, smiling, round, red-faced man of forty-five, full of good intentions but lazy, too fond of wine and really nothing but a cheerful nonentity. His wife, Moussia, was a very different type, however. Of medium height with brown hair and enormous eyes, she was younger than Alex, had good looks, a good figure and fine delicate hands, and above all, a tremendous personality. She spoke perfect English, learned as a small girl at school in England and at the Smolnia, the leading Russian girls' school in Petrograd. She also spoke Japanese which she had acquired while nursing in the East in the Russo-Japanese War.

Like many others of their society, she and Alex had decided to move from Petrograd as a result of Kaledin's promise of safety and, train-hopping during the autumn of 1917, they had made their way south. Alex, from being a wealthy officer in a crack regiment, was now dependent on the small wage he drew from his position on Bogaievski's staff, but it was enough to buy them food and in this they were probably luckier than many. They had sold almost everything they possessed, however, and now lived in a very small house with a daily help. I was to become great friends with them.

This particular evening the party was a large one, and included Count Bezobrazov, an old Chevalier Guard officer, and his wife, one of the most beautiful women of Russian Court society; Madam Bogaievski, wife of the Ataman, and her daughter by her first marriage; Madame Pashkov, who used an eyeglass and a perfect English drawl; her son Alexis, another

Chevalier Guard officer, educated at Cambridge and now one
of our liaison officers; Helen Abramov – no relation of the
other Abramovs; Alexis Aladin, a representative of the Labour
Party in the First Douma about whom I had already been
warned at headquarters; officials of the Don Government; and
Rechitovski, a staff officer, and his beautiful wife, a woman
with snow-white hair and the features of a girl, who was
quietly but elegantly dressed in black and looked as if she
might have stepped straight out of some eighteenth-century
French picture. She spoke French fluently and I was lucky
enough to sit next to her at supper.

The first introductions, which involved shaking hands with
everybody in the room were rather alarming and, as I was not
yet conversant with the "rules of procedure" of a Russian
supper party, fears of doing or eating the wrong thing entirely
spoilt the first few minutes of the meal. Madame Rechitovski
was quick to put me at my ease, however, and I soon got going
in my villainous French. Born a Romanovski, Madame
Rechitovski had lived mostly in Moscow and had been forced
to flee to the Cossack country with her husband to escape
certain death.

I managed to talk with all the other guests who spoke
English or French and especially with the dubious Aladin. He
was obviously unwilling to leave the safer channels of un-
important chit-chat but he was a strong personality, though he
was inclined to talk so lengthily round the point under discussion that it invariably disappeared from view. Possibly this
was intentional, but both then and later I adopted with him
the method of going straight to the point, because I knew that
once I got involved in conversational fencing matches with a
man of his ability, it would be all up with me. We became good
friends and I held him in great esteem without ever getting to
terms of the slightest mental intimacy. He always professed
the strongest anglophile sympathies, and associated himself
with all charitable organisations for the good of the soldiers
or the refugees, but, owing to his personal friendship
with the Ataman, the Generals of the Don Army, and

in fact with everybody of note, he frequently acted as a go-between between the authorities and dissident political parties.

He was very firmly on the bad books of the Mission Headquarters on account of his association with the First Douma and the German occupation forces with whom he was reported to have been too friendly. Keyes, in particular, was very antagonistic towards him and his attitude was always, "Keep away from him. He's one of those pro-German swine!"

The talk was nostalgic and the women sighed for pretty clothes which were not only unobtainable but entirely beyond their means. Moussia Smaguin probably possessed very little other than what she stood up in and, though she and her friends sometimes tried to sew clothes, they were not always very good at it. They had previously always employed seamstresses but they could no longer afford them as they had had to sell almost everything they possessed just to keep themselves fed.

Everyone was remarkably cheerful, however, but occasionally there were odd little gaps in the conversation, hastily covered with a quick smile, which showed how pathetically the circumstances of most of the guests had changed. Their minds were full of their hopes and fears but they tried desperately hard not to bore one with them, and they always changed the subject with a toast – "*Na Moskvu,*" To Moscow, or "Moscow by Christmas."

Most of the parties were merely tea-drinking or supper parties, where there was a volunteer amateur guitarist who would intermingle conversation with a chord here and a few lines there of some of the most popular Russian gypsy or national folk songs.

Ochen Tchornya, which we all knew, was always popular, as also was *The Song Of Stenka Razin,* a pretty ballad which became extremely popular with the British. It related the activities of a famous seventeenth-century Don Cossack who captured a lovely Persian princess in a raid. Becoming enamoured of her, he found he was neglecting his band of brigands, so, rather than desert his faithful men, he threw his beloved into the Don where she drowned.

Occasionally the parties took place in small cheerful restaurants, decorated with tapestries and rugs and – considering what had happened in Novocherkassk – with a surprising amount of assorted silverware and white linen. There were always a great many officers there with their women, most of them senior officers who never seemed short of time to relax. Occasionally mazurkas or country dances were performed but, though they were pretty, they weren't much in my line. However, from time to time, I got going in a polka or a Viennese waltz, and my partners always appeared satisfied, though I determined that I must teach somebody a two-step.

To pay the bill, you had to produce sheaves of paper money, most of which was pretty valueless. There were Kerensky roubles, Romanov roubles, and Denikin roubles, all printed by different governments, but most of them had been around so long it was becoming difficult to get them exchanged, and people were already preferring to barter instead.

Supper cost about 160 roubles but, as before the war, the rouble was 10 to the pound and had since jumped to 40 and then to 80 and finally to 165, one needed a great deal to pay the bill, particularly if it were for a party. In these restaurants, the drink was a little stronger than tea from a samovar, and nostalgia and Crimean wine worked on each other in a vicious circle so that the toasts – always including *"Na Moskvu"* – were drunk faster and faster as the music from twanging balalaikas and beribboned accordions grew louder and more insistent. Invariably the younger members of the party eventually lost control.

On one occasion in a small restaurant patronised by refugee society, toasts drunk to the Tsar, to the British, to Denikin and others, became noisier and more hysterical until one of the orators, who had drunk too much Abrau Durso, the Tsarist champagne, collapsed across the table, crashing crockery and glassware to the floor amid storms of applause.

No one turned a hair as he slid slowly from his chair and disappeared out of sight.

My next-door neighbour, Princess Tchebyshov beamed.

"How wonderful it is," she said proudly, "to see someone so gloriously drunk they cannot stand up. It is in such a good cause."

CHAPTER FOUR

From the first day of my arrival at Novocherkassk, the world-famed hospitality of the Russians was always in evidence. It was the custom of the country that unless a guest was considerably the worse for wine on his departure, he was not considered to have been honourably entertained, and I certainly left many functions very much the worse for wear.

"I wish the government at home could realise," Keyes said, "how often I have to get drunk to get anything done at all."

At every party I visited, however, I always felt I was being entertained by the best host in the world who had specially laid himself out to do me honour. The Russian excelled at this, and even when in the lowest of water would always submerge himself to try to give pleasure. Only the best was ever good enough to offer, and I had to show enormous tact. Like Keyes, I found that unless I was prepared to drink as much as my companions I was not likely to command any esteem from them or get much co-operation in my work, and I therefore made it a rule to do my best on the first meeting to conform with the custom, and, having proved my ability, to make excuses on subsequent occasions. I might otherwise never have recovered.

In addition to private parties, we were also invited to an incredible number of official banquets, the first and most impressive of which was given for us by the Ataman and the staff of the Don Army in the hall of the Ataman's palace, right next door to the room where Kaledin had shot himself.

The guards were drawn from the Regiment of Cossack Bodyguard to the late Tsar, whose remnants were now incorporated in the Don Cossack Army, and carriages had been arriving for some time when we appeared. Guests in blazing uniforms, studded with decorations and glittering with jewels, epaulettes, brilliant sword-hilts and polished boots, stared with curiosity at our drab khaki jackets and lack of ostentation as we entered the hall. The banquet was attended by about a hundred and fifty generals, staff and regimental officers, some of them from the highest of Moscow and Petrograd society; members of the Douma; government officials; and church dignitaries, with the Bishop himself – in full robes, too! – to pronounce the Blessing.

The first half-hour or so was occupied in eating "zakouskis" or hors-d'oeuvres – a meal in themselves – standing round a large table in a separate room. Only the most important guests were admitted to this room and every friendly greeting had to be responded to with the ubiquitous glass of vodka. The table was covered with caviare of all sorts; radishes and butter; hot slices of tender mutton baked with cabbage and carrots; kidneys; pancakes; and hot potatoes covered with white sauce.

Throughout these preliminaries Count du Chayla was constantly at my elbow, presenting me to first one and then the other much-decorated general or colonel with a breastful of orders and a clanking sword. I thought I should never get through it, but at last the signal for a move was given by the Ataman and we filed into the banqueting hall where dinner was prepared on two long tables stretching the whole length of the room. I was on the left of the Ataman, who sat at the head of one table with Sidorin on his right, and Angus Campbell was on my left to do any translating which should be necessary. The other British officers were scattered throughout the company with an interpreter handy to each. At the end of the hall to sing a choral grace was the Cossack choir from the Cathedral, about sixty men and women in long blue surplices with silver girdles and trimmings. Without any orchestral accompaniment whatever, they also offered selections of old Russian folk songs, Cossack melodies and national dance tunes which they sang with tremendous dash and in perfect time.

The thought of responding to the official toasts under such impressive circumstances quite ruined the meal for me and I hardly tasted the food that followed. Then I remembered that no one would understand a word of what I said till it was translated by Campbell, and it seemed to me that he had the worst job of the two of us. The Ataman led off with a welcome and ended by calling for the health of King George and the British Mission. The wildest enthusiasm greeted this toast which was honoured with the drawing and flourishing of swords, and a great deal of cheering and clapping which lasted several minutes. It was exciting to find myself on my feet to reply, standing in the great hall of the Cossack Chief's palace with its walls covered with pictures of past Atamans of the Don, and with its magnificent crystal candelabra blazing with light. Looking down the long table I saw uniforms of all sorts, generals of the staff, Cossacks from the Caucasus and Terek, ex-Imperial Guard Cavalry officers, officers of the Line regiments, priests, the British in their khaki jackets, and, at the far end, the blue-and-silver-clad choir.

Every eye turned on me, and what a strange line of heads there seemed as I looked down on them! Mostly close-cropped crowns surmounting black- or brown-bearded faces wearing an air of sympathetic tolerance for the eccentricities of a few enthusiastic representatives of Britain, who actually felt they could reorganise and re-equip the armed forces of South Russia in a matter of weeks. Most of these men had held big commands and high official positions under the old regime and were not Cossacks, and there was still a feeling running through them all – many of them officers of the Empress's Lancers or the Chevalier Guard – that the Cossacks were their inferiors, the frontier guards of the Empire who were called in to do the dirty work of the capital. These officers had originally only joined the Don peasants because of Red hatred or because of something they had done against the Bolsheviks in Moscow or St Petersburg, and an element of snobbishness still existed. A humble battery commander like myself would not normally have received much consideration from them.

I think Angus Campbell was even more nervous than I was but, as he spoke in a rather low voice, his translation was possibly not heard at all. I made no mention of monarchy or politics or of the Don Army being separate from the Armed Forces of South Russia, but our joint effort was received with cheering and more drinking of healths. The British National Anthem, the Don Cossacks' Hymn, and – inevitably – "Tipperary" were sung, followed by speeches by the Bishop, General Konovallov, the crack cavalry general of the 2nd Division, and others who were keen to say something kind about us. Between speeches, the choir sang Russian songs.

By this time many diners were becoming rather noisy and about midnight, some of the more reckless were conveyed limply home and the lower ends of the tables were removed to leave half the hall vacant. Several of the choir girls then threw off their surplices and, egged on by the rest, gave examples of Russian dancing, and four soldiers of a Caucasian Cavalry Regiment also did the famous *Lisgintka* or Caucasian national dance. They were bearded ruffians in long-skirted reddish brown coats, or *tcherkasses*, with golden cartridge cases across their chests and inlaid swords and daggers and long flat-heeled boots. They danced to the music of accordions, violins and balalaikas and, as the music grew faster and faster, they performed extraordinary feats with their razor-sharp daggers which they clashed together while holding them in their teeth or balanced behind their necks, while the audience beat time, clapped and sang.

The music ended with the usual wild toasts of "Christmas in Moscow," everybody banging their fists on the table and cheering, and it was daylight before I got away.

I was glad it was only two hundred yards to my quarters.

*

Soon afterwards I had to attend a banquet given by the Society of Landlords in Novocherkassk, which followed a dinner given by the Ataman to Keyes, who came up from Rostov for a few days to see how things were going with us.

"Sometimes," he said, "I wonder if we're here to eat or fight our way to Moscow."

The affair was held in the house of Professor Ilovaiski, one of our interpreters, and clearly the main idea was to impress upon the British the importance and goodwill of the aristo-cratic land-owners who were watching with interest the de-velopment of the land laws with regard to expropriation and the division of their possessions among the peasants.

This question of the land was always a stumbling block between Denikin and the large bulk of his supporters – espec-ially the Cossacks, who longed to control the large stretches of countryside which had previously belonged to the land-owning classes. It is possible, in fact, that the uncompromising attitude of Denikin's government on this question lost him much support and when, in the following spring, he conceded points to the peasants on the subject, it was too late and the damage was done. Needless to say, the Society of Landlords were strong champions of the retention of the land in the hands of its original owners, and every effort was made by them to pre-vent Denikin passing any laws to expropriate it. By getting on the right side of the British officers they thought that their cause would receive the support of Mission Headquarters.

At this affair I met a few new friends such as Princess Volkonski, who had written several articles for the London papers under the pseudonym of "Russian Patriot", and who, with her two daughters, was living as a refugee in Novocher-kassk. Her son had been killed on the German front and she, like all the others, had lost everything she possessed. Her jewels were now being sold, piece by piece, to provide food, and her daughters were endeavouring to make a little money by typing whenever they could obtain employment. The Princess was one of the most bitter anti-Bolshevik speakers and writers I ever met but her opinion of the Reds was always so forcible that it detracted from the literary merit of her articles.

The usual toasts were proposed and small speeches made, but Keyes, knowing quite well we were in a hot-bed of monarchists, was especially careful not to give any sign of sympathy with that particular sentiment. It was a point on which he had always given me most emphatic orders, though I often found it very hard to carry out these instructions without a feeling of disloyalty to my own King.

This evening was an unlucky one owing to the exuberance of one of our interpreters, Prince Lichtemberski, a cousin of the Tsar and an officer of the Cossack Guard Regiment. He was only twenty-three and was one of the first officers to be attached to our Mission. He had fought with distinction on the German front, but like many of the ill-fated Romanovs, he displayed a fanatical tendency towards religion and had passed various degrees of proficiency for high office in the Church. He was a pale, wild-eyed boy, with a passion for music and played the piano beautifully. He was also an expert player of the chimes in the Cathedral, and performed this duty for many of the most important church services when he could be spared from his work – and often when he couldn't, so that if he were urgently needed, we got into the habit of listening if the bells were ringing or not. I went with him once to watch him and it was extraordinary to see the absorption he displayed when manipulating two sets of chimes with his hands and one or two of the larger bells with his feet. The biggest one of all was so large it took a full-grown man to swing the tongue enough to give it a regular peal twice a minute.

These monastic pursuits, however, did not prevent him from being an excessive "bon vivant", and this particular evening was no exception to the rule. With each glass of liquor he drank, his devotion to the late Tsar and his advocacy of a restored monarchy became more pronounced and, after the first two or three toasts, he rose to his feet and demanded the silence and attention which his rank and name would have received under any conditions in any corner of anti-Bolshevik Russia. In halting English and with a pathos that can only be understood by those who knew how these Russian nobles had suffered, he put forward his feelings.

To the old nobility, the Tsar was the very basis of the

society they belonged to but he had been murdered with his family and several of his entourage at Ekaterinburg just beyond the Ural Mountains, where they had been taken to avoid rescue by the Whites. They had all been brutally shot in a cellar and their bodies had been thrown down a disused mine shaft. Fragments of their corpses and other relics had been later rescued and identified as the Reds had been driven back, but their deaths had left people like Lichtemberski rootless and aimless and highly unstable, and they were ripe for plots and intrigues. We well knew there were always people like him who were acknowledged monarchists and were only lying low until the Romanovs returned, but until this particular evening I had never realised just how emotional they were about it and knowing our professed policy of neutrality in this matter, I was horrified as Lichtemberski spoke.

"Once upon a time," he said, "we had a Tsar as great and as good a man as the English King we have been toasting. We also had a country, beautiful, rich and covering half the world. Now we have nothing. Our Tsar has been murdered, our cities have been ruined, our lands are in the hands of Jews and convicts, and are overrun by Chinese soldiers." He paused. "We still have something left, however. We have hope and I call on you all now to drink with me to the future Tsar!"

The wildest enthusiasm greeted the speech, and people leapt to their feet and to their chairs to raise their glasses, their faces flushed with patriotic fervour – and more than a little wine. Glasses flew and the place became like a madhouse for a while, then as the crashing and the cheers died away, Lichtemberski turned to a band of Cossack musicians who, so I understood, had very democratic – if not actually Bolshevik – sympathies, and ordered them to play the old Russian National Anthem, which had been forbidden since the Revolution. It was sung by the whole company, some standing on chairs and some on the table, and as they resumed their seats, Lichtemberski gave an excellent display of Russian dancing.

I shot several looks at Keyes during this period. He was obviously tremendously angry at being associated with the gathering and he never forgave Lichtemberski, who went to join Alexis Aladin on the already long black list of people associated with the Don Cossacks.

*

The banquets we were expected to attend were far too numerous for my liking and involved sitting up much too late. At another dinner party a week later, given by Sidorin, sentries were even posted to clear the streets between his house and ours, to prevent us being jeered at or accosted by the townspeople on our return.

"Enjoy yourselves, sir officers," he said gaily, giving that curious attractive chuckle of his. "And have no fear. I am posting men along the route to your hotel in case you should be embarrassed on your way home."

At this party, I made the acquaintance of the widow of General Kaledin, who had shot himself in the Ataman's palace the previous year as the Bolsheviks were entering the town. She was charming and half-French and had suffered terribly during her husband's struggle to save the Don from the Reds.

I also met Madame Sidorin, a Siberian woman, and Colonel Agaiev, Sidorin's A.D.C., who became known to us, because of his dubious loyalties, as Dirty Dick. He was a very difficult character to deal with and was devoted to Sidorin, with whom he seemed to share a strong distrust of the British. Although our opening talks – conducted through interpreters – were hesitant, however, we somehow found that our ideas struck a mutual chord, and in the end we became fast friends, despite the fact that I never really trusted him and that we never understood a word we ever spoke to one another without the aid of an interpreter.

I was growing wholeheartedly tired of parties and celebrations by the end of May. Only the guests and the surroundings varied – never the toasts, the wild enthusiasm for "*Na Moskvu*" or the amount of drink that was offered – and I was becoming desperately anxious to do some real work now that the diplomatic overtures were behind me.

Throughout the last week of the month and during June, however, British stores of all sorts began to filter up to Don Army Headquarters, and six batteries of 18-pounders and two of 4.5 howitzers had been equipped and were en route for the front. Some naval guns had also been handed over for use on power-driven armed barges on the Don, and others were being mounted on armoured trains. A good supply of Vickers and Lewis guns was also appearing at the front, together with quite a show of khaki uniforms.

The morale of the troops had improved considerably in recent weeks, too. Wrangel had won a tremendous cavalry victory at Veliko Knyazhesk, on the railway to Tsaritsyn, and the Reds had been driven northwards again. Tsaritsyn, Liski, Kharkov and Poltava were now the objectives of the main operations of the White Armies, and already the Donets Valley and the network of railways south of Kharkov had been cleared of the enemy. A successful rising of Cossacks on the North Don had cleared a large area round Ust Medvyeditsa of Soviet troops and Mamentov's Cavalry Corps of Don Cossacks had broken through on the Likhaia-Tsaritsyn railway and joined with the insurgents. They had been followed by the 1st and 2nd Don Corps, who were clearing up the country, collecting recruits and advancing north-eastwards of the Likhaia-Voronezh railway in an endeavour to clear the whole Don area and consolidate the railway line from Povorino to Liski. The 3rd Don Corps, having crossed the Donets at Kamenkaya and Lugansk, were advancing in line with the 2nd Corps, north of the railway line. Wrangel was preparing for the capture of Tsaritsyn on our right flank; and Mai-Maievski with the Volunteer Army was going strong on our left, assisted by the redoubtable Skouro with the Caucasian Cavalry Corps, including his own famous "Wolf Pack".

Short, weatherbeaten and sporting a long yellow moustache, Skouro was one of the characters of the Civil War. Never without his wolfskin cap and the red, blue and white ribbon of the Volunteer Army on his sleeve, he was a Caucasian from one of the mountain tribes, savage and cruel as the best of them,

and his regiment of three to four hundred cavalrymen all wore
wolfskin caps instead of astrakhan wool. They had their
headquarters in their own special collection of railway trucks,
on which were painted a pack of wolves in pursuit of prey,
and they were a particularly fierce and relentless collection of
mountaineers, carrying the usual armoury of a *kinjal* or dagger
at their waist, a sword slung over the shoulder, a revolver
whenever possible, and rows of cartridge cases for rifles across
each side of their chests. Skouro was undoubtedly a great
cavalry leader but, as we'd been told, he was also a bit of a
brigand and, on one occasion, accompanied by three or four of
his officers, he entered the ballroom of a big hotel in Rostov
where dancing was in progress and invited all the guests to
contribute in jewellery or cash towards the maintenance of his
Wolves. Confronted by glittering eyes beneath the shaggy
wolf's hair and remembering the Wolves' reputation for ruthless pillage and lack of mercy, no one argued. He made a very
successful haul.

Not only in the immediate north were things going well.
News from the Siberian front indicated that Kolchak was also
sweeping all before him in his drive across the Urals, while the
Ural Cossack Corps working up the eastern bank of the Caspian
Sea was making good progress to get in touch with him.

Things were beginning to look much better for the Whites,
it seemed, but, to a close student of the situation, it was still
quite obvious that full benefit was not being derived from the
very large amount of war material which had by this time been
landed at Novorossiisk. The railways were in a hopeless
muddle because, though the officials remained neutral and
claimed to favour neither side and only carried out the orders
of the occupying troops, there were many with Communist
sympathies among the workers who didn't hesitate to throw
things into confusion whenever they got the opportunity. In
addition, since the revolution, older men had been replaced by
newcomers who weren't so skilled, and there was a great deal
of thieving by junior members of the staff at the ordnance
stores, and by officials on the railway and at the dumps.

Everyone was aware of this but we were also aware that there was no means of stopping it. As a British officer, I could do nothing except remonstrate when it was discussed, and feel miserable when I had to meet men who were devoid of even the simplest necessities.

On one occasion when I was to inspect a parade of fighting soldiers, I had dressed in my best uniform which included a very smart pair of boots. Angus Campbell was horrified.

"You can't wear those boots," he said. "Some of these poor devils haven't any boots at all!"

Despite the number of old British uniforms which were beginning to pour into South Russia, surprisingly few ever found their way to the men who needed them most. Apart from the pilfering, the love of Russian officers in charge of stores for getting them filled and *keeping* them filled was allowed unlimited licence, and the water-tight compartments in which all branches of their staff worked resulted in the enormous accumulation of spare parts for artillery, uniform and hospital equipment at Novocherkassk, Ekaterinodar, Rostov and Novorossiisk. Nobody would give orders for its distribution at all and, added to all this, the whole policy of the British Mission was at fault in that once stores had been landed at Novorossiisk they became the property of the Russians to handle and distribute as they liked. The assistance of the British officers was only given when asked for, which was not often. We had no authority to interfere in the appalling muddle which existed, even though we saw our good equipment rotting in the goods yards, or spoiled and wasted by the inexperienced and never over-energetic Russian officers at the bases.

There were, however, nothing like enough British officers to make much headway in the work, and any effort on the part of individuals to take a strong line or to visit the front to study the conditions was severely squashed by Mission Headquarters Staff, and the policy of masterly inactivity which ruled at Ekaterinodar where headquarters was established never looked like being the right one to meet the situation. The policy commended itself to the Russian High Command, however, because this was very largely composed of ex-Imperial Officers brought up in the old Russian School and the policy did not demand much personal supervision on the part of officers of exalted rank, or for that matter of any rank at all. Thus, what would have appeared to British officers as a lack of initiative, was regarded as entirely the correct attitude – and a very commendable one, too! – by many Russian senior officers whose personality alone made them popular to Denikin and his staff.

To be fair to them, however, our Russian friends had been soundly beaten on most fronts by the Germans, had lost all their possessions, many relations, and most of their country, and had barely escaped with their lives from one of the bloodiest revolutions on record. They were ill-equipped; they drew barely enough pay to keep body and soul together; and they were placed haphazardly with all sorts of troops – mostly deserters from the Red army – whose loyalty was by no means assured. They had no railway communications worth speaking of and only such telegraphic and telephonic liaison as could be adapted from existing arrangements. They had no hope of running anything successfully without strong leadership.

Who should have insisted on action I don't know, but I do know that the lack of a definite policy and the British "Let Russia work out her own salvation" idea, which was carried out to the last letter of the law, very nearly wrecked everything in the early summer of 1919.

Though for the moment the Reds were retreating northwards, things were nevertheless becoming very critical for British prestige when an unexpected change took place at Mission Headquarters, and General Briggs, who had requested to be allowed to go home, was replaced by Major-General H. C. Holman. Adjutant and Quartermaster-General with the British Fourth Army in France, Holman was a man who was known to be an expert Russian-speaker and to have a great deal of sympathy with the country, and we suddenly began to hope for big things.

*

During the month of May I made a trip by train to inspect the equipping of a 4.5 howitzer battery. In the middle of the steppes, the engine – an ancient model with a funnel like a six-foot bucket – broke down and we came to a stop miles from anywhere. After the clatter of the wheels, the silence seemed ominous and the steppe around the track seemed bare, lifeless and depressing. During the journey we had seen little life beyond the drab brown villages with their square thatched wooden houses, and the emptiness of the steppe seemed eerie.

"What's happened?" someone asked.

"Engine's given up the ghost," came the reply.

Prince Lichtemberski, who was with us as an interpreter, decided that the cause was lack of fuel and struggled manfully to persuade the engine driver to stoke up with wood from a stack beside the lines. It was a losing battle, however, and he finally returned and reported cheerfully that the engine refused to respond to *any* type of fuel.

"Now the train is entirely broken," he said gaily, "so we must wait for another one."

As we knew that Communist cavalry patrols had cut through in the neighbourhood and had been trying to destroy the line, this suggestion had little appeal.

We stared across the empty steppes. There was nothing to see except grass and flowers, and an occasional partridge, and nothing to hear except the slow escape of steam over the singing of the larks.

Eventually someone chivvied the engine crew into making repairs, bullying them when they preferred to flap their hands and blame everyone but themselves, and we managed to start again. I wasn't sorry to reach our destination.

*

I regularly sought out Keyes for advice and information. He lived in a very pleasant flat in Rostov near the river and was assisted by Captain Walker, of the Bays, and Captain Ivanyenko, a Russian cavalry officer with an international horse-show reputation, while his clerical work was in the hands of

Princess Cantacuzene who, as well as being very beautiful and amusing, spoke amazingly good English and organised his office with great skill. His flat was a resting place for any British officer held up at Rostov overnight, whether he was there himself or not, and his hospitality was proverbial.

In contrast to most of what I had already seen of the British Mission, Keyes was essentially the man of action, and in June he was named Political Representative for the British Government at Rostov, which meant that he did everything, went everywhere, and carried out liaison duties of all kinds. More than most things, he was involved in the organisation and control of the Intelligence Branch which was endeavouring to combat the skilful propaganda carried out by numerous German and Bolshevik agents in the town.

I often suspected Count Du Chayla and Alexis Aladin of German sympathies and for a time even suspected Du Chayla of being a German agent.

There were certainly plenty about, because the struggle of the Don Cossacks against the Bolsheviks had always been maintained by outside aid which had come originally from the Germans, either directly from occupation troops, or from the Ukrainians who had received it from the same source. The Don Army was even organised on the German system and they certainly had a very strong admiration for German efficiency. Many of the German officers who had been in the occupation forces at Novocherkassk and Rostov, in fact, had spared neither money nor trouble to ingratiate themselves with all classes of the inhabitants, and they had taken over the railway and telegraphic systems and introduced into them more efficiency than ever before. With the Bolsheviks they had dealt sternly and drastically.

Added to this, Russia had always had a great admiration for German art and the German system of education. The two races had intermarried a great deal because of their geographical position, and many of Russia's greatest rulers, including the great Catherine herself, came of much purer German than Russian blood. Despite the Great War, there had always been a strong Germanophile party throughout Russia, and a million and a quarter pure-blooded German colonists had been introduced into the country by Catherine to set an example in tidiness, thrift and agricultural efficiency. As a community, these Germans had been ultra-loyal to Russia throughout the war, but individually many of them were before all else Germans, and the Fatherland had always held the uppermost place in their hearts. Among them there was soil by no means ill-suited to the ever-diligent sower.

Georgia, Batum and Constantinople were still full of German prisoners and swarms of sympathetic citizens were ready to carry on propaganda work for her, so that although she was in no position herself to exploit any channel of colonial aggrandisement which might be open, she could still prevent others from doing so. Every malcontent in the Middle East was, therefore, encouraged to stir up civil wars and local insurrections in the hope that the principal combatants would become weaker and weaker, while France, Great Britain and Italy, whom the greatest diplomacy had barely succeeded in keeping united during the Great War, would gradually become antagonistic to one another.

Because of all this, we knew the German agents were working on the pro-German sympathies of White Russian officers caused by birth or education, and their jealousy of the British; of the Don Cossacks; of General Petr Wrangel – who was of German descent – and many old regime officers under him in the Caucasian Army, many of whom considered Denikin far too democratic; and of Georgia whose dreams of independence had been spread by German ex-prisoners of war to excite the people against both the British and Denikin. In addition, we had to contend with German instructors with the Bolshevik armies; with the presence of German personnel fighting for the Ukrainians against Denikin as well as against the Bolsheviks; with German assistance to Nestor Mahkno, who was running the bands of insurgent peasants in the Ekaterinoslav area; and with the rumoured presence in Rostov of Kochenhausen, former Chief of German Secret Police, who eluded all efforts to bring him to book.

There was a tremendous undercurrent of pro-German sympathy running through the Don Army Staff, and the intrigues were enormous; and it was never possible to tell who really believed what. The ramifications of South Russian politics always bedevilled everything we tried to do, and I finally came to the conclusion that the chief agent for this particular type of nuisance was the smiling and debonair chief of the Political Section, my friend Count Du Chayla. Of his constant profession of devotion to England and assiduous efforts to help me and follow me round – which usually ended in my work being interfered with – I soon became very suspicious.

Eventually, though it took me a long time to become convinced of it, I decided that rather than being pro-German by sentiment, he was essentially "pro-Du Chayla" and had realised that conditions in Russia were eminently suitable for a political adventurer of his type. He threw himself heart and soul into fostering the spirit of dissatisfaction, therefore, labelling himself for the purpose a democratic Don Cossack, who hoped for the eventual autonomy of his country.

Keyes had an intense dislike for him from the beginning, but so strongly was he fixed in his post under Sidorin and Khislov, the latter of whom especially was noted for his Don Separatist sentiments, that two successive efforts on the part of British Mission Headquarters, one of them direct from Keyes himself, failed to get him removed or even curtail his activities. Owing to his friendship with Sidorin he was, of course, on good terms with Lambkirk, the part-Russian British officer who was running the machine gun school at Novocherkassk with great success, and this combination of unfriendly spirits, though on the surface they were my most devoted friends, was a nasty thorn in my side. Lambkirk was not associated with Du Chayla's political aspirations, of course, but he was more friendly with this little group of Russians than he was with his brother officers, and so acute did the situation become at the end of June that I was forbidden by Keyes to meet Du Chayla again.

One afternoon, however, I saw him in the Central Hotel. He had evidently drunk a good deal of wine, and contrary to the orders I had received I decided he might be more communicative with just a little more. I invited him to split a bottle of wine with me in my room, and, as I had anticipated, he finally became quite wordy and told me who was on whose side, who was to be trusted and who was not, how much Sidorin had co-operated with the Germans and how much he was still influenced by them – the sort of diplomatic gossip I could store away for future use. In addition, I found some of his tips about the officers of the British Mission, who were beginning to object to the positive way I was working for the Cossacks, surprisingly useful.

Finally he vowed his eternal friendship, and begged me to dine with him the following day as it was his name day and he was intending to have a small celebration.

I arrived at his house at 8 p.m. To my surprise I was the only English officer there and I began to grow a little suspicious immediately. A good deal of wine was drunk, Du Chayla himself surpassing all his guests. Among these was Abramov, an interpreter, a clever little man but of no military ability at all. Like most of the guests, he worked in Du Chayla's office and was no relation to the Abramov banking family or to General Abramov, in command of the 1st Guards Division, whom I later met.

His presence there made me even more dubious about the gathering and I was not particularly surprised when during the evening a quarrel started and ugly words were exchanged. Abramov and Du Chayla came to blows and, as Abramov tried to leave, he was followed into the street by Du Chayla.

Without thinking, I followed them with another guest to try to separate them and found them standing in the darkness under the trees away from the lights, arguing bitterly. Du Chayla was excited and shouting and, as I approached, he lifted his arm and I saw he was holding a revolver. A shot was fired and a bullet came closer to my head than I liked. As we grabbed his hand, Abramov ran away in the darkness, shrieking with terror, and Du Chayla flung us off and struck an attitude of indignation and rage.

"I'll fight a duel with Abramov or you or anybody else," he shouted.

He seemed more than eager to put a bullet through me and it suddenly occurred to me that the whole affair was a put-up job to involve me in a scandal which would result in me being moved from the Don Army group. If I were not there Du Chayla might manage to get me replaced by someone more easy-going and not so likely to interfere in his obstructive activities.

From being an amusing and interesting evening – though one which was made a little tense by my suspicions and the apparent dislike flickering all the time between Du Chayla and Abramov – events had suddenly taken an ominous turn.

"You'd better go," one of the other officers advised me while Du Chayla was still prancing about under the trees in an attitude of hostility. "There's going to be trouble and you'll be well out of it."

I took the hint and vanished and when I went next day to make a formal protest to Sidorin and the Ataman, I received an apology from the latter, but almost complete indifference from Sidorin. Curiously enough, two days later, a request came officially from the British Mission (which I am sure emanated from Keyes's office) that Du Chayla should be dismissed from his position on the Don Staff. Naturally there was no result.

It was about this time also that I began to hear rumours that our equipment was giving dissatisfaction to the Russians, and Norman Lack claimed that Du Chayla was behind these, too.

Since some of the equipment which arrived – apart from portions of it having been pilfered on the way up – had previously been used in Salonika or Egypt, he was spreading wild tales about the "cunning British" exchanging useless and worn-out war stores for concessions in oil, coal and corn which would cripple the new Russia for many years to come. In addition we were accused of deliberately obstructing their artillery officers from taking their batteries to the front. This no doubt arose because I had asked for at least two weeks' battery training, terminating with two days' firing practice under the supervision of a mixed board of British and Russian gunnery instructors. I had been refused, of course, on the grounds that the guns must go to the front at once, but as day succeeded day, for one futile reason or another the batteries remained, wasting time in the back area stations doing very little training.

Partly, this was due to the Russian officers. Some of them were just not sufficiently trained, but many – in personally-designed uniforms made from British khaki – had no intention whatsoever of going to the front and, keeping one eye always over their shoulder on their line of retreat, found every excuse they could to hold up their departure.

I was, therefore, determined to kill the stories of British indifference and mismanagement, and went to Sidorin and demanded a parade of British-armed batteries.

"We must show the population what's already been done," I insisted.

Sidorin nodded. "It is a good plan," he agreed. "I will arrange for the two Boguchar Batteries to be inspected by the Ataman and blessed by the Archbishop in the Cathedral Square, before leaving for the front."

The inspection took place before an enormous crowd and the troops were blessed by bearded priests in long robes, their ringleted hair curling to their shoulders. The batteries made a good show with their British guns, harness and uniform, and we all worked hard to see that the turn-out was more or less correct.

The parade was held outside Novocherkassk Cathedral, and horse-tail regimental standards, which were precious to the Cossacks, were on show. The ranks stretched from one end to the other of the huge square where an altar had been erected in the middle below the statue of Ermak, and the priests, in glittering robes and surrounded by acolytes, performed their offices to the sound of bells rung by Lichtemberski with superb precision. The solemnity of the service was intensified not only by the crucifixes but also by the magnificent bass voices of the choir in their Gregorian chant and by the amazing finale by the trebles.

The Bishop wafted his whisk around to splash holy water on the horses' heads, while above him Ermak looked on with iron eyes from his plinth as the religious canticles soared up into the peaceful air. The *Te Deum* was followed by the presentation of flags and, as the banners changed hands, the officers receiving them dropped on one knee with bowed heads. There were more rumbled prayers and more choral singing, and a great deal of holy water flung about among the rising blue smoke from the swinging censers, then the units marched past the saluting base, their steps firm and vigorous. As the Cossacks cantered off, they broke into song, their officers conducting with *nagaikas* or whips from the front.

It was an impressive ceremony which seemed to indicate strength and stability. Had I only realised it, however, it did neither and it was really the last settled moment I was to have in Russia. As the war began to reach its climax, I was to travel hundreds of miles by horse, car, rail and even air, and I rarely knew from that time onwards until I left Russia where I was to sleep the following night.

CHAPTER FIVE

All this time I had been desperately wanting to reach the front and the fighting troops to see how the batteries we had trained were behaving in action.

The parade was a great success, however, and when Ataman Bogaievski asked me to tea afterwards, even Du Chayla approached with a grin, his fat face sly.

"Mon Commandant," he whispered, *"c'est votre triomphe aujourd'hui, le mise-en-scène était parfait."*

I was glad to get away from him and visit my friends, the Abramovs, the Rechitovskis and the Smaguins, who took me to the hospital run by the Ataman's daughter, Countess Keller. Count Keller had been assassinated in Kiev.

I lunched with the doctors and drank tea – Russian fashion, in glasses from an enormous samovar – with the patients, for whom I was able to produce a thousand English cigarettes. They included a general, a colonel who sang Cossack ballads to a guitar, a private of only fourteen who had been wounded three times, and two Kalmuk troopers who were practically Chinese. Officers and men were in the same room, forty-two of them, with only two girls and a few Bolshevik prisoners to run the show.

Two convalescent officers sang and played for us and the patients gave a concert which included a native dance by a Kalmuk orderly. The Ataman's daughter ran the place efficiently, and her patients were devoted to her and the two sisters who helped her. They were desperately short of medicines and bandages, however, and it only served to make me more eager to get to the front.

I was silent on the way back and when Alex teased me about it, Moussia chided him gently.

"It's always painful to see how desperately we're in need of help," she said.

She talked for a while of the conditions in the hospitals in the East during the Russo-Japanese war and I decided that, *whatever* help was given, somehow the Russian lack of method would always fail to make the best use of it. Even in *that* war they had been unprepared and had been defeated through the same lack of leadership and corruption that was ruining everything they did now. The selfishness and indifference of the officers, which was proverbial and always part of the old Imperial system, never gave even the best of them the unswerving loyalty of their men, many of whom could have become fine soldiers with the right officers.

These men were patient, good-humoured and hard-working but they were largely despised by their officers and treated abominably. It took a great deal to discourage them but their officers *did* discourage them and they deserted constantly in ones and twos and groups; and, sometimes even, when attacks were pressed by shouting staff officers on excited horses, they simply rose up en masse, murdered their officers and walked over to the enemy.

Leadership at all levels, in fact, was dreadful, and with the poor example set them by their officers, the men had no heart for fighting their own countrymen. Those who didn't desert were often sent home from the front line suffering from self-inflicted wounds. If a man was caught after deserting, he was usually shot and I heard there was even a practice of offering rewards for anyone who brought in a deserter, alive or dead. This did little but encourage murder, as all sorts of people were killed down dark alleyways, dressed in a rag of uniform and hauled before the authorities for the reward. All it did as far as the deserters were concerned, was encourage them to disappear in even greater numbers for their own safety.

As for the leaders, their decisions were always wrong. Right from the beginning, the statesmen – Russian and Allied alike – guessed wrongly. If the Allies had been wholehearted about their anti-Communism and had sent sufficient troops in the early days, they could have walked into Moscow, because at that time the Reds were as demoralised as the Whites and a few battle-trained regiments could have cut through the defences like a knife through butter. But the statesmen tried to keep up a pretence of neutrality to the rest of the world, and everything was only half-done or not done at all.

In addition, the colossal financial problems of the White governments never diminished, so that the printed paper roubles, though they looked smart and crackled encouragingly, depreciated so rapidly there was a saying that Denikin could not turn the handle of the printing machine fast enough. Finally, his commanders rarely showed much imagination. No general liked to be led by another general, and as they all had too much power, there was never any unity of command. They could have held out for years if they had retreated to strong points or co-ordinated their efforts, but they were always plagued by ambition or laziness, which persuaded them to do too much or not enough, or by sheer unadulterated indifference.

We all knew that places on trains which should have been given up to the wounded were sometimes occupied by women who had no right to be there, living in comparative luxury under some general's protection, while injured men dragged themselves along on foot. Whole trains were occupied by influential officers who should have been with their men, while sick and wounded officers in the hospitals were refused places and were sometimes even left behind to be murdered by the advancing Reds. One French general called these trains "bordels roulants".

I was fully aware of all this corruption and laziness, and the way jokes were made.

"How do you think General Asnikov's girl friend looks in that cloth that was sent out for the Red Cross nurses?" I heard for instance, and we all knew that, like many others, she wasn't a nurse at all and only adopted the disguise to enable her to remain with the general at his headquarters. However, my attitude was that it was the worst possible form to criticise a people who had suffered so severely, and I managed to avoid seeing some of the worst excesses. I just didn't want to see them, in fact. I was already greatly attached to the Don Cossacks and preferred not to look. And as many of the British officers who made the remarks were doing pretty well, thank you, with the whisky, I felt that we had no right to be sarcastic at the expense of those who had endured more than we could ever conceive.

My letters home probably bored to tears everyone who read them. They probably thought I had lost all my sense of proportion, but I felt terribly involved with the sufferings of the Russians and wrote constantly to my mother asking her to help with comforts for the refugees or in trying to encourage British politicians to do more.

*

I was still wretchedly aware that I was doing little to help and constantly demanded to be allowed to go to the front. About the most I had done was inspect the British-armed batteries of Semiliatov's Don Partisan Division and even this had not been a great success. I was supposed to have gone in a special train but, thanks to one of Du Chayla's triumphs of disorganisation, I had ended up in a bug-ridden third-class carriage on a troop train. Even the official luncheons I had to attend didn't always work out properly. At one of them, a Russian officer I had had to take with me to interpret instead of Campbell, found it necessary to faint three times, not from the vodka, as might have been expected, but presumably from the sun coupled with some sort of emotion at the importance of the occasion. There hadn't been another soul present who could speak English and only one with as much French as I had myself.

I was in low spirits and thoroughly unhappy with some of the officers under my command and aware of a certain amount of bad feeling towards me because they preferred the old easy-going way of running things. I was even beginning to sense that the Mission was also growing tired of my enthusiasm and, when I finally received an invitation from the Ataman to go with him to the front I was delighted at the thought of leaving.

On referring the matter to Headquarters, however, I was refused permission, but Keyes finally relented and made another
suggestion.

"I'll take you myself," he said and, without asking leave, we
set off for the 3rd Don Corps Headquarters at Lugansk.

We had barely started, however, when Keyes was recalled
urgently by a panicky message about intrigue at Rostov which
had begun there immediately after his departure and which he
alone could deal with, so he stopped at Novocherkassk on his
way back and asked Sidorin, who was himself due to visit the
front, to take me with him.

I was told to be ready to leave immediately on the Commander-in-Chief's train together with Cuthbert Hargreaves,
who was an old pre-war friend of mine, and an interpreter.

Angus Campbell was not well and Lack was not available
and a hurried search was made for Lichtemberski. The cathedral bells were ringing, and I was just wondering if I had
time to have him called when Lambkirk appeared and said *he'd*
been asked by Sidorin to go along. I wasn't very keen on Lambkirk because he was too much a crony of Sidorin's, but it
seemed I had no choice and I hurried away to pack my suitcase.

"Mission Headquarters won't be sorry to see me go," I said
to Hargreaves as we climbed into the waiting car. "They don't
like me very much and, as I'll be getting the sack when I return,
I might as well enjoy myself."

We roared through the streets to the station, where we were
met by Colonel Agaiev, Sidorin's A.D.C. and I was shown into
my coupé on the special train, which consisted of a saloon car
with a kitchen and an open platform at the end, and four or
five coaches, with another coach attached for sleeping. There
were also trucks for Sidorin's car and other transport, and
accommodation for horses and Russian grooms and orderlies.

The train moved off during the night and by the following
morning we were already past Likhaia Junction and steaming
quickly across the bare steppes eastwards for the point where
we were to strike inland to join the Headquarters of the 1st

Don Corps, at that time holding the right of the line in touch with Wrangel's Caucasian Army which was working up the Volga front. We had with us on the train two cars, a Packard and a Fiat, and two lorries for transport, as well as horses for all and an escort troop of Cossacks, all over six feet high and mounted on wiry ponies.

We arrived at Surovikina in the evening. As we halted outside the town to wait for a clear track, barefooted girls harvesting the sunflower seeds stopped work to watch us, and alongside the carriage appeared the vendors of enormous green melons in whose delicious pink flesh the germs of cholera were all too often lying dormant. Bearded Cossacks were working in little patches of soil along the sandy, clayey ground round the village orchards, but the burning wind had scorched the earth. The grass was shrivelled yellow, and in the road alongside the track there were huge cracks across the dried ruts that stretched across a rolling prairie empty of everything but tawny grass and clumps of birch and alder.

After a series of jolts, we got going again and the train eventually eased into the station between ugly buildings and the haphazard houses of the poorer quarters of the town. Immediately, it was besieged by people eager to shine shoes, carry bags or sell food. One or two men dropped to the platform to stretch their limbs but Sidorin was determined to move on as soon as the vehicles could be made ready and we packed ourselves into the cars, with the servants and most of our kit in the two lorries. I insisted, however, on sticking to my tin basin with its canvas cover, in which I kept my shaving and washing things, and it proved a wise move as, throughout the whole trip, the lorries were seldom less than three days' journey behind us and on the return journey my suitcase disappeared entirely for three weeks. Generals Sidorin and Alfuerov and Colonel Agaiev and I went in the Packard, and General Semiliatov, Captain Dudakov, Lambkirk and Hargreaves went in the Fiat.

It was a lovely evening as we struck off into the steppes. The sun was setting on our left and a heavy dew was rising, making the grass sparkle with moisture. No maps were used and the chauffeur appeared to be driving haphazardly along the rough tracks beneath the empty sky. Often there was no road at all and the wheels of the car ground the scent from the wild thyme so that it rose all around us. Rapid discussions and wild gesticulations from car to car told me that nobody was sure of the way and we made several bad "casts" in an endeavour to find it. Once, even, while apparently completely lost, we tried to get in touch with some wild Kalmuk shepherds, but they fled from us in fear that we might be Bolshevik armoured cars or – equally unpleasant – loyalist recruiting agents.

The Fiat and the lorry fell far behind. The lamps were lit and burnt themselves out, and the short summer night began to pass. Finally, on top of some rising ground, we saw two blazing headlights from a car sent from the 1st Corps Headquarters at Ust Medvyeditsa to meet us, and as we followed it to the top of the hill, to right and left, as far as the eye could see, I made out the river Don winding along to the horizon through the vast rolling steppes.

Twice as broad as the Thames at London, it lay shining in the first light of a glorious summer sunrise. Immediately below us was the stanitza – or village – of Ust Medvyeditsa, the very heart of the Don Cossack country – a "stanitza of stanitzas" with its great domed churches looming far above the heavy, wooden, flat-topped, single-storied houses of which it was chiefly composed. As we exchanged greetings with the staff officer who met us, the sun itself appeared at the very spot where the river met the skyline, and long crimson splashes lit up the silver of the water and threw pink light over the great bare landscape. I felt that it was the biggest place I had ever seen, and even India had never impressed me so much.

With this impression came the feeling that here was a setting fit for an adventure far greater than that provided by the crowded trench warfare on the Western Front – far more exciting than stalking game in the plains of India or the mountains of Kashmir. Here, I was alone in the midst of the mysterious steppes, associating with all types of Russian people

– not the over-civilised product found in the great capitals of
Europe and on the Riviera before the war, but real honest-to-
God Russians reacting to the impact of nature on their lives in
a way that laid bare their national characteristics as clearly as
anyone was ever likely to see them. Here, I was meeting all
grades of society: Generals and junior officers; priests and
simple Cossacks; ladies of the court of the late Tsar and
ordinary country girls nursing in the hospitals; Bolshevik
prisoners; Bolshevik deserters; loyalists who had been
prisoners with the Bolsheviks and had escaped; relations of
victims of Bolshevik massacres; and men ready at any time to
massacre again and join the Bolsheviks, should their prospects
improve thereby. All of them had passed through conditions
and scenes which to me would have appeared horrifying, even
after France, and to a certain extent they were all a little demoralised. But they were all longing for the sort of liberty that
few individuals in Russia had ever had the chance to enjoy;
and I, a young and inexperienced officer, was almost alone
among them, and by virtue of the uniform which I wore, I was
entitled to their consideration as the representative of my
country.

*

We didn't wait for the other cars to arrive before we drove
down the hill into the town. We could see the lights of the
Fiat coming in the far distance, but of the lorries we had no
hopes. On arriving at our billets, I was given a pleasant room
to myself in a medium-sized house with a pleasant garden.
The furniture was all wooden, crudely carved and painted in
bright blues, reds and greens, and there were the inevitable
ikons in the corners or on the walls or above the huge pot-
bellied stove which was always a feature of Russian houses. I
had hoped to turn in and was just preparing to do so when a
messenger arrived from Agaiev.

"The Sir Officer," he said, "is asked to get ready for supper!"
The time was about 4 a.m.

The meal consisted of caviare, vodka – of course! – and

sterlet, the boneless fish peculiar to the Don. To finish there were masses of strawberries and cream. Our hostess made us welcome in the usual Russian way, though she had only just recovered from typhus, and her hair was still cropped like a boy's. She wore a simple Cossack countrywoman's dress and was busy every day nursing in a local typhus hospital. She was evidently a great local organiser and she noticed that I was pretty tired and remarked on it to Sidorin, who seemed prepared for a late sitting. Eventually she came over to me and said in all the English which she could muster: "The English officer is tired?"

She beckoned me to follow her to my room, then, putting her hands under her cheek like a child when it goes to bed, said, "*Spee, spee*" – "Sleep, sleep." And did I sleep!

The arrival of Hargreaves with the lorry left me unmoved and it was around 9 o'clock with the sunlight pouring through the windows before I became aware of the coppery jangle of a church bell over the dozing village. Everything was sultry heat and silence, and the shuffle of feet stirring the dust. As I climbed out of bed, a Russian officer came to tell me to get ready for a parade in half an hour. By the time we were dressed the sun was blazing down and I was very glad of my Indian solar topi which I had brought with me. Agaiev, who was in charge of us, led us into the town after Sidorin and the other generals.

In the absence of General Mamentov, who was at the front, the first Don Corps Headquarters was represented by a General Alexeiev, his Chief of Staff. We were also accompanied by the Ataman of Ust Medvyeditsa and by two members of the Don Kroug who represented the district – both of them out-and-out Don Cossacks. They had both taken a leading part in the anti-Bolshevik revolt which had cleared the Reds out of the district and, bit by bit, I was able to get the story of it out of them and their comrades.

The regime of the Bolshevik commissars, with its brutality and licence, and the continual seizure of corn, cattle and horses from the peasants, had provoked the Cossacks almost to desperation during the first months of the district's occupation. They soon repented of the thoughtless way in which they had been gulled by the Bolshevik propaganda into relinquishing their struggle for freedom, but small risings and acts of insubordination were immediately suppressed with the utmost cruelty. Torture was common. Men and women suffered the notorious glove-and-stocking treatment – their hands or feet dipped in boiling water and the skin stripped completely off – or they were burned with molten metal, beaten up or whipped across the face with a Cossack short-handled leather whip called a *nagaika*. Murder was common.

Nevertheless the Cossack spirit had been roused and, after a few months' secret preparation, a revolt broke out in several stanitzas simultaneously. Ust Medvyeditsa was the centre of the disaffected area, and here, as in many of the villages round about, the commissars had been killed and many of the Bolshevik troops had joined the insurgents, who eventually mustered an army of about 3,000 men with two or three machine guns.

They had been commanded by an ex-Imperial N.C.O. called Otlanov, a splendid soldier and organiser, and not only had they beaten off all the attacks the Bolsheviks had sent against them, but they had driven them out of an ever-increasing area on the Upper Don. From every stanitza which was freed, more and more Cossacks came in to fill the ranks of Otlanov's force, and in the middle of June, Mamentov's 1st Don Corps had broken through the Red troops which separated the insurgents from the main Don Army and joined hands with them. This had coincided with the crossing of the Donets at Kamenskaya and Lugansk by the 2nd and 3rd Don Corps, and when we arrived in Ust Medvyeditsa, the front was still being pushed forward about sixty miles north of us.

The troops were fine soldierlike men wearing the grey-green *rubashka* – or high-necked shirt-blouse – blue or green trousers with a wide red stripe and the typical Cossack love-lock hanging from under the side of their caps, which they wore, like all Cossacks, at a rakish angle. The younger Cossacks were very

proud of these lovelocks and, whenever they took out combs
at the end of the day and proceeded to comb them, you always
knew they had a date with one of the village girls.

Our first function of the morning was an inspection of two
sotnias of these men who had been issued with British khaki.
They were very smart but preferred to wear their own Cossack
caps to preserve their individuality. Sidorin spoke to them,
and asked me to say a few words which I managed with the
assistance of Lambkirk. It was unfortunate that Lambkirk, of
all people, should have been the only interpreter available, as
whatever he did was done with a sulky and resentful air, and
although I did my best to ignore his unpleasantness and asked
him for as little assistance as possible, he made a point of being
as difficult as he could throughout the whole journey.

After the inspection we attended a thanksgiving service in
the church for the deliverance of the town from the Bolsheviks. We were blessed by the priest and a prayer was
offered for the Allies in general and ourselves in particular. As
we entered, we passed by a sacred shrine enclosing one of the
many ikons which had supposedly miraculous powers, but
before doing so all weapons were discarded, and a heap of
swords, revolvers and daggers was left at the entrance. The
choral music as usual was beautiful and was offered without any
orchestral assistance. The Cossacks were extremely musical, and
although, as in all Russian music, the minor key seemed to be
predominant in their songs, the soldiers had excellent voices
and sang persistently on the march.

On leaving the church, I was presented with a bunch of
flowers by an extremely pretty Cossack girl and more flowers
were thrown at us as we came out into the road. By this time,
having had no breakfast, I was becoming extremely hungry
but there was more ceremonial still in store for us, and we were
taken to the Town Hall, on the steps of which we were
photographed with a group of Atamans from all the small
villages in the district.

Here the ceremony of presenting bread and salt and a speech
of welcome from the Cossack civilian administration had to be

endured and I was given a loaf of bread with salt on top as a token that I was an accepted guest. Lambkirk looked at it as hungrily as I did.

"I'd give a good deal to take a bite at it here and now," I said.

After more speeches and introductions, we went at last into an enormous lunch at the Town Hall, at the conclusion of which I was again forced to give a speech on the British constitution. The afternoon was spent on visiting hospitals.

These were full of patients, mostly with typhus, lying on straw in bare rooms, the dark reddish-brown rash that always came with the disease spreading across their entire bodies. Many of them were in a coma and raving, but there were no beds or even mattresses, and sick and wounded lay side-by-side. They were dreadfully crowded and the atmosphere was stifling, and swarms of huge flies perpetually settled in the eyes and noses of men who were gasping for breath in the last throes, or groaning from the pain of flesh and bone smashed by shell splinters or bullets. None had been washed since their arrival and, still in their infected clothing, they lay covered with dust and caked with sweat. No anaesthetics were available to help them through any operation except the most severe amputations, and such instruments as were available were blunt, dirty and unserviceable, so that there were many cases of gangrene. Bandages and lint simply didn't exist and their place was taken by wads of straw, lumps of cotton rags, and strips torn from old tablecloths or dresses.

In one room, a dead man was lying mixed up with the living, probably until then unnoticed, and totally insufficient staffs of doctors and young medical students tried wearily to cope with the situation, though without the necessaries of hospital work they could do little. Each hospital had a matron, who, with the small staff of Cossack girls, seemed perpetually to be moving from room to room, trying to encourage a few of the more despairing to live. They all had bare legs and walked on wooden sandals because they had had no shoes or stockings for some time for the simple reason that they just could not be bought. They wore their hair cropped close to their heads like a boy's, and spent much of their time carrying water in tins to the patients, holding them up to drink and driving away the flies with small branches cut from the bushes in the garden.

Wherever we went we were explained as "the English officers who had come to help them," and all eyes followed us round curiously, and such questions were asked as "Was the war over in the West?" "Was the Tsar in America?" "When were the British troops coming to fight the Bolsheviks?" and "Were the British soldiers as big as the Russians?"

Before leaving the building, a little party of weary-looking sisters, a matron and the chief doctor timidly asked if they could speak to the English officers, and in a few simple sentences unburdened themselves to me.

"You have seen our hospital?" the chief doctor said. "It is not as good as yours in London. But what can we do? We have no bandages, no lint and no medicine. There are only a few beds and even the sheets for these have been torn up for bandages. Two of our doctors died of typhus last week and – " he pointed to a ghost-like child of eighteen with eyes like burning coals – "this little sister only recovered the other day." He shook his head. "It is not long since we had a Cossack brought in with his leg cut open from top to bottom by the Bolsheviks to imitate the red stripe he wore on his trousers. He died of gangrene." He spread his hands in appeal. "But now you are here, will you help? Will you get us just a little material to carry on with? England is so rich, surely she can send us bandages, at least?"

I was in and out of hospitals many times in the next month and always found myself involved in heartrending scenes of this kind. But this, my first impression of what civil war and class hatred, worked up by a semi-criminal, semi-educated, self-seeking class of political agitators, could produce, stamped itself on my memory for ever.

How *had* I helped up to then, I thought bitterly. Principally by attending banquets notable only for the orgy of food and speeches, by receiving flowers and drinking healths! Not a very creditable record, I decided as I left, and shame and rage combined together to produce in me a tight feeling at the collar.

After leaving the hospital, I was able to get a little rest and, in spite of another dinner party and dance in the evening we got to bed fairly early. The next morning was occupied by a memorial service on the hill above the town.

"At the beginning of the civil war," I was told, "before the Bolsheviks began raising recruits, the Red Army was composed largely of escaped convicts, out-and-out riff-raff and the scum of the old army. They robbed and massacred the populace, killed off the wounded and raped the women. The service is in memory of the victims of their massacres."

A large Greek cross had been erected on the highest point near the town and several wreaths of wild flowers were placed on a mound at the foot. We went from here to a large monastery close by, occupied by some three hundred nuns under a Mother Superior who had been a great friend of the late Tsarina. They all wore black cloaks and hoods and there was a lovely underground chapel with blue walls, where a short thanksgiving service was held. Here, as in all churches, when we entered we had to remove our side-arms and lay them behind the altar.

The Bolsheviks had not molested the place during their occupation of the area and we were given an excellent lunch in the private quarters of the Mother Superior, who spoke perfect English and French. We also met some of the older members of her staff – ladies of seventy and upwards who showed great interest in the British officers. I was given a loaf of white bread baked by the nuns, and we were again pelted with flowers as we walked along the uneven dusty streets and planked sidewalks of the little town.

After a good deal of delay we got away the next morning but began to suffer from tyre trouble before we had gone many miles. There was no question of changing the tyres because there weren't any more in the whole of Russia, and the damage had to be repaired on the spot. It was grillingly hot and while the unfortunate chauffeurs were replacing tubes in one car, we slept in the shelter of the other.

The steppes were lovely at this time of the year, full of larks' songs and covered with long grass and masses of wild flowers of at least ten different kinds, with here and there clumps of birch and alder. They were a rolling prairie very much like Salisbury Plain in many ways, with no made road of any kind, but covered in patches of golden sunflowers. In other parts there were huge patches of blue and pink and our nostrils were filled with perfume for mile after mile, with never a soul in sight.

We arrived at Ust Khopersk about midday and after the usual ceremony of welcome and speeches, we were given lunch by the local Ataman. We heard more details of Bolshevik atrocities and I met a magnificent old soldier of seventy-two years of age who had been in the Cossack Bodyguard of the previous Tsar, and now turned out in full uniform with medals. Despite his wrinkled face and white hair and long curving moustachios, he was erect and smart in his coat with its richly ornamented belt, and looked as though he could still be a formidable warrior.

After lunch, we pushed on to Jelenskya, the home of Otlanov, the leader of the Cossack insurgents who came to meet Sidorin and make his report. He was a smart soldier-like man with a strong personality, and he showed me their secret arsenal, where they repaired salvaged rifles, made saddles, harness and even bullets in crude moulds. He gave me a saddle and seemed very keen to have a souvenir of the British Army, so I gave him one of my 'Ubique' gunner's badges. Peasants stood on the fringes of the crowd watching us as we talked, manure still on their boots and holding pitchforks – bearded, ragged and ugly, only their eyes attractive with the innocence of people who had no idea what was going on.

We spent the night at Jelenskya after supper with the local Ataman. "The German word 'uhlan' or 'cavalryman armed with a lance' is derived from the name of this village," he said proudly. "We have provided many famous Cossack soldiers."

Next morning we drove on to Veshenskaya, a much larger stanitza, where we were shown, among other things, a wireless receiver captured from the Reds.

"The operators obviously know their subject," Hargreaves said. "It's in damn' good order."

The hospitals here were in a dreadful state, and as we went through them in the hottest part of the afternoon it very nearly made me sick. Hargreaves always came with me through all the typhus wards and his elementary knowledge of Russian was tested to the full. Sidorin himself also went through all the wards, but the members of the party who were not actually needed usually awaited us outside with their handkerchiefs to their noses.

It was about this time that I was inoculated against typhus.

A Russian doctor approached me shyly. "Would you like to be inoculated against typhus?" he had asked.

I was startled at the suggestion because I knew there was no serum, but he insisted that he had some. "I've made some from the blood of a man who's just died," he said.

I shrugged. "Very well," I said. "Anything once."

He therefore injected me and, whether it was due to his serum or not, when I came to catch the disease I didn't die.

We stayed the night at Veshenskaya and before supper we had our first chance to bathe in the Don. The river was a little muddy, but cool and swift-flowing with sandy banks. After the heat it was very welcome but none of the Russian officers made the slightest attempt to dry themselves after coming out of the water and simply put their clothes on while they were still wet. They seemed to regard me as a little mad because I used a towel.

Next day we went on to Migulinsk, stopping on the way at a village where, during the insurrection, the women themselves, itching to repay a few debts, had caught the commissars as they tried to flee and murdered them with farm tools and kitchen knives.

At Kazansk we crossed to the north bank of the Don and, as we had a long journey to our next stage, we spent two days here. We had some splendid bathing in the evening which gave the lorries a chance to catch up. I also had my first chance to write some letters, though when and how they were to be posted was quite another matter.

We had now done about a hundred very rough miles along the south bank of the Don and the next morning started north on a further journey of eighty miles, which we hoped to complete in one day, to bring us to Uryupinsk, the Headquarters of the 2nd Don Corps. At a small village near Solonka, where we stopped for lunch, we found the remains of a French light tank captured by the Bolsheviks after the French retreat from Odessa and now abandoned. During the afternoon we stopped to drink large quantities of fresh and sour milk given us by the Cossacks, who always seemed to have a supply kept ice-cold in deep underground cellars.

To my intense surprise, we arrived at Uryupinsk on time, more dead than alive, and after being shown to our billets and fed as usual on eggs and black bread and butter and gallons of Russian tea, we dropped on to our beds and fell fast asleep, exhausted by travelling tightly-packed over dusty tracks for eighty miles along the steppes, with no protection from a semi-tropical sun.

Hargreaves, Lambkirk and I were in a billet owned by a Russian widow with a pretty daughter of nine, both of whom spoke English. As it was Sidorin's plan to spend two or three days at Uryupinsk we were allowed to lie in most of the following morning, and began our inspections with the usual church service at noon. We lunched at Corps Headquarters, and on our way there, we were presented with flowers. The Corps Commander's A.D.C. asked me how I liked them.

I carelessly replied that though the flowers were pretty, the sixteen-year-old girl who had presented them was prettier still. Immediately, to my intense embarrassment, the girl was sent for and introduced to me.

"She will be your partner at a dance tonight at the Officers' Club," I was told.

As we had been promised, the dance was held after a dinner

Bogaievski drinking with the Kalmucks

Cavalry parading for blessing before leaving for the front

Troops crossing the Don by rafts

at the Officers' Club, and I sat next to the schoolgirl I had met in the morning. She was the daughter of a professor in Moscow and had seen more of the Bolsheviks than we had, as the stanitza of Uryupinsk had only come into our hands in the last week or two. Contrary to regulations, I offered her the fellow of the badge I had given to Otlanov, and as the Bolsheviks shortly afterwards re-captured the stanitza, I often wondered if it was found in her possession and, if so, if anything happened to her.

The promised visit to the front was to have been made the next day and we went off by train to Borisoglyebsk, about twenty miles north-west, which had been captured by the Partisan Division of the 2nd Corps two days previously. On arrival there, however, to my intense disappointment, we merely inspected troops in reserve and wasted most of the time in the usual big lunch at Headquarters. We were also informed that we must be back on the train by 7 p.m. as Bolshevik forces were driving in our advanced troops about six miles outside the town.

By this time I was growing furious with all the inspecting and eating and drinking and was fairly bursting to see some real soldiering. But there was no opportunity of going against Sidorin's instructions or I would have found myself abandoned in the middle of the steppes without transport.

The news of the Bolshevik advance had come in on the telegraph but, for some reason, Sidorin preferred to keep the news to himself and I only found out about it because I had all along been badgering Lambkirk to keep me informed of what was going on.

The troops I saw at Borisoglyebsk had been fighting the day before, and they were very badly equipped. Only thirty per cent had boots, and they had no machine guns whatsoever. The faces of the men, under the covering of wind-blown dust, were blank and haggard, and you could see their knees and elbows through their threadbare uniforms. Shirts were discoloured and threadbare, and many of them, in fact, lacked shirts altogether and wore woollen vests. There was no sign of any British uniform or equipment, and some of the men actually wore spiked *pickelhaube* helmets left behind by the German army of occupation.

There was a fatalism about them as they stood in the hot sun, their rifles by their sides, their rolled blankets over their shoulders. Yet during the rising they had captured Uryupinsk with only seventy men and had killed over a hundred of the enemy. When they were driven out again shortly afterwards, the Reds had retaliated by murdering about 200 schoolboys and girls.

They were now exhausted, however, their expressions apathetic, and it was clear that just then they hadn't much interest in who was winning the war, and I remarked bitterly that it would be better for everyone if some of the khaki worn by the Corps Headquarters troops comfortably ensconced in the rear areas were sent up to the front line.

I was growing more disgusted every day at the way the trip was turning out. Try as I would to get to where something definite was happening, I could never escape from the supervision of Sidorin or his staff, and we returned to Uryupinsk late at night, with the next day again spent wasting time as usual, although the arrival of one of the lorries with my long-lost suitcase gave me the chance of getting some clothes washed. Late in the evening, news came in on the telegraph of severe fighting.

"The Reds have been driven out of Balashov," we were told. "It's an important railway junction fifty miles to the north-east. The Cossacks have been joined by a large body of Greens."

"Greens?"

My informant shrugged. "Bandits. Discontented Bolshevik soldiers. They deserted two months ago. They've been wandering about in the wooded districts of the Tambov area waiting for us to arrive. They're very democratic and refuse to acknowledge officers with any respect, but they're also bitter anti-Bolsheviks, and useful fighting material."

Sidorin had decided to go to Balashov to see the Greens the

following day, so we packed up again and, escorted by an armoured train, arrived about four o'clock in the afternoon. This was the farthest point north that the White Armies ever reached on the Don and Volga, and with its capture, the whole of the Don Cossack country and a good bit of the Tambov district as well was cleared of the Reds.

At the station we were met by a guard of Don Cossacks of the 2nd Corps, mostly in khaki, and a detachment of Greens, commanded by a man called Voronovitch, drawn up alongside them. The Greens had practically no uniforms at all and wore mostly peasants' clothes with tweed caps or shaggy sheepskin hats ornamented with a cross of green cloth. They carried a plain green flag and appeared a well-built and strong body of men. After leaving the station, a quick review was held on the station platform, and the Greens were harangued and reviewed by Sidorin, who gave them a good supply of decorations to encourage them to further efforts on our behalf. Their loyalty was short-lived, however. They preferred their own company and soon went back either to the Bolsheviks or to the woods, where they could hide and rob the peasants with impunity.

Mahkno, the man who had organised the first of these bandit bands, had been serving a prison sentence in Siberia when the Revolution started but on his return, he had begun to organise his groups of bandits who perpetrated every conceivable horror on the South Russians. He flew a personal flag of black and fought everybody, striking terror into the hearts of the peasants. Towns, universities, museums and art galleries alike were destroyed by him. The Greens, whether under Mahkno or not, were unlikely ever to take to military discipline and no one seemed very surprised when they left.

Among the things they left behind in Balashov was a large munitions dump, formerly belonging to the Reds. In it I found quantities of British ammunition and stores, probably captured on the Northern Front or part of the supplies sent by us to the Russians in 1916 and 1917.

Nearby I also saw the 3rd (4.5 Howitzer) Battery which had

been equipped and trained in Rostov and was the first battery armed with British howitzers to appear on the Don Front. It had apparently been most successful, and the instantaneous action fuses had been a revelation in destruction to the officers, who asked for nothing else to be sent in future. Our harness had caused them a lot of trouble, however, as it was too large for their small horses and they had had a terrible number of sore backs and collar galls. The ample supply of ammunition which was available had caused them enormous joy, however, and they claimed that they now understood all there was to know about their equipment. Unfortunately they were losing four to five men a day with typhus.

We dined at the house of a dentist. Unlike some of the other houses we had seen, it showed no sign of damage or occupation.

"I am a Jew," the dentist explained. "So the Bolsheviks have not worried me."

I was very tired and ready for sleep, but I noticed a great deal of hurrying about going on outside, and I had scarcely undressed in my billet when Agaiev appeared at the door with an interpreter.

"We're leaving," he said.

"Now?"

"Yes. The General's train's leaving in two hours. There has been a Bolshevik counter-attack outside the town. We expect them to break in at any moment."

He turned away as I dived for my kit and began to throw it together. Two days later, in fact, the Bolsheviks did recapture the town, but not before the Cossacks were able to remove a considerable quantity of munitions from the dump and a lot of much-needed sugar and white flour.

The hurried retreat, with everyone flinging kit aboard the train in a wild scramble, was another blow as I had hoped to get up to the real front the following day. I had realised, by this time, however, that so long as I trailed round with Sidorin I was never really likely to do much good for anyone or be able to make any efficient investigation of the forward area. All

I wanted now was to return to Mission Headquarters and send more letters home asking for help for the hospitals.

On our return to Uryupinsk disquieting news from Army Headquarters at Novocherkassk awaited Sidorin, and without further delay he got into one of the old unarmed Voisin two-seater pusher aeroplanes which the 2nd Corps possessed. As the ancient aeroplane waltzed into wind and buzzed into the sky, we made our own way home by car and lorry to arrive at Millerovo on the Likhaia-Voronezh line just in time to meet Sidorin's train, which had come all the way round from Surovikina to meet us. With it came the news that the baggage lorry with all our equipment was completely broken down sixty miles out in the steppes, so, reluctantly regarding my elusive suitcase as lost for ever this time, we set off south the same night for Novocherkassk.

CHAPTER SIX

My first official visit to the front had been a most disappointing affair from the military point of view, though every moment had been full of interest. The extraordinary contrast between life at Headquarters and that of the wretched workers, soldiers and patients in the hospitals had made a great impression on me.

It had been hard work, however, as we had been nearly always on the move, and had covered a good deal of country. The heat had been intense and the flies had been very bad and, since I had lost all my kit, the thought of a week at Headquarters seemed a very pleasant prospect for a change. Nevertheless, I could have shouted for joy when, on arriving, I was given a telegram which had appeared the day before.

"Proceed at once to Mission Headquarters Ekaterinodar to accompany the Chief of the British Mission on an extended tour of the entire front probably lasting six weeks."

"This really is the goods!" I shouted enthusiastically.

I borrowed another kit bag, replenished my changes of clothes from my trunks, and was off the next night to report to General Holman. Before I knew where I was, I was having tea on his train in Ekaterinodar Station.

The first two days at Ekaterinodar were spent in fitting out the train with provisions, loading up the horses and inspecting and equipping the grooms and the escort of one sergeant and three Cossacks. During this time, I heard a lot of discussion among the officers about the new system inaugurated since Holman's arrival, and the criticism was not by any means always favourable. My own opinion was that the great "volte face" in the Mission's policy which Holman had insisted upon was considerably upsetting the easy life of many of our Headquarters staff, Russian as well as British, and I personally felt it was quite time that something did.

However, I remained quiet and watched events, feeling sure that sooner or later I should see tremendous results from the energy and dash which was now being displayed by Holman and his supporters. The sooner the discontented ones went home the better it would be for all of us, I thought, but it didn't concern me so long as he would help me and my Don Cossacks, and get me certain unsatisfactory officers replaced in my group.

Holman was a tall burly man with white hair and a merry twinkling eye. I was not small and he dwarfed me. He had been a brilliant administrator during the recent war and he had not taken at all kindly to the situation he had found at Mission Headquarters. In spite of Russian efforts to stop him, he was determined to get to the fighting troops in the forward area, and he discussed with me the steps necessary to make the Mission into a more lively affair.

He had arrived at Ekaterinodar with a special briefing from Winston Churchill himself, who was one of the prime movers in the intervention and the allied attempts to prevent the spread of Communism. I had served under him as a junior staff officer with the Fourth Army in France and the fact that he sent for me was particularly encouraging as, under the previous regime, my rather pro-Russian activities were not popular at headquarters and I had even been expecting to be recalled on my return to Novocherkassk.

The party consisted of Holman, with Colonel Dmitri Svegintsev, a charming, educated officer of the old Romanov Chevalier Guard – though not at all a ferocious type – who was Chief Russian Liaison Officer and interpreter; Major Wynter, of the Worcester Regiment, with Prince Obolenski as his interpreter; two Russian-speaking captains, Harvey and Roberts; and myself.

To my deep concern, I had found on my return to Novocherkassk that Angus Campbell had been evacuated during my absence seriously ill with typhus and one of the sergeant instructors was ill with cholera. Whilst typhus normally resulted from bites from lice on dirty bodies, it more or less died out by the spring but there were still many cases of it which were usually fatal and frequently resulted in homicidal mania and sometimes caused nurses to be killed by patients. Cholera, on the other hand, spread quickly during the summer and, while there was no known serum to deal with typhus, inoculation against cholera was possible. The local habit of eating large quantities of melons grown in the most unsuitable ground was a contributory cause to what was known as·"cholera stomach", which died down as fruit became scarce. I was inoculated against cholera and did not catch it.

Since I had to find a replacement for Campbell, I got in touch with a Russian officer, Peter Gytkov, who had been a military instructor at one of the schools and had a considerable knowledge of French which I also spoke. I had been to one or two parties with him and his friend, Alexandra Timofievna, the widow of a Cossack officer, a very pretty girl whom I admired more than a little. Gytkov was a smart officer and helpful but was often very moody and seemed to feel he was not treated with enough deference compared with the other more senior interpreters.

Holman's train, like Sidorin's, consisted of four or five cars with a truck for his motor car and accommodation for horses and Russian grooms and orderlies. It was quite comfortable for two or three days at a time and carried an authority to be attached to any train that Holman's liaison officer, Svegintsev, demanded.

Our first stop was at Rostov, and here we lunched with Keyes, now a general, and picked up Harold Williams, correspondent of *The Times* and *The Daily Chronicle*, who had a life-long experience of Russia. He spoke the language perfectly, and had married a Russian woman of considerable literary talent.

We spent the afternoon in the propaganda bureau of the

White Armies. In addition to cartoons and posters designed and executed by volunteer workers, we were able to see a private exhibition of propaganda films captured from the Reds at Kharkov. In contrast to the Whites' unsophisticated efforts, there was no mistaking the cunning of their preparation or the appeal to the uneducated and morbid minds of the people whose sympathies the Bolsheviks were striving to enlist. The first depicted in serial form the misery of the life of the Russian peasant dragged from his home and family to fight a cruel war for the benefit of the brutal capitalist, who was represented by a callous land-owner, an immoral officer, and an overfed and luxurious plutocrat.

Between each scene the screen became blank and a hand appeared shaking a knout or holding a pair of hand-cuffs – the insignia of slavery – and at the end, on a perfectly blank screen, appeared a tiny red spot which grew in size until it finally covered the whole screen with the red five-pointed star and the motto "Give your money and your life for the sacred ideals of the Soviet Republic."

This was followed by a similar serial depicting the wretched life of a factory hand who loses his arm to defective machinery while working for the idle capitalist. In addition to these films, there were several short ones showing the infamous Trotsky and others of the Republican Government inspecting troops, haranguing the people, and at work; and a film of a parade of the Officer Corps of the Red Army showing what I had to admit was a very well equipped and well-set-up body of men.

After this we saw other films which were propaganda for Denikin. Most of them were of inspections of troops by large staffs of aristocratic-looking generals who exuded the atmosphere of the old regime with every movement they made. Then there was the triumphant entry of the ferocious Skouro into Kharkov escorted by his famous "Wolves" – extremely savage and picturesque-looking but not inclined to soothe the nerves of a hardly-tried anti-militarist population. Field court-martials were also depicted, in which Skouro, sitting at a table in the open, condemned to death whole strings of Bolshevik prisoners with a stroke of the pen. These certainly were mostly ex-Chinese Labour Corps and renegade officers, but it did not seem very good policy to complete the ugly side of civil war by photographing the actual executions. Nothing was omitted, however, and an unfortunate Chinaman, climbing on a chair, putting the noose round his own neck, and jumping off into space, was portrayed in every detail up to the last expiring convulsion of his death agony.

Films were also shown of Generals Alexeiev, Kornilov, Denikin, Wrangel and Romanovski, and of a few short manoeuvres by the British tanks which had already been put into commission. I also saw a collection of photographs of mutilated corpses which had been dug up at Kharkov after a particularly atrocious massacre accompanied by more than usually cruel torture, committed under the direction of the chief commissar just before we captured the town. These evidences of Bolshevik civilisation nearly made me sick and I heard that they were sent to England to be circulated there to show those really interested what might be expected of the "Dictatorship of the Proletariat". Holman was much impressed by the efficiency of the Bolshevik film propaganda, though our own films appeared more likely to alienate public sympathy than to enlist it, and he used his influence to have the execution of the Chinaman and the more reactionary of the films suppressed.

We left shortly afterwards for Losovaia, which was supposed to be the headquarters of the 1st Corps of the Volunteer Army under General Mai-Maievski, and as the General's special train had a "clear the line" order throughout, we arrived there about noon the following day.

I was looking forward to meeting Mai-Maievski. I had heard a lot about him and seen pictures of him, and had wondered how any man who was as fat as he appeared to be could be a good leader. We expected to hear news of where to find him and what was to be the programme, but late at night Svegintsev received a telegram that the corps headquarters had been moved to Kharkov, and we were expected there.

This did not suit Holman, who had already shown signs of impatience at the persistent efforts to waste his time which the Russians always made under the guise of lavish hospitality and courteous respect. He cross-examined the Staff of the Station Commandant as well as Svegintsev, who was undoubtedly better informed than he pretended, and discovered that an offensive operation was about to commence against Poltava, in which a portion of Mai-Maievski's army was to take part. This was due to start in the vicinity of the station of Kegi-chevka the next day.

Holman nodded. "Very well," he said, "we'll go and see it."

So, despite the remonstrances of Svegintsev, we ordered the train to be ready. At last we were going to the real front.

*

The train appeared, pulled by a ninety-ton monster of an engine, decorated in red and black and liberally sprinkled with flags. There were more flags on the front and rear of the train and on the corners of the carriages. Everyone climbed aboard, crowding into the coupés, filling the windows of the saloons which were furnished with tables and chairs and even potted plants, and hanging over the rails on the platforms at the end of the carriages. A few women waved, the wheels spun and there was a roar of steam, and we were away.

Next morning found us at Kegichevka, once more just too late to catch Mai-Maievski, whose headquarters had moved on to Balki only that day.

The operation which was just developing was a thrust in a north-west direction with Poltava as the main objective, and was carried out by three principal columns, the first consisting of the Guard Corps under General Baron Stackelberg, with the 8th Kuban Plastoune Brigade under General Gaiman, in re-serve; the second, consisting of the 7th Division and a battalion of Ossetine Infantry from the Caucasus Mountains; and the third consisting of Skouro's savage cavalry division, now composed mostly of Cossacks and Mohammedans from the northern slopes of the Caucasus.

The central column was to advance along the railway via Constantinograd and Karlovka, and had two armoured trains to assist it. Owing to the fact that most of the fighting took place up and down the railway lines, the first long-range contact between two opposing forces usually involved an armoured train action.

There were dozens of armoured trains operating south of Moscow, some belonging to the Reds, some to the Whites, some to the Green Guards, who belonged to neither side and preyed on both, and a few to private and uncontrollable armies with very dubious loyalties. The railway staff stayed neutral for safety and dealt with the lot, working points and changing signals often at the point of a gun, and one of the more interesting pastimes was trying to decide just where all these armoured trains were – an important point if you had one of your own.

The generally adopted formation was to have a lightly-armoured repair truck then a truck with machine guns. Next would come the train itself with a light field gun and more machine guns, heavily-armoured, and an armoured truck full of troops ready to reinforce the leading group. Finally, in most cases and sometimes taking the place of the field gun, would come a heavy naval type of gun which could indulge in long-range slogging in those cases when lightly-armoured leading formations were not available. Bodies of infantry usually advanced in country carts along roads close to one flank or another of the railway tracks whilst the cavalry formations covered the flanks for considerable distances over the steppes. For short reconnaissances, the train might consist of the armoured engine with one truck carrying a field gun or even only men with machine guns. Opposing armoured trains seldom came face-to-face with one another at short range, though the crews always kept their eyes well peeled for booby traps or wrecked tracks ahead of them.

In this case the left column was advancing on a parallel line about twenty miles to the south with a view to converging on Poltava from that flank simultaneously with a frontal attack by the Guard Corps. The right column, being the most mobile, was coming in from a westerly direction from Starovierovka to cut the railway communication between Kharkov and Poltava, the only remaining railway by which the Reds could escape to Kiev.

"We'll see the operation through with the central column," Holman announced, and, having called on General Gaiman whose train was in Balki Station, we awaited the return of Baron Stackelberg, the Commander, who had gone forward a few miles to see how his troops were getting on. All our horses were unboxed, saddles fitted, and forage and baggage carts – which we had brought on the special with us, complete with Russian horses and drivers – packed and got ready for a cross-country march. Holman's Vauxhall was also taken off the train, as it was to be used for quick liaison work in case we needed supplies. (As the Reds were rumoured to have cut important bridges, it might be several days before the trains could catch us up.)

We could distinctly hear sounds in the distance of armoured trains in action, covering a bridge across the river Berestovaya. This was about a mile and a half east of Constantinograd, which it was most desirable the Reds should not destroy.

Gaiman's staff were very cheerful and seemed to like Holman who quickly made use of the fact.

"I'd like to move on ahead a little," he said and they promptly insisted on mounting him on one of their own horses; and he and Svegintsev and I, with a group of Kuban Cossacks and a small escort, rode off about four o'clock to a village called Dobrenka. This was supposed to be the battalion head-quarters of a regiment who were working up to the bridge from the south to try to capture it before nightfall.

As we advanced, we heard rifle fire and occasional machine-gun fire. The armoured trains were apparently indulging in a long-range duel by the harmless method of "chuck and catch it". On arriving at the village we found that the battalion commander had moved closer to the bridge.

"We're going to rush the bridge after dark," an officer,

commanding what I imagined was a company in reserve, told us. "For the moment, though, we're only keeping the Reds away with rifle fire to prevent them destroying it."

At that moment a Red battery commander must have taken it into his head that the Whites were using a church tower as an O.P. – which was probably true – and proceeded to fire spasmodically into the village. The principal danger of this kind of bombardment was its extreme inaccuracy, as the shells fell in all sorts of unpredictable places. The inhabitants appeared to be fairly apathetic about it, however, but took the trouble to drive the children indoors. When several old men appeared to see what was happening and to stare at the British officers, Holman questioned them about their attitude to the Bolsheviks. They seemed quite indifferent.

The bombardment stopped after half an hour and, as there were no signs of the battalion commander's return and it was getting late, we set off back to the train. On our return we found the column commander there.

"How best can we continue co-operation without interference?" Holman demanded.

The Russian, of course, tried to put him off, but he wasn't having any.

"I intend," he said, "to see every branch of the Russian service at work, both on the march and in action, as well as at stores, railheads and headquarters."

We all listened with due deference and although Svegintsev and the Russian generals, backed at times even by some of the dissident British officers on our train, did their best to keep Holman out of the forward area and confine him to liaison duties pure and simple, the next few days gave him a reputation among all ranks for dash and determination, coupled with an air of confidence and enthusiasm which strengthened his hand enormously when dealing with dangerous and difficult situations.

While his conference with Baron Stackelberg was still going on, a staff officer came from Gaiman's train to ask some of us to dine with him, so taking Gytkov with us to interpret, Harvey, Wynter and I went over.

Gaiman's establishment was of the type to which I later grew accustomed, but at the time it appeared to me very strange.

Every Russian general holding a command of any size invariably lived in an "echelon" or train, which consisted of four or five carriages comprising a dining-room, kitchen, offices and sleeping quarters for himself, his staff, a small escort and his transport in case he had to go across country. This did not often happen, as in the vast country over which we were fighting, the lateral supply of stores and ammunition would be so complicated that military operations were practically always confined to areas extending ten or fifteen miles on each side of the railway system along which the groups of troops moved. The intervening spaces between were occupied and watched by small forces of cavalry living entirely on the country and, because of the distances, seldom in touch with similar enemy formations.

Gaiman's train was nothing like so luxurious as many others, but it seemed very comfortable. Presiding over the kitchen, the waiting, and the general comfort of all was a Russian girl, dressed as a nursing sister with the black *kazinka* or hood, which all Russian nurses wore. She looked tidy and quiet and was evidently extremely popular with officers and soldiers alike, all of whom addressed her as "*sisteritza*" or "little sister'. She would not eat until she was sure that everything possible had been done for the guests, then she sat down and joined in the general conversation.

"She is a skilful doctor," we were told, "and such medical stores as the brigade headquarters possesses are distributed by her to any sick or wounded as come her way."

She belonged to the headquarters staff as their "nursing sister" and, in addition to her medical duties, she ran the mess.

She told me her father had been a landowner in the Ukraine, and that she had been taken prisoner by Nestor Makhno, the peasant brigand and leader of the Green Guards. She had managed to escape, however, but had been shot in the leg while doing so, so that she still limped badly. She also had a curious black smudge across the bridge of her nose.

"It was made by a blow from one of Makhno's officers on Makhno's order," she said. "Because I would not sleep with him."

After her escape she had found her way to Nicolaevsk, where she had hidden for some time before getting herself attached to Gaiman's staff as a means of obtaining food and clothing and of following the advancing troops back into her own part of the country.

*

Before turning in, Holman took me on one side.

"The advance is going to be continued in the morning," he said. "So we should all get out early with the attacking troops. It's hoped to capture Constantinograd by evening. Wynter and Harvey are to take the armoured train which is supporting the attack, once the bridge has been rushed, and you and I and Svegintsev are going with one of the Guards Battalions. They have two 18-pounder batteries working with them on the north of the railway so they might be glad of your help."

It was a perfect morning and I felt just as though I was going out cub-hunting as we rode out of the station compound with our little escort of bearded and fierce-looking Cossacks, and made for a small village about three miles north-east of where the column was starting. We caught up with the tail of the column just as it was leaving the village, trailing a vast cloud of golden dust behind it in the still air. The transport consisted entirely of ordinary open country carts drawn by one or two ponies, and we found a couple of our field medical panniers on one of them, though the man in charge knew nothing of the contents or who was supposed to use them.

About eleven o'clock we heard the unmistakable sound of 18-pounders firing a short distance away on our flank. Heads jerked round as horses were reined in, there was a short discussion, then we went off at once at a gallop in the direction of the shooting and found a battery in action in a cornfield

The first train into
Poltava after its
re-capture

Funeral procession
of two white officers,
Novocherkassk
1919. Note horses
draped in white
sheets

Camouflaged transport train

Watering cavalry in a Cossack village

about 3,500 yards from the Reds. There was a great deal of excitement among the Russian officers.

"They're in full retreat across the river into Constantino-grad," we were told.

Apparently the target was good as a rapid rate of firing was going on, the guns banging away noisily. But the gunners, having only received the equipment a month before from the artillery school at Armavir, were not very well trained and within ten minutes of our arrival three of the guns were in difficulty, one with a hopelessly jammed cartridge which had been thrust into the breech still covered with sand. Another had an overrun trigger, and the third had such weak springs in the buffers that the gun had to be pushed up by hand into its cradle after each round.

In no time at all, the gunners were staring blankly at their silent weapons while the officers, who probably didn't know very much more about them than they did, cursed and waved their arms.

Holman looked at me. "Can't we fix this?" he asked.

"I think so, sir."

"Let's try."

We took off our coats and got two of the three guns into action again, whilst all ranks of the Russians looked on from behind in amazement.

"A general!" I heard them saying. "A general who knows how to put a gun right himself, and doesn't mind doing it!"

As we worked, the Battery Commander appeared. He disdained to ride a horse and drove up to the position in a small and very shabby two-horse victoria, and he now began to protest violently at our undignified conduct.

"An officer does not serve a gun!" he insisted indignantly, almost spitting with rage. "That is the job of the men!"

We managed to calm him down, especially as the guns came into action again, and shortly afterwards we left the battery and made for the railway bridge across the river, where fighting was actually in progress. As we came in sight of the lines we saw Wynter's armoured train being bombarded by the enemy.

After six or seven rounds had fallen within fifty yards of it, however, it got up steam and the wheels began to spin. To my intense surprise, though, instead of retreating, it *advanced*! The bridge was apparently safe, but our infantry could not push on and were waiting for a flank attack on the town along the ridge running into it from the north-east.

Meanwhile the infantry on our immediate front, covered by the fire of the 18-pounder batteries, were crossing the river at a ford. A shell fell in the river and flung a geyser of black water upwards, then we saw more shells exploding on the opposite bank. The sound was muffled by the distance and the mushrooms of smoke seemed to rise silently into the air, caught by the sun, curling lazily upwards and hanging for a moment before collapsing. They seemed quite harmless at that distance and we could see no return of fire, but there were huddled shapes of casualties sprawled in the grass.

For about an hour, the advance was held up, then the arrival of a flank attack, the men running in over the folds of ground, resulted in a "sauve qui peut" on the part of the Bolsheviks, and we saw them streaming out of the other side of Constantinograd. They were hastened on their way by the armoured trains which steamed across the bridge, clattering and roaring, their machine guns rattling away, and dashed into the station, capturing about fifty prisoners and hunting the retiring Red train as far as ten miles further west.

*

As soon as we could, we led our horses across the railway bridge and climbed on to a pilot engine which had come up. Leaving our horses with the escort, we steamed triumphantly into Constantinograd almost in line with the infantry. Holman sat on the front buffer with a Lewis gun in his arms and the rest of us hung on to odd valves and bits of machinery or stood on the platform round the boiler. We arrived amid cheers.

In the station master's office, we found several of our soldiers amusing themselves by covering the faces of their prisoners with burnt cork. It was difficult to see the reason for it and we asked each other cheerfully if it came within the terms of the Geneva Convention. It seemed harmless, however, and there was a great deal of laughter going on.

"It makes them look pretty ridiculous," Holman said. "But it hardly comes under the rules of war."

By the next morning they had all been recruited into the White forces and were good Volunteer soldiers – until next time!

We had an early dinner of goose provided by the Cossack escort – they were a pretty wild-looking group and one only had to ask and the meal appeared, and no one asked any questions – but preparations were made for an early start next day to keep in touch with the retreating enemy, and if possible capture Karlovka the same evening.

"The Reds are receiving reinforcements," we were told. "They intend to hold Karlovka at all costs."

Karlovka could only be approached across marshy ground and stood on a hill beyond the river Orchik. The distance to be covered was about seventeen miles, so it looked like being a longish day.

The Guards Regiment, which comprised most of General Stackelberg's command, was to march in two separate columns parallel to, and north of, the railway, and converge on the town towards evening, in the vicinity of the only causeway and bridge which could be used. The Kuban troops were to follow the line of the railway on the South, supported by the armoured trains.

"They'll not be much help, though," one of Stackelberg's aides told me quietly. "The bridge at Fedorovka's badly damaged and it'll require several hours' work to repair."

The artillery opened the attack and the colours were unfurled. The men were drawn up in battle array to the sound of music; bugles rang out, and the standards floated on the breeze. Swords flashed and a cheer went up, and the men moved forward in a cloud of dust. War, before the advent of the aeroplane, the motor car, the tank, and barbed wire, must have been like this, I thought as I watched them. This was what it

must have been like even as far back as Napoleon when men
in gorgeous uniforms charged with snapping banners over
green meadows against enemy batteries.

For a variety of reasons, the majority of the British officers
had to remain with the train, so I found myself alone with
Holman and Svegintsev riding at the head of the main body of
the left Guards column close to the railway line, clattering and
jingling alongside the gleaming metals. Behind us, the column
advanced with a steady swish-swish through the long grass,
flowers and wild thyme.

The whole body of troops was 'mobile', and numbers of
country carts had been commandeered. In them the infantry
was carried – about eight men in each – and in addition to a
battery of 3-inch Russian field guns, we also had two batteries
of British 18-pounders, one battery of 4.5 howitzers and a
section of curious little 1½-inch Martini infantry guns fitted to
galloping carriages.

I was surprised that no artillery was sent with the advanced
guard, which consisted of about one company of infantry –
all in country carts – and a squadron of cavalry which was split
up into patrols in front and on the flank to keep in touch with
the other columns. It was blazing hot and I soon had my coat
rolled up and across the saddle, riding in shirt sleeves.
Immediately I became aware of raised eyebrows from the officers and grins from the men. One of the officers explained:
Taking my coat off struck them as very curious, as they
considered it a most improper state of déshabillé for an
officer.

About midday we came under fire from a Bolshevik
armoured train out of sight on the far side of Fedorovka
Bridge. There was a distant thud then a whistle, and a shell
tossed up dirt and stones a hundred or so yards away. It was
followed by another and another, and there was a hasty conference among the column officers as a great delay would be
caused if they were obliged to deploy their men. Skilful use of
the folds of the ground, however, succeeded in getting us out

of the sight of the Red gunners, and they gave up searching the bare countryside for us. Probably they were as short of ammunition as we were.

Later we bumped into a group of Red cavalry but they made no attempt to interfere and we lunched at a little farm with the commanding officer of the artillery attached to the column, who was very cheerful and keen and seemed very capable, and it must have been nearly 7 p.m. when, breasting a patch of rising ground which we had been climbing for some time, we suddenly saw the ground sloping away from us down to a swampy-looking valley. There, on the hill beyond it, was our objective – Karlovka, about three miles away, a small Russian village with low heavy-shouldered Russian houses with carved eaves and dashes of gaudy paint.

Dusk fell very rapidly, and this no doubt prevented the enemy seeing us, but we almost at once heard machine gun and rifle fire coming from the direction of the bridge where our advanced guard was being fired on at long range. We could also hear firing on the right, as though our neighbouring column was also meeting with opposition.

As I looked at the position in front of us, which we had to take with about 2,000 troops at the end of a hard day, it struck me that it was as nearly impregnable as possible, and could be held by a man, a boy and a catapult if the defending force had one atom of pluck or skill. I was very anxious to see how the Russians would tackle the situation.

The column commander, the O.C. of the Guards Battalion, didn't appear worried in the least, however, nor did he think it necessary to halt his column or make any new disposition. There was no reconnaissance, no fire plan, just a few verbal orders and in half an hour all the batteries were firing away anyhow, while the infantry edged up to the causeway. The sound of the Guards' little battle became quite pronounced, and we could see shell flashes clearly in the deepening darkness along the lower edge of the village.

Suddenly, the column commander halted his men, called up several of his officers, held a hurried discussion and, before I realised that anything could possibly happen, the column was off again. Two companies trotted up from the main body in their country carts with two Lewis guns and dashed down the hill in support of the advanced guards in great style, rattling and clattering past, the carts bouncing over the folds of ground at top speed and flinging up stones and great clouds of dust, the men clinging to them for dear life, clutching their weapons. A few men were hit and two horses, which brought their carts to an abrupt stop. One of them overturned, its wheels spinning, flinging the men out in a heap, but they merely scrambled up and set off after the others on foot.

The little Martini battery went after them in approved Horse Artillery style, clattering and bouncing over the rough ground, and the remainder of the main body moved forward again at a steady pace, with the 18-pounders and 4.5 howitzer batteries deployed to right and left of the road and coming into action with a rattle and jingle. Within ten minutes, sharp cracking explosions showed that the Martinis were in action in close support of the advanced guard, while in the distance we could see the flashes and smoke of bursting shells, as the field guns searched the far end of the bridge and the outskirts of Karlovka with a slow rate of fire. They were using instantaneous fuses and covering as much of the area as possible, with a view to flushing the enemy from posts which he might have established.

It was now almost dark, and it seemed that the entire centre of interest must be the causeway over the river and the bridgehead, so Holman and I and Svegintsev cantered on till we were among the troops, who had dismounted from their carts by this time and were slowly feeling their way forward. The resistance seemed very indifferent, but quite a lot of shells came spinning over us, evidently extremely badly directed.

After wandering to right and left of the marshy ground, we suddenly came upon the causeway leading across it. A few of our men were already waiting there, and at the same moment, to our intense delight, we saw a party from the column which had been advancing on our right, part of which had already forced a crossing at Varvarovka and had come to help us at the exact moment we wanted them.

All this time, our guns were steadily probing the far side of the river, but we wanted to stop them so as to try to rush the bridgehead. As there was no telephonic communication of any sort, a complicated kind of Very pistol and some very damp-looking cartridges were produced from somewhere. The Russians looked blank.

"*Chto takoe*? What is it for? How does it work?"

None of them knew how to use the pistol until Holman showed them, but it was eventually fired off in the hope of attracting the gunners' attention and getting them to stop firing. A reinforcing party of three cartloads of infantry were prepared, and then our artillery fire suddenly stopped.

"They've seen the signal and understood," someone said.

Knowing the Russians by this time, I was more than doubtful but we decided to chance it. So off went the infantry, scrambling up and running at full speed over the causeway, and all shouting and cheering for all they were worth. By some marvellous coincidence those who had already worked up to the Bolsheviks at the far end elected to cheer and make a rush at exactly the same moment and we could just make them out pouring forward, waving flags and sweeping towards the Red positions in a swarm.

Holman and I, with about twenty cavalrymen, rode after them. We were inclined to be more cautious, as the causeway could have been swept with fire if properly defended but we were carried away by the others and found ourselves clattering forward into the village surrounded by wild-looking horsemen waving sabres and discharging rifles all round us. There was some erratic firing in front, which seemed to go whistling well over our heads, then we swept into the outskirts of the village.

I saw the flash of rifles and men running ahead of us and disappearing round houses, then a saddle just in front of me emptied as its owner rolled over his mount's rump with whirling arms and legs and landed flat on his back with a thud and a jingle of equipment in a cloud of dust. Whether he was dead or wounded I didn't know, because as we swept down the street, we were all too excited to care.

Before long, I knew, someone would have to do something about bringing some order to the attack, because the whole thing at that point seemed to be a little out of control, but the Bolsheviks had had enough, and we began to hear the unmistakable sounds of success – continuous bugle calls, cheering and the wild sound of horses' hooves clattering over a stony road. Then the rifle fire began to die down into sporadic outbursts until it had almost disappeared. The "impregnable" position of Karlovka seemed to be ours. It had not proved such a very hard nut to crack after all.

We were all a little relieved that so little resistance had been put up because, rather against our intentions, we had found ourselves in the van of the attack, and charging into the place with the first of the cavalry, and we pulled up, panting, to make sure that neither our horses nor ourselves were hit. Apart from the man I had seen fall, we didn't appear to have lost anyone.

Collecting ourselves together, we decided to move into the centre of the village, particularly as the light had by now almost gone and we felt it might be wiser to be nearer the bulk of the troops. The Bolsheviks had a nasty habit of sniping round corners.

Skirmishing was still going on ahead of us and there were still corpses in the streets, together with dead horses and overturned wagons. As they heard the sound of bugles, however, the citizens came out of doors, laughing, weeping, singing, clapping and cheering, and offered wine, cigarettes and money as the Cossacks galloped about.

We quickened our pace, but in the dark I became separated from Holman and suddenly found myself galloping along one of the streets with a strange party of cavalry. They were a pretty excited-looking lot, hung about with all sorts of weapons, and they challenged me fiercely.

"*Stoy*! Halt!"

"British officer," I offered uncertainly but they drew rein and gathered round me and I found myself staring into the muzzles of several rifles.

Dark bearded faces stared at me in the dusk and I heard the grating hiss as one of the long curved swords was whipped out of its scabbard. These swords were sharp as razors and I'd seen what they could do, and it didn't ease my spirit much as I thought of it.

"*Angliski! Anglichanie!*" I racked my brain for the few words of Russian I'd managed to pick up and flapped my arms a lot, pointing at my gunner's buttons.

I found myself quite unable to explain who or what I was but, in the end, they seemed to realise I was only one of the "mad English officers", and I gathered they wanted me to go off on a foraging expedition with them. I was worried about having lost the general, however, and much preferred my own company to theirs and I decided to look for the column's head-quarters, which by this time should have been establishing itself for the night in the village.

I found it round a large crackling bonfire in the middle of a grass patch where a few orderlies held dark, steaming horses for officers seated at a table, as messengers came and went. A man was cooking and a second was up-ending a bottle of wine. In the shadows a group of men trudged wearily past and a fur-capped Cossack, probably a member of one of the escort troops, was honing a vast sabre to the edge of a carving knife. It glittered redly in the firelight and he bent over it with an in-tense dedicated expression on his face.

Holman and Svegintsev were among the officers round the fire and they greeted me with relief, as they were beginning to wonder where I had got to. It was now 11 p.m. and we were all dead beat, so, having seen to my horse, I dropped down and slept on the floor of a cottage, mixed up with all sorts of strange officers and men, shuffling and muttering in a variety of foreign dialects, and smelling of horses and leather and the oil with which they cleaned their guns. No outposts of any kind were put out, or the smallest steps taken for security – so much so that a Red armoured train which had lost touch with its own troops, was in the station for half an hour after we arrived before slipping away quite unmolested!

By that time, however, I couldn't have cared less. I was tired and delighted at last to have reached the front.

CHAPTER SEVEN

Next morning we were up early, intending to push on at all speed to capture Seleschina Station by nightfall. During the night, a Bolshevik officer had been found hiding in a cottage, and before we left he was tried by a drumhead court martial and, on the evidence of the peasants, was condemned to death and shot. He was a brave man, but for the leaders in the civil war there was no mercy, and he dug his own grave with considerable sang froid before he died.

The previous day's advance had done my horse in completely, so for the moment I was dismounted but I succeeded in getting a seat in a small carriage belonging to a battery commander who was supporting the Guards Regiment.

It was quite refreshing to advance as in the days of Marlborough, in a carriage drawn by two fast trotting ponies, side by side with the Russian commander, whose flag – of colossal dimensions! – floated from a pole on the box seat.

The advance guard was only one company of infantry with a few cavalry scouts and no artillery. The main body, however, had two 18-pounders and one 4.5 howitzer battery with it, while the rest of the guns were allotted to another column.

The bridge beyond Karlovka had not yet been repaired and was still a twisted mass of broken and splintered beams sagging into the water, or floating among the reeds, so we had to advance without the support of the armoured train. I decided that, because of this, the Red trains would probably act boldly if they got half a chance, and hold up our advance by coming to closer range. It seemed, in fact, an opportunity – if we could only get our field guns well forward unnoticed – to surprise them. Since the advance guard, which was already a mile ahead, also had no close artillery support, it seemed an opportunity to kill two birds with one stone.

Holman, who was riding at the head of the column, was talking to Colonel Sachs, the artillery commander, so I borrowed a horse and rode up to him and broached the subject of sending up a section of 18-pounders to join the advanced guard. After a lot of discussion through interpreters, he turned to me.

"Can it be done with an 18-pounder and an ammunition wagon?" he asked.

"I think so, sir."

"Have a go."

Accompanied by an officer in a country cart, the detachment was made ready to push forward without escort and join the advance guard. I naturally considered I should go with it and jumped on the limber.

By the time we had caught up with the advance guard, they were moving towards the edge of a small village shaded with cherry and willow trees in a hollow near the railway line, which could be seen stretching for nearly two miles away to the horizon.

"If we can get the gun concealed just short of the village," I explained carefully, "we should be well placed to face the Red train as it comes down from the skyline. It's bound to try to prevent our infantry passing through the village."

I outlined my plan in painstaking French to the Russian subaltern in command, and climbing off the limber, left him to get his gun into position and arrange his observation post and communications, while I did a little liaison work with the officer commanding the advance guard. He had halted his men on the crest and was watching his scouts through his glasses as they entered the village, apparently without opposition.

I remained with the advanced guard for a while, sitting smoking among the men, and when I looked round a little later for the gun, I found to my horror that it was sitting perched up in full view on a forward slope. The team and the outriders' horses were grazing quietly beside it, and the officer's little carriage stood close by, *all* of them in full view of the opposite high ground held by the Reds. I cursed and rushed off in a fury and with some vehemence and a great deal of gesticulation got the horses under cover and ran the gun a short distance further forward till it was partly hidden by another fold of rising ground. We then decorated a country cart with "corn stooks" and made a very fair observation post out of it. We were now about 2,000 yards from a curve of the line along which a hostile armoured train was bound to pass if it came. Thinking all was well, I walked on to find Holman, who was now with the advance guard, to tell him what was going on.

I had hardly been gone ten minutes, pushing through the long sweet-smelling grass and scrub, when, sure enough, I saw the Bolshevik train appear over the brow of the hill and slowly begin moving down the slope in front of us at a distance of about 5,000 yards. On it came, stopping only once to fire a few rounds into the village, until as far as I could judge, it must have been in the very spot where we had expected it to be. I waited in a tense silence, watching it carefully as it halted again, the snouts of its guns moving slowly in search of a target. Over the still air, I even heard the clang of a gun port as another gun was prepared for action. There was a Russian word, probably the name of the train – they all had sonorous and war-like titles – painted on the side in Cyrillic letters, and I could almost smell the metal and see the eyes peering nervously through the gun slits.

"Come on," I murmured, still waiting for the crack of an indignant 18-pounder. But nothing happened. What was wrong? In a rage, I ran back to the gun position.

The column was waiting for its lunch and the gunners were *all asleep* in the sunshine!

I kicked them awake, livid with fury.

"Get this damned gun going!" I stormed as they scuttled to their posts. In a rage, I made my way back to the observation post where the officer, who had been told that the mad Englishman was looking for him, was slowly stretching himself after a midday nap. He had decorated his carriage with corn stooks and had slept contentedly out of the sun underneath it.

We climbed on to the box seat and stood side by side looking through our glasses over the pile of corn. There, quite plainly, was the train, already firing with its 3-inch gun at a ridge to our right over which some of our troops had appeared, scattering them in little running groups and driving them down to the cover of the lower ground.

The Russian subaltern gave his orders – in Russian, so I could not be absolutely sure of his method, though he certainly got on the line of the target very well – and in two or three minutes had obtained a fairly satisfactory short bracket on the train. Two shells hit it and I saw a piece of metal go whirring away from somewhere near the front turret to land in the long grass, and a cloud of steam burst from the engine.

The hit on the armoured truck had knocked it out and its crew ran like hares back to a loose engine which steamed up to see what the trouble was. This was a bit too quick on the move for us to hit that, too, because the service of the gun was dreadfully slow, and just as I was hoping for some effective shots against it, the Bolsheviks decided that the "cause of the trouble" was somewhere in our direction, and a good supply of both shrapnel and H.E. from the armoured train's after gun began to fall along and behind the ridge where our observation post was. Earth and stones were flung up about fifty to a hundred yards away. I saw men scatter, and a horse covered with blood galloped off. Nearby another, its legs broken, struggled to rise, flinging up its head with a snort, its shoes skittering on the stones.

Despite the firing, I was just beginning to enjoy myself when, for some unknown reason, having obtained two direct hits on the train and stopped it dead, my friend alongside me on the box seat of the carriage changed from high explosive, which would have blown it off the rails, to shrapnel which was quite useless even against the thin armour of the carriages. He was wasting a valuable chance of doing some serious damage, and I remonstrated with him wildly!

"For God's sake, not shrapnel!" I shouted.

But in vain. I could see he was getting a little sulky at my constant interference, especially when I tried to hurry him with his orders, and I wondered what certain well-known instructors at the Gunnery School at Larkhill in England would have said at the sight of a British Gunner standing on the box seat of an ancient two-horse victoria under a broiling sun in the middle of the Russian steppes endeavouring to knock out an armoured train – momentarily stationary and quite helpless – with the assistance of a range table and shrapnel! However, it was the Russian's gun, not mine, and the combined efforts of us both had at least succeeded in silencing the enemy, who apparently had a nasty pain in the engine and the forward gun turret.

I made one last appeal. "Try high explosive," I said.

"We prefer shrapnel," the Russian replied.

"It'll do no good."

"It can kill the engine crew."

"Damn the crew! We can smash the whole train and capture the whole lot of 'em – crew, troops, everybody. Now's the time to knock him out before he can make repairs!"

I had finally managed to persuade the Russian of his lethal potential when one of his sergeants appeared on a horse and began to shout something to him. The subaltern gave me a quick look that might well have been of triumph, then he turned again to the sergeant. He had a pale face as long as a fiddle and commenced to jabber away in Russian again.

"Sir Major – " the Russian Commander said, turning to me, "our small stock of ammunition is finished. Not a round is left!"

I felt like exploding, but the gunners appeared to be again thinking of going to sleep in disgust and a few of them were already making themselves comfortable on the ground. There seemed little I could do with them, so I borrowed a horse and went off at full speed to look for Sachs to ask for more ammunition or for another battery to come into action and mop up the train. Running into him unexpectedly, I dragged him to where he could see the stationary train, which was now firing only with machine guns at long range at our infantry – *their* heavy ammunition was probably expended too! – while engineers worked round the engine trying to repair it sufficiently to move it.

"We must bring the 4.5 howitzer into action and smash it up," I said.

He laughed gaily. "Oh, no," he said cheerfully. "It's not necessary. The train's already finished. Our infantry will capture it now."

I didn't agree and, sure enough, in a quarter of an hour's time smoke appeared from the distant train and, slowly and silently, it steamed away with not a single shot fired after it to hinder it. I was livid.

It had been an exciting and hysterical little duel while it lasted, and to have obtained so many hits, as well as finding the range and line with no more than fifty shots from such woefully inefficient gunners, was, in spite of my rage, really quite satisfactory. The enemy's retaliation against us was much too well directed to have been pleasant, and the armoured train gunners on both sides were always picked men. The enemy's shrapnel, however, burst very high, while his H.E., unless within twenty yards of you, was not very dangerous as, owing to faulty construction, it didn't explode well and broke up into small pieces. The procedure had been completely unorthodox, however, with the Russian soldiers far more concerned with sleep than with battle.

The retaliation of the enemy's train had been chiefly directed against the infantry and the few shells flung in our direction were quite ineffective, yet they could easily have put us out of action if they'd shot straighter. And I had been sitting up on the box seat of an ancient victoria in the middle of a cornfield which had been hopefully disguised with corn stooks but still flew a huge red, blue and white flag. It was really quite ludicrous – a bit of opéra bouffe – though in fact it was probably more hair-raising than I realised, and would certainly have been very dangerous if the enemy had taken it into their heads to use any initiative and had advanced past our infantry.

*

The artillery seemed to think they had done enough for the day. I joined the leading company commander of the main body of infantry to move ahead, but while waiting just short of the village, a Bolshevik battery, which must have been firing at extreme range, began searching and sweeping the tracks along which we were about to pass. So, while shells exploded nearby, throwing stones and earth into the air, or the duds skittered along the ground away from us, we sat down behind the wall of a small compound to eat our lunch. It took me back to the baking days of open warfare in September, 1914, and my companions might almost have been the officers of a British battalion with whom I was doing a little liaison work.

The fire soon slackened and we pushed on again through the village, where I found Holman in a very forward position with the advance guard, towering above everyone else and thoroughly enjoying himself. Despite the minor hold-ups, the column had never halted for long or been compelled to deploy, but we still had a good journey to complete before getting to our objective for the day. The batteries came into action again to engage any target which appeared and to cover the advance of our infantry, but we managed to push on without interference apart from a little sniping at the scouts.

About 4 p.m. we found ourselves approaching a small village two miles short of Seleschina, and for some reason that I could not fathom the whole column suddenly started trotting and soon we were entering the main street at full gallop. The wheels of the country carts made a tremendous dust and clatter, sending chickens and livestock bolting between the houses, and through the dust I saw the frightened faces of women. Then, above the exhilarating clink and jingle of accoutrements and the shouts of the troops, I heard the relieved laughter of civilians that suddenly fell silent as a village cart went past. It contained the torn body of a man who lay with his arms flung out, his head bouncing up and down on the boards, his face carved up by a sabre, his cheek hanging loose where it had been cut away by the slash of the curving blade.

Holman and I again joined the advance guard and pushed on with them, until the station for which we were making was clearly visible about a thousand yards away. Some desultory firing was taking place, and a house was blazing. The smoke was filling the street, but it looked as though the enemy's rear-guard were not going to make much of a fight and the men were eager to press on.

The day had been hot and we were all very tired, especially the Russian officers, who *always* seemed tired and were already comfortably tucked up in their country carriages, but I rode off to the left to have a look at the country on our flank. I was also interested in the railway line and wanted to see it, and suddenly I spotted a Bolshevik armoured train standing quite still only about seven hundred yards away, apparently in a position to enfilade the whole advance guard as it passed. The Reds must have been sleepy, too, however, as they never saw me and I clapped heels to my pony, wheeled it round, and dashed back to Holman. Pointing out the train to him and the Russian commanding officer, I persuaded the Russian to deploy his men to the right and get them under cover.

At this very moment, each side became aware of the other's presence and we had to dive for cover as heavy rifle and machine gun fire was opened on us. We immediately replied, and our batteries and the main body of troops all came into action at once against the train which, deciding it was out-matched, steamed quickly away. In another half-hour the advance guard, with Holman and I riding in the middle of the firing line, drove the few remaining Reds from Seleschina station and captured it without difficulty.

After the capture of the railway station, a thorough search was made for any Bolsheviks who might be hiding in the vicinity, and the troops began to push through the houses, their weapons at the ready. Walls and windows were broken and the floors were fouled by horses and stank of human excrement. Furniture was hacked by sabres, mirrors smashed and books charred, and from the wreckage one unfortunate commissar was discovered. His identity was proved beyond all doubt by the papers he carried and by his red star badge of office.

Under escort of an N.C.O. and two soldiers, the wretched man was brought to a group of three officers with whom I was talking. It was useless for him to deny his position and he could never have expected to escape with his life. Immediately, two of the young Guards officers with whom I had worked and fought during the last forty-eight hours seemed to cast from them the cloak of refinement which they had appeared to wear so naturally, and the primitive man, embittered by the hatred of civil war, came into evidence.

The trembling commissar was beaten across the face and head till the blood flowed and he was abused and reviled and threatened with the pains of hell. It was plain that he was about to undergo untold and indescribable suffering and I remonstrated with one of the officers, and finally drew my revolver and said I would no longer witness this type of brutality. The officer turned angrily on me, beating down my right hand.

"We are proud and grateful to have you fighting with us and helping us," he said sharply, "but you do not appreciate the circumstances from the Russian point of view."

Each of the three men standing with me, it seemed, had lost relations and friends, as well as property, under the most brutal circumstances at the hands of the commissars, of which this man was a typical specimen.

"If we were to fall into the hands of Bolsheviks," he went on furiously, "we should be tortured. *We* are not torturing the commissar, only frightening him in the hope that he will betray other Bolshevik sympathisers in the neighbourhood."

They all referred to the massacre of naval and military officers by the men of the Black Sea Fleet at Sebastopol, where the wretched victims were lined up on the decks and given the choice of "dying hot" or "dying cold". If they chose "hot", they were tied to planks and fed inch by inch into the ship's furnaces. If they chose "cold" they had iron bars tied to their feet and were dropped into the sea. They also excitedly related to me some of the appalling atrocities which had been perpetrated against their women relations at Petrograd in 1917 and 1918, and claimed that the prisoner was the type of man who had instigated and encouraged these actions, and was, therefore, more guilty than the ignorant soldiers who were led on by the agitators.

"It is," the first speaker claimed, "just a personal question between ourselves and him. When this sort of thing happens in England, perhaps you will be able to understand it better! For the time being, please mind your own business!"

Looking at it impartially I had to agree with them, but as we had become very good friends during the last two days, I prevailed on them not to touch the man again and he was taken away and hanged without more ado.

*

It was now fairly late, and we were all pretty exhausted, so we billeted in the village close to the station, intending to advance on Poltava early the following morning. About 8 p.m., however, Svegintsev arrived in the Vauxhall in a state of extreme agitation. Reports had been filtering back to Karlovka of Holman's continuous presence in the firing line and the enthusiasm with which the Russian troops were greeting him.

Both he and Wynter tried to persuade him to keep out of the next day's fighting.

"The General is too important a personage to take the risks which this sort of civilian guerilla warfare entails," Svegintsev explained.

Then he went on, looking a little sheepish. "Besides," he said, "Russian Generals do not make a habit of frequenting the forward positions and they might feel hurt. It would be more suitable for the Russian Command to carry out the final capture of Poltava on their own and for the General to follow on as their guest, rather than precede them with the fighting troops."

Very regretfully, therefore, we packed into the Vauxhall and drove back to Karlovka where we climbed on to the train again. Late in the evening, receiving news that the First Guards Brigade were already on the outskirts of Poltava, we moved forward and arrived in the station early next morning.

It was nearly midday, however, before we were allowed to go up into the town as there was still a good deal of "mopping up" to be done, and Toporkov's cavalry were still collecting stores and prisoners whose escape to the north had been cut off. We also collected three armoured trains and several engines.

Men appeared carrying boxes of ammunition, weapons, clothes and food. One or two even had a dead chicken hanging at their belts, with the owner protesting loudly just behind. Prisoners appeared, kicked and pushed and stumbling under the blows of rifle butts, some of them wounded and all of them terrified.

"I remember finding the corpses in Migulinsk," someone said bitterly. "Their fingers were cut off and their eyes were gouged out. They buried half a score of men alive."

Many of the prisoners had considerable sums of money on them and their officers' baggage was packed with all manner of things like sugar and tobacco, furs, rugs, cut glass, furniture and even pianos.

Despite the wreckage caused by shellfire, the collapsed houses with their wailing owners, and the occasional sprawled corpse, there was a lot of laughter and bottles and cigars were passed around, and fierce eyes grinned at me from beneath the fur Cossack caps. This was what it must have been like through the centuries, I thought with surprise. This is how the Cossack raiding parties must have entered the border villages to collect their loot and snatch the women. It seemed incredible that I was taking part in it in the Twentieth Century.

Poltava was a pleasant large country town with the usual park and gardens where the people still promenaded as though nothing had happened. Despite the column of prisoners moving off, the bivouacking troops in the streets, the horses quietly cropping the grass, and the blue smoke of cooking fires, the women in their country dresses were still taking their children for walks. About a dozen urchins, the eldest not more than fourteen, appeared shouldering Bolshevik rifles as big as themselves and said they were going to hunt down Reds. One of them, not as big as the weapon he carried, claimed to have shot several.

We were all invited to a dinner party and concert in our honour and told to assemble at the "Hall of the Nobility" (lately called by the Bolsheviks "The People's Palace!").

On arrival, we each had to enter singly while the band played the usual welcoming tune and our hosts clapped their hands noisily together. The big hall looked impressive with its walls hung with massive gold picture frames filled with torn portraits. In the old days these had held the images of local notables and landowners, whilst one at the end of the room from which the double-headed eagle had obviously been detached, had clearly been occupied by a picture of the Tsar himself. The original occupants, however, had been torn out in the early days of the Revolution and been replaced by the popular heroes of the new democracy – Lenin, Trotsky, Tchicherin, Lunacharski, Zinoviev and Dzherinski, who in their turn were now hanging in dejected strips where they had been slashed by the bayonets of the infuriated White soldiers or used for pistol practice that very morning. Someone had neatly shot out Lenin's eyes with a rifle.

At one end of the room was a concert platform and the rest of the space was occupied by two long tables joined by a headpiece at which the guests of honour sat. The band which welcomed us had played for the Bolshevik administrators only forty-eight hours previously, while the artistes who were to entertain us had done the same. These included a very attractive Polish lady, who I was told was very well-known in Moscow and who, as well as singing extremely well, whistled to her own piano accompaniment. There was also an excellent tenor, and two violinists who would not have been ashamed to play to a picked London audience.

The most touching part of the evening to me, however, was

the delight of our hosts, and their joy at being free from the rule of the Soviets. Many members of the best-known families in Russia were there. Old generals had dug out their faded uniforms and put on their badges of rank, orders and epaulettes, which since the Revolution had been carefully hidden away. Jewels and dresses of three, four and even five seasons before were unearthed, and cultured and attractive women who had suffered appalling losses and hardships again indulged in the pleasure of dressing up. Most of them had spent the last eighteen months in hiding, working as maids or servants in their own houses to avoid the attention of the ubiquitous "Extraordinary Commission for the Combating of Counter-Revolution", which so diligently sought out the supporters of the old regime, trumped up false charges against them, and condemned them ruthlessly to imprisonment or death.

They were all doing their utmost to show their appreciation to anyone who had in any way contributed to their deliverance, and about 11 p.m. the tables were cleared and the dancing began, and it was 1 a.m. before I left with two of the officers on General Gaiman's staff. Our car would not start, however, and we were walking down the hill to the station when, with a rattle and a ringing of bells, an unexpected vehicle dashed past us. The Poltava fire-engine was like most others, though a little old-fashioned, but the Russian firemen – complete with brass helmets – seemed rather inclined to make use of this opportunity to search other people's property in the hope of taking a share of the loot that had been left behind. This was not altogether appreciated by the unfortunate house-owners, and a great deal of arguing and shouting was going on, while the fire, which had been started in the Jewish quarter shortly after the arrival there of Toporkov's Caucasian Cavalry, burned itself out.

I decided I'd better keep out of the dispute and went on alone to the station. Coming out of the gate, looking very fresh and dainty, I saw Gaiman's lady mess caterer who, I discovered, was just off to the market for vegetables, bread and eggs to replenish the train's supplies. Thinking it was now too late to go to bed, I offered to help and made a point of obtaining a good share of the produce for our own mess.

Returning to my coach, I was called to Gaiman's train. Two or three of the Kuban officers were still awake and I found myself sitting down to hard-boiled eggs, radishes and vodka – at 6 a.m. on a hot summer morning, after three of the most exciting days one could imagine! I was dog tired, but the whole atmosphere was so full of novelty, pathos, adventure, and all the sensations which went to make life worth living, I dared not go to sleep for long in case I missed some still more engrossing experience. I got to bed for a few hours soon afterwards knowing we were due for an inspection of troops at one o'clock, and a presentation of British medals by Holman to officers and men recommended for conspicuous service during the operations.

This took place before an enormous crowd on the parade ground, and was, of course, accompanied by the usual solemn open-air thanksgiving service. So great was the enthusiasm for Holman he was accorded the enormous but uncomfortable compliment of being thrown up three times in the air and caught again by a muscular party of young Guards officers.

When we got back to the train we were absolutely exhausted. There seemed nothing more to do in Poltava, so our entire party, horses, carts, etc., were collected and entrained. Ling and his interpreter had arrived from Kharkov to report, so, saying goodbye, we turned into our coupés, and decided to remain in them until such time as an engine which was taking to Kharkov the armoured train to which we were attached, should get going.

Holman did not want to spend much time at Kharkov and got through his official visits to General Mai-Maievski and General Bilaiev in two days. I had heard a lot about Mai-Maievski but he was even better than the descriptions. If he hadn't worn a uniform, he would have been taken for a red-nosed comedian from a provincial English theatre. He was perfectly round in shape, had a chubby face and a bulbous nose, but he was reputed to be a good officer, though he was a tremendous drinker and his drinking bouts were considered outrageous.

We also visited the scene of the massacres carried out by the Bolsheviks before they had left the town. A great many men and women had been shot and buried in a communal grave and horrifying photographs were produced for our inspection.

I excused myself to visit a railway repair shop, which was desperately in need of many very important necessaries, and later, while wandering round the town, I found some excellent Hungarian Tokay which had been left behind by the Reds, and was able to buy several bottles very cheaply. We were all, however, very anxious by now to get to another front as the General was beginning to realise the existing liaison system was defective, and was anxious to re-organise the whole Mission on a more practical basis.

He went straight to Ekaterinodar from Kharkov, dropping me off the train at Rostov whence I returned to Novocherkassk. He promised to pick me up again in a few days' time on his way back to visit the Don Army to compare it with what we had just seen of the Volunteer Army.

He had already made a decision to ask for more officers from England and to get rid of all the unsuitable ones already in South Russia.

CHAPTER EIGHT

Back in Novocherkassk I found more batteries had gone to the Front and equipment arriving more satisfactorily. The sergeant instructor had died of cholera, however, but Angus Campbell was now well over his attack of typhus, and had gone to the base en route for England. The Don Army were still pressing steadily towards Liski and the north, and all sorts of supplies had arrived at Novocherkassk, though they were only being distributed very slowly.

I went to see the Abramovs and the Rechitovskis and to call on Alex Smaguin and his wife.

There had been a new batch of refugees from the north and the talk was all of old friends. There was an undercurrent of doubt, however, as they talked of hopes and fears, but when Alex passed round the vodka, as he always contrived to do, everyone's spirits picked up at once.

"*Piet odnya*," Alex said. "Drink now! To Christmas in Moscow!"

Everyone drank cheerfully enough but the doubt managed to remain.

"Suppose the Bolsheviks come here?" Moussia said.

"They won't," I said firmly. "We're moving north."

"We've moved north before," she pointed out. "What if they *did* come?"

"You'd be all right," I said. "We've undertaken to look after you all. All you'd have to do would be to pack your baggage –"

She laughed but there was a tinge of sadness in the laughter. "I have no luggage," she said. "None at all."

She showed me a bracelet full of exquisitely enamelled miniature Easter eggs by the famous jeweller Fabergé. "This is my luggage," she said. "I can get it all into my pocket. The only safe thing to have these days is jewellery. You can always eat if you have it. I've kept mine as long as I can."

She fingered the bracelet. "These were always a popular Easter gift in Petrograd society," she went on. "We all had them. This will probably be the next to be sold."

I saw a lot of the Smaguins in the next few days because I knew that as soon as Holman turned up I should be busy again, and, sure enough, as soon as he arrived I was dragged off to lunch with Sidorin at his house, and went the same afternoon in Holman's train to the headquarters of the 3rd Don Corps, at Kantimirovka. We had a short interview with the Commander, General Ivanov, and tried to make plans for our trip. We were put off as usual.

"The whole front is on the move now," Ivanov said.

The Corps staff were very reluctant as usual to let us into the forward area, but they were finally persuaded into giving us an extra escort of an officer and fifteen Cossacks, and more country carts, and we set off northwards the same evening.

We were hung up, however, by the railway bridge across the Tchornaya Kalitva which had been blown up and was still under repair, and, at some risk of breaking down the temporary trestle bridge, which had been put up by the Cossack sapper battalion, we man-handled Holman's train across, one carriage at a time, and eventually pulled up the following morning at Saprina station. Here we found a battery of 18-pounders, who had received their British guns about three weeks previously. On going over their equipment for them, however, we found it in a parlous state. They had lost (or never received) all spare springs, they had no buffer oil, and the top of their director was missing. The Battery Commander appeared to take little or no interest in getting matters adjusted or his battery into a fit condition to fight, and he was subsequently removed from command.

The headquarters of the 5th Division were at Saprina village, where we lunched with the Divisional Commander. He had only about 2,000 men under him, split up into groups working up the right bank of the Don and trying to keep in touch with the 3rd Division whose headquarters were at Pavlovsk. Their orders had been to capture Losevo, cross the river Bityug and clear up the country between there and the Don, and eventually advance on Bobrov.

Losevo had apparently been captured during the last twenty-four hours, but the right flank of the 3rd Division was somewhat in the air owing to the uncertain movements of the 1st Division on that flank and to the reports of a Bolshevik regrouping of forces farther still to the right in the neighbourhood of Buturlinovka.

Holman's A.D.C., Roberts, and Harold Williams followed us with the transport, while the General with Svegintsev and myself pushed on in the car to arrive at Pavlovsk in the afternoon. We had a good deal of difficulty in getting across the Don by the main trestle bridge, a temporary trellis of wood put up to replace the original piers, as the sentry was very obdurate.

"*Angliski*," we kept saying. "We're English officers."

The sentry was either very stupid or enjoying the discomfiture of senior officers because he refused to budge and it was only when Svegintsev got angry that he allowed us to pass.

Leaving the car at Pavlovsk we started next morning for Losevo. 3rd Divisional Headquarters had moved forward again between the Don and the Bityug, however, and we eventually caught them up at Beresovo, about nine miles farther on, late in the evening. General Krievov, the commander, gave us all the news about the division.

"We are very low in strength," he said, "and we have had no British uniforms at all, nor any British artillery or machine guns."

This seemed to be the usual story. Though Don Army Headquarters claimed at one time to have 100,000 men under arms, I visited all the fronts and there were never more than three or four thousand troops in any one forward area at a time, all very badly equipped.

Krievov, in fact, gave us the impression that his division had been badly neglected because of their position so far from rail-head. They were due to attack Osinovko next morning, but our horses were too beat to get to the front to see the operations. Owing to a rain storm and the fact that sixty per cent of their home-made Russian shells did not burst, these ended in failure. We went up, however, in the morning, and met General Philimonov, commanding the 2nd Infantry Brigade, and General Igonmonov, whose regiment the 12th had carried out the attack.

Philimonov, a cautious, weak-willed man, was very bitter. "We failed because of the failure of the artillery," he said. "There were never enough shells."

Some of the criticism came my way, of course, for no other reason than that I was a gunner.

From their trenches we could see the Bolsheviks about 1,000 yards away on the other side of a valley, but neither side appeared to have any further hostile intentions for that day and Holman asked to see a platoon of the 12th Regiment so as to form an idea as to their equipment. Twelve men were paraded straight from the trenches and I have never seen such a miserable sight in my life. They only had *five* boots among the lot, one man had no rifle, and that of another was clogged up with dirt. Their clothes were hanging in rags, one man had no trousers and wore woollen underpants, and they looked half-starved. How could men so ill-equipped fight? With so much British uniform coming into the country, surely these were the first to have been equipped, not the clerks at Headquarters or the embusqué officers at Novocherkassk.

In a fury, Holman turned to his staff. "We'll go back at once to Taganrog and Novorossiisk," he said. "And see if we can't speed up the distribution of stores."

We hurried to the railway via Pavlovsk but here, unfortunately local hospitality had prompted a dramatic effort for our entertainment and it was difficult to turn them down. It was a Chekov play – but we were rather exhausted and, as it was in Russian, I slept through most of it.

On arrival at Novorossiisk we spent three strenuous days collecting stores of every kind. Holman was determined to take up complete field ambulances as well as medical equipment on his visit to Wrangel's Caucasian Army which he proposed to see next. He also collected 2,000 complete sets of uniform and equipment in an incredibly short time, hoping to fit out one or two of Wrangel's units. I collected a lot of gun stores, bandages and hospital necessities and bought a lot of rations such as tea, sugar and tinned milk, and every pound of tinned food, jam and sweets, that the base canteen would allow me, so that as soon as my trip with Holman was over, I could do the same thing on my own for the Don Cossacks. One very important thing, whisky, was almost unobtainable, although I noticed there appeared to be plenty for the inhabitants of the base.

We were back at Ekaterinodar by August 19th when I was inoculated for cholera. I was just looking forward to starting when I received a bombshell from Holman.

"You'd better return to Novocherkassk," he said, "and prepare things for the arrival of the trainload of stores being organised at the base for the Don Army. I shall be taking all the things we've already packed up to Tsaritsyn for Wrangel."

I saw myself done out of my trip to the Tsaritsyn Front, as well as my stores for the Don Cossacks, but next morning, as I sat at my usual place for breakfast in Holman's dining car trying to look as little mutinous as possible, Holman came in. I rose to say "Good morning," and sat down again in gloomy silence. He eyed me for a while in silence then I heard him say slyly, "I see Williamson sitting there as though he had decided to come to Tsaritsyn."

I pretended to pay no attention and he eyed me for a while.

"How will things get on at Novocherkassk if you are away much longer?" he asked.

"Everything will be fine, sir," I said, and the subject was dropped and I stayed on the train.

We started the same night, and arrived at Beketovka on the 23rd, where we found "C" Flight of 47 Squadron, R.A.F., and the 1st Kuban Flight of Nieuports, both of which were working with Wrangel's Caucasian Army. We moved into Tsaritsyn in the afternoon. It had been in an appalling state when captured by Wrangel's troops. Many of the people had been murdered and the houses and shops looted, and there were epidemics raging everywhere. The mortality had been heavy and thousands of corpses had been thrown into a gulley outside the city. It had taken a week to bury them all and clear the streets of dead horses, of which more than 400 were taken away, but Tsaritsyn was alive once more now, its shops and restaurants open. The bishop, who had to hide in the suburbs with the other priests, had just been released from prison and had conducted a Te Deum in the Cathedral.

Unfortunately, the town remained dirty and dusty with unswept streets, and no renovation or repair work seemed to have been done on any buildings for years, and there was no organisation for the disposal of garbage. Owing to its position at the big western bend of the Volga, it had always been a great market for goods passing from East to West and vice versa, but it certainly had few natural merits.

We saw Wrangel and his Chief of Staff, General Shatilov, that afternoon, and both seemed very energetic and able. Wrangel was an enormously tall man, lean as a greyhound, with a tremendous personality, who seemed well able to control his troops. During the first days of the revolution he had been in Petrograd and, while other officers wore red ribbons to save their lives, he had resolutely refused to do so and faced up to mutineers and revolutionaries, his height and commanding presence being sufficient to keep him from being harmed.

When he was eventually arrested and imprisoned in a dirty custom-house with other generals, young officers, students, and common loafers, the sailors and Red Guards outside had wanted to execute him, but his wife, who refused to leave his side, saved him from joining the prisoners who were being shot outside the door. More than a thousand officers were murdered and their bodies thrown in the water but Wrangel was freed, and when money, clothing and jewellery were taken away from those who had them, he saved his own family jewels and money by hiding them in the stomachs and heads of his little daughter's dolls, and their furs and laces under a heap of charcoal.

His troops adored him but he had no time for deserters and when Bolshevik regiments came over to him, he recruited men by the simple method of shooting all the officers and non-commissioned officers on the spot and telling the rest to take their choice. Most didn't hesitate.

The situation on this front at the time of our arrival was still very uncertain. Our old friend General Gaiman, of Poltava, had returned to the Caucasian Army, but had been held responsible for the loss of Kamyshin, an important town 100 miles north of Tsaritsyn on the west bank of the Volga and, since he had been suspected of speculation in flour looted at Poltava, he had been deprived of his command. In addition, the Bolsheviks, supported by heavily-armed river steamers, were advancing rapidly down the Volga, and our fleet of barges and armed steamers seemed unable to stop them. Though bombed every day by both British and Russian Air Forces, they seemed to be keeping determinedly on.

On Wrangel's left, the right flank of the Don Cossack Army was also falling back on the Tsaritsyn-Povorino railway line, and news had just come in on the telegraph of the loss of three armoured trains with their entire personnel. It was a favourite trick of both sides to go into enemy territory early in the morning and, under cover of darkness, widen the lines by about a foot for a distance of ten to fifteen yards, and it was assumed that this was what had happened.

South of Tsaritsyn, affairs were no better, and several efforts on the part of the Caucasian Army to capture Chernyi Yar and advance on Astrakhan had been driven off, although the troops had been closely supported by British airmen with bombing raids and machine gun fire. The Bolsheviks had dug themselves well in north of the village, and could not be shifted. To the east a body of Denikin's troops had crossed the Volga, and cavalry was moving towards the Astrakhan-Urbakh railway line, searching for Kolchak's advanced patrols from Siberia, which had been reported approaching the railway from the Urals to link up with the southern armies. No trace of them was ever found.

Though we didn't know it at the time, of course, the tragic retrograde movement of the White Army in Siberia was already commencing. The last we heard of Kolchak was that he was in possession of Omsk and was heading for Cheylyabinsk, but the green and white flags were now in retreat everywhere and the rearguard were just waiting their chance to desert to the Reds without trouble.

Wrangel was frankly worried when he arrived for lunch and a conference in Holman's coach next day. He was thin with sparse hair, an aristocrat with all the haughtiness of his class. For twenty years he had been an officer in a Cossack regiment whose uniform set off his commanding figure to great advantage. He was no mean strategist either and the morale of his Caucasian troops was high. The green crescent flags of his Mohammedan regiments had moved steadily forward but they were strictly disciplined, and one of his commanders, Ulegai, had been known to hang men for stealing chickens.

His excitable temperament made him a first-class cavalry leader but he was in a gloomy mood as he sat down. We knew nothing of what was happening in Siberia, of course, and he was only concerned for what was happening in the south. Everything seemed to depend on Denikin and he was being stubborn.

"He should recreate the old regular cavalry," Wrangel insisted. "We have the necessary men and many officers serving as privates to lead them, and *this* is a cavalry war."

Unfortunately, Denikin, like his advisers, was an infantry officer and nothing was being done.

Wrangel was also bitterly critical of the army as a whole. By this time he was no longer showing his former unswerving loyalty to Denikin. He thought Denikin was wrong and said so and from this point on he was never able to give him his full support.

There were, he said, too many disagreements among the senior officers and the ferocity of the war was dimming the flame of enthusiasm in the men. He also felt that Denikin's advance had reduced the army's effective force.

"Its rear is too big," he said. "And it's fast becoming a collection of tradesmen and profiteers instead of soldiers. Regimental rolling stock has grown to enormous dimensions. The troops are becoming demoralised."

What he said was unfortunately true and many senior officers *were* setting a bad example with gambling and drinking, while their troops were neglected and becoming utterly exhausted.

"The bitter truth," Wrangel went on, "is that there is no longer a compact army and the enemy are rapidly becoming aware of it."

Again what he said was true. Due to a lack of trained men to send as drafts to the front, some brigades were only as big as battalions. And some batteries, due to lack of organisation and a general shortage throughout Russia, had only enough horses for one or two guns.

He had registered protests to Denikin, and had advocated the evacuation of Taganrog and Rostov and had been promised action, but nothing had been done and Rostov was left un-organised and undefended for a tragedy that, had we only known it, was to take place only too soon.

During the lunch break, General Pavlishenko, a Kuban Cossack from Umanskya, was presented to Holman. Aged only twenty-seven and wounded seven times, he had always fought with great gallantry and, with huge delight, he departed with a British D.S.O., given him in the King's name by Holman.

At the afternoon conference, I suggested that to hold up the Bolshevik advance, the artillery should use mustard gas. A large number of these and other gas shells had been dumped at suitable railheads, but for political reasons they had not been used up to that time – not only to avoid killing harmless peasants but also because the personnel of the White Army were rather nervous of handling them. As the loss of Tsaritsyn would be a very severe blow to Denikin's cause, it seemed a suitable moment to bring this very powerful agent into use. Gas was a horrible weapon but it had been used constantly in

France since 1915 and was still regarded as a normal adjunct to war, and the occasion seemed to demand it.

Wrangel accepted the idea with keenness. Holman, too, was enthusiastic.

"You'd better go at once to bring them up," he said. "You'd better also help the Kuban batteries with them. It's a rather technical type of warfare."

I was, of course, delighted, and was eager to start at once, but, to my surprise, I was told to get into the Vauxhall with Holman and we drove straight off to the aerodrome at Beketovka where an up-to-date D.H.9 piloted by Captain William Elliott, a cheerful R.A.F. officer from 47 Squadron, R.A.F., with a curious bird-like appearance, was put at my disposal until the job was complete.

I had no idea at what dumps the gas shells were stored but thought I'd try the Don Army first as I knew they'd let me have anything they had at Novocherkassk without further trouble. We started at dawn next morning, and flew across country on our 250-mile flight, following the line of the Tsaritsyn-Likhaia railway. The weather was hot and we never had to fly high and, as there were no enemy aircraft about, I thoroughly enjoyed myself.

Almost before we knew how far we had come, the five golden domes of Novocherkassk Cathedral appeared in the south-west, and after circling two or three times round the town we landed comfortably on the racecourse, at that time used by the Don Flying School as an aerodrome. Elliott decided to check his machine while I borrowed one of the Russian cars and rushed off to my headquarters to find out where I could get the gas shells.

"There are none in the Don Army area," I was told and the only suggestion that could be offered were to try Bataisk or Umanskya.

It was too late to start that night but as soon as the machine was tuned up next day we flew straight to the new Mission headquarters at Taganrog, which I thought would be the best place to get the most accurate information and the necessary authority to draw the ammunition. We flew via Rostov, down the Don and along the edge of the Sea of Azov. This was like an inland lake off the Black Sea but it was totally devoid of shipping. I lunched with Keyes, then we started off for Rostov again in the afternoon, where we had to find General Kirey to give us the rest of the information and the authority we required. It was too late to find him that day so I passed a note over to Elliott suggesting flying to Bataisk and landing there to see whether there were any shells at the dump in the railway station.

We landed on open ground close to the station amid great excitement, as Elliott did a little light-hearted stunting first, but when we searched the ammunition dumps and wagons, there were no shells there, though the officer in charge said he was sure there were plenty in Umanskya.

It was already dusk as we left for Rostov and, although it was only a ten-minute flight, we had to have a good look on arrival for the racecourse which was the only suitable landing place we could think of. It grew darker and darker, so Elliott decided to chance any unseen obstacles, and down we went and pulled up without mishap in the long grass. We climbed out of the machine and received something of a shock when we saw that the whole area was strewn with wooden benches about two feet high, which would surely have wrecked the undercarriage if we had hit one. We commandeered a group of Russian soldiers to guard the machine for the night, and made our way to the British Mission.

Next morning we completed our business, getting all the necessary signatures from General Kirey and his staff, and decided to start for Umanskya about sixty miles away. At the racecourse, however, we found a meeting in progress and a large crowd watching trotting races run on a dust track of good width.

Elliott grinned. "The track's the only place we can take off safely," he said. "Think they'll let us?"

"We can try," I said and we accordingly approached the stewards and asked them to stop the races for half-an-hour while we got away. Despite protests by the bookmakers, we prepared the big D.H.9 for the flight and man-handled her on to the straight while the race-goers of Rostov had to wait.

At Umanskya we were lucky to find the officer commanding the dump at once. He was a little Cossack Colonel called Archipov, and to our delight, as we had no interpreter, his wife, an attractive girl who had followed him all over Turkestan and a lot of Central Asia while his regiment had been on frontier duty there, spoke English perfectly.

Archipov had the shells we wanted and we made arrangements for loading them and sending them off next morning, and as I had so many written orders for wagons to be expedited by every railway official that they were to approach, I decided to leave them in charge of a Russian officer to bring along, and to fly straight back to Tsaritsyn, to give a little instruction in their use to the Russian artillery, and to make plans for a good concentration of British guns to give the Reds a real good dose.

We were to start in the afternoon so as to arrive at Tsaritsyn in the evening, and Archipov and his wife came down to see us leave. Elliott went through the usual preliminaries of sucking in, and we started swinging the propeller in turn. I had taken my swing and was just clear of it when I heard several explosions and, looking round, saw Elliott lying on the ground on the point of fainting. He had forgotten to switch off before swinging the propeller and the engine had picked up.

His arm was badly smashed above the elbow, and the badge had been torn out of his cap by the tip of the propeller. I had only escaped because the engine had mis-fired while I was handling the blade, and picked up when it came to Elliott's turn.

Madame Archipov was splendid. She had a rough splint on him in ten minutes, while Archipov dashed off and returned with a bed and eight Cossacks to carry it to the village hospital about two miles away. A doctor was sent for and he examined the fracture and reported it as very severe. Elliott suffered terribly while it was being set, but he was remarkably cheerful and Madame Archipov sat up with him all night. I went off to the station and managed to get a horse truck cleaned out and detailed for the next train to Sossika, which was not expected to be until next day.

We carried Elliott to the station and got him into the truck but we were kept waiting nearly a whole day and would never have got the truck attached to the Rostov train if Archipov had not finally drawn his revolver.

"This truck will be attached to the Rostov train," he said firmly, flourishing it under the nose of the Station Commandant.

"Your Excellency," the Station Commandant stammered. "I have my orders and the engines have only a limited capacity."

"One more truck won't make any difference," Archipov insisted. "As the trains only move at walking pace, they couldn't go much slower."

"Excellency – "

"I give you thirty seconds to make up your mind."

The Station Commandant's eyes rolled and he swallowed with difficulty.

"It shall be attached," he agreed.

It was important to get Elliott to Taganrog into the British Hospital there, if there was to be any chance of saving his arm. He was still suffering a great deal, and owing to the heat and the disgusting state of the railways and the lack of sanitation, the flies were almost unbearable. I was anxious to go with him to Taganrog, but apart from companionship, I could do no more for him and I ought already to have been back at Tsaritsyn, so I reluctantly parted from him at Rostov, giving a letter to Archipov to be delivered to Keyes at Taganrog. I had no kit, except my razor and a pair of socks, no interpreter and no ticket, so I just boarded the first train which I saw pointed eastwards with Tsaritsyn written on it, and trusted to luck.

The big engine was already tossing out a streamer of white smoke and the driver was in the cab adjusting the valves and I expected it to leave at once. But like all trains, it was terribly crowded and covered with feather beds, pots and pans, and the organisation of getting it started was immense. Russian trains in the summer always seemed to carry as many passengers on the roofs of the coaches as were huddled inside, and more often than not the coaches were really only horseboxes called *terplushkas* from the warmth they derived from the brazier fire burning inside them. These stoves burned an enormous amount of wood and, in winter, people grew frantic trying to find enough fuel to keep from freezing. Sanitation was nil.

Crowded trains were a feature of the civil war and the compartments were always packed to suffocation with refugees, and with far too many soldiers on leave, who appeared to be making the fullest use of such few trains as the shortage of fuel allowed. Most of the engines had to use wood, as the supplies of coal and oil were limited for lack of means to transport them to the depots, and since the track across the steppe was single, when they broke down or came to a halt through lack of fuel, so did all the trains behind them. It wasn't at all unusual to see whole strings of motionless trains winding across the folds of the steppes. However, it was still summer and nobody worried. There were larks above the flowery plain and occasional coveys of partridges bursting upwards and the children could play games alongside the stalled trains, while the dogs were given walks and women changed their clothing.

The train I was on was no exception to the rule. It consisted only of cushionless third class carriages but I succeeded in impressing the guard of the post van with my importance.

"Courier," I kept saying, and got myself tucked up among some indescribably dirty letter bags. This was very different from travelling in Holman's comfortable special, and it was appallingly slow, and I had to fight with the crowd at the station food markets to get even a glass of disgusting-looking milk. At Torgovya, however, I managed to buy two cold roast chickens, one to eat and the other to barter with my fellow travellers for anything desirable which they might possess.

As we moved eastwards, rumours came floating down the

telegraph wires that the Reds had appeared just outside
Tsaritsyn, and that Wrangel's headquarters had been forced to
move to Sarepta, and by the second day when we reached
Kotelnikov, refugees began appearing in crowds with wild
stories of the loss of Tsaritsyn.

Several trains had been leaving the city every day for some
time, they said. The first had carried the war material, then the
civil and military administration had followed, and lastly those
civilians who wanted to leave the town. There was luggage
room for one trunk per person but the trains were crammed
with merchandise of all kinds. One passenger train, in fact, was
full of pianos, mirrors and valuable furniture and Wrangel had
had it all thrown out and smashed. Then he had discovered a
train with locked carriages which were said to be loaded with
ammunition, but they were full of passengers, mostly Jews,
who were hoping to get their merchandise away, and had
bribed the stationmaster. He had flung them all out on the track
and hanged the stationmaster.

The news made me more eager to get back to the front but
the train ahead of us on the single track had come to a stop so
I left the post van in which I was riding and installed myself in
an open truck on the train in front but, on seeing still another
train in front of that, moved up again. Eventually I moved up
five trains till I found myself on a troop special on which was a
regiment of Kabardine Cavalry, about 200 strong, all of them
the most evil-looking ruffians I've ever set eyes on.

Dark, unshaven men with Afghan appearance, they wore the
long black waisted coat peculiar to the Kuban Cossacks, black
or grey sheepskin caps, and an array of black-and-silver inlaid daggers, swords, old-fashioned pistols, and the usual
decorative line of cartridges across the chest. Many had red
bashliks, or hoods, hung round the neck to introduce a
touch of colour, but all wore the red, blue and white chevrons
of the White Army. None of their officers could speak French,
and I could barely understand a word of their Caucasian patois.
Once they discovered I was not a Bolshevik in disguise, how-

ever, they treated me very well, but because I wasn't armed to the teeth, they seemed to find me an object mostly fit for derision! They were absolutely wild, and at every one of the numerous long halts which the train made, they always brought their band into action and indulged in a display of barbaric dancing.

I felt very much alone – particularly when they started brandishing their swords and daggers and shouting at me. As they had a plentiful supply of vodka, it was difficult to be quite certain if their gestures were always as friendly as I hoped. One of them, while dancing in the horsebox in which he lived, fell out backwards and broke his neck, but nobody seemed to mind very much.

After considerable delay, I arrived at Sarepta. There was a trainload of newly wounded men in the siding. They lay in crowded wooden cars largely untended, crying out for water, help, or relief of any kind. The stench coming from the train was appalling. From their overworked attendants I tried to get information of what was going on.

They stopped long enough to try to enlighten me.

"There's been heavy fighting," they said. "There are more Reds than we expected and they've pushed us back."

"Where from?"

"The Tsaritsyn area."

This was as much as I could discover in my hesitant Russian but a young Russian cavalry officer, seeing me in difficulties, helped me out.

"If Tsaritsyn falls," he said, "there will be only isolated areas of resistance between there and Saratov to the north. The 10th and 11th Soviet Armies are attacking the city at this moment. Only a few Kuban regiments are in control of the Kotluban area."

He had a friend with him who had been wounded that morning and I shared with them all the food we could buy in the station, and the one thing which till now I had kept up my sleeve – my last drop of whisky. With a little of this inside them my friends grew more talkative.

"If Tsaritsyn goes, all to the north will be cut off," they said. "But don't let's be too pessimistic. Let's forget all this talk of a move south. It hasn't happened yet. Wrangel's still in Tsaritsyn, though it's true the Bolsheviks have inflicted heavy losses on the Caucasian Army."

They seemed unduly optimistic, almost as though we'd won a victory.

"Are we still falling back?" I asked.

They exchanged glances and their smiles vanished. "Yes," they agreed unwillingly. "We are."

Late in the evening, I arrived at Beketovka, riding on the engine of an armoured train, which was coming up to reinforce, and went in search of the R.A.F.

They were under the command of Raymond Collishaw, who had been one of the most successful of the British fighter pilots in France, and were a crack group. They had an engine and tender, two pullman cars, a mess car, and assorted box cars and flat cars for their ground crews, workshops, ammunition, oil and provisions, and for their machines when they could not be moved by air. They were flying Camels, one of the best of the scout planes available at the time, and had done stout work for Wrangel's armies. Their mess car was austere but comfortable, and against one wall was a bar.

I gave them as much reassuring news as possible about Elliott and in return received news of Holman.

"He's left for Taganrog," they said to my astonishment. "He got an urgent message from Denikin that he wanted to confer." They also said that General Mackiev, Chief of the Artillery of the Caucasian Army, wanted to see me next day.

I had a bath, tidied up, found my kit which Holman had left for me to pick up, and felt like a new man. Scarcely had I completed all this, than a message came over from the Russian Flying Corps' train asking me to dine with them as it was the name day of one of their officers. After climbing up the ladder to the end door of a long dining-car, which was evidently their mess, I found myself in surroundings which by their very contrast to the squalor of my last four days seemed all the more grotesque.

The interior of the dining-car had been transformed into a combined sitting- and dining-room. A piano was at one end and a long table stretched down the middle, while at the rear end, by which I had entered, were loose seats, a screen, and a small shrub in a pot. On the walls and screen were numerous pictures and cartoons, some done by the airmen themselves, others cut out of newspapers, but all portraying girls in advanced stages of déshabillé, or pilots and aeroplanes painted in fantastic colours. It was just like a French battalion headquarters dugout in France, with the exception that here also, sitting round the table, were five extremely pretty Russian girls, all very young. They were all well dressed and one was playing a guitar, while another accompanied her on the piano, and the rest of the party were singing a Russian folk song very popular in the Caucasus.

"Of course, they are all married," one of the senior officers informed me gravely. "Or are soon going to be, at any rate."

After my last few days of flying, travelling in horse trucks, and train hopping, during which I had covered nearly 900 miles, I was very grateful for any comfort that was going and the evening went quickly, though only one or two people could dance at the same time in the somewhat restricted space. It was one of those moments when I had to pinch myself to make sure that I really was in the middle of a bitter civil war with Bolshevik advance guards only thirty miles away, and nothing between myself and them but a few thousand ill-equipped and ill-armed Kuban Cossacks, many of whom were of doubtful loyalty.

When I reported to General Mackiev, I found him in a very difficult frame of mind and not very appreciative of my efforts over the shells.

"The British-armed batteries are scattered," he said. "Although the gas shells have arrived, it will take so long to distribute them it is hardly worth having them."

I felt deflated after all I had put into the scheme, but I didn't argue. The Caucasian Army was not my business and Holman had gone back to Taganrog and I wanted to get back to my Don Cossacks. So I said goodbye, found a place in the first reasonably clean train I saw heading for Rostov, and after three days of dusty, disgusting travelling, arrived back at Novocherkassk.

CHAPTER NINE

When I returned to Novocherkassk, there was a great deal of gloom about the place and it was full of wild stories that Tsaritsyn had finally fallen.

"The hospitals there were overflowing with typhus victims and men with wounds," I was told. "It must have been impossible to move them all before the Reds arrived. There were never enough orderlies and doctors, and most of their time was spent moving the dead. God knows what happened to them all. They must all have been murdered when the Reds arrived!"

There was little I could do, but the news was sickening.

People were already packing and preparing to move south and, when I went to the Smaguins, I found that, true to her beliefs, Moussia had only a few clothes packed but what remained of her jewellery was carefully stowed away ready for the "off". At government headquarters there was already a great deal of alarm and much ostentatious destroying of records.

The whole town was crowded with people from the north. They were already starving and beginning to die like flies of typhus, because there was no fuel and no organisation and only the strongest and most ruthless could hope to survive. A long string of box cars waited on sidings outside the station, loaded with refugees who were cramming the compartments, clinging to the doorways, crowded on the roofs and on little platforms built between the buffers. As these trains rounded corners, someone was always likely to fall off, and either to be killed or to be left standing, dusty and dazed, in the middle of the steppe, miles from anywhere, while the wailing relatives watched the figure growing smaller and smaller as the train drew away. The trains never stopped for incidents such as this, and the station

walls were always plastered, alongside the claptrap the staff
put out about the low morale of the Reds, with tragic little
notices for people who had become separated from their
families.

"*Mikhail. Your family is in Rostov.*" "*Piotr – look for us in
Taganrog. We will wait.*" "*Dear Masha. Wait with the children in
Tikhoryetsk.*" There were never any surnames because no one
dared to give them.

Despite the gloom, however, I was still optimistic, and,
though the refugees' fear depressed me, I was young enough to
feel we could still win, especially as details were just beginning
to come in about a tremendous cavalry raid launched by
General Mamentov behind the Bolshevik front which had inflicted severe casualties on the enemy. In its scope, it matched
the vast cavalry raids of Stuart and Forrest in the American
Civil War. This kind of fighting suited the Don Cossack well.
He did not like holding a solid line of trenches but preferred
to advance, dissolve and reform, in alternate waves of élan
and depression.

The raid had been launched across the Khoper and had been
intended to form part of the summer offensive which Denikin
hoped would reach Moscow. I had tried, in fact, to accompany
it but had failed to get myself included. It seemed to exemplify
all the good and bad qualities of the Cossacks.

By the beginning of July, 1919, Denikin's three armies had
been strung out along a line which ran intermittently from
Tsaritsyn through Bielgorod to Ekaterinoslav. British equipment of all sorts, artillery, small arms, ammunition, uniforms,
and hospital requirements were by now reaching the fighting
units, and everything seemed to be building up for the long-
dreamed-of "March on Moscow".

"*Na Moskvu,*" everyone said. "To Moscow." It was a
wonderful slogan and everyone believed it and in the cafés and
public gardens, you could see people greeting each other with
it or raising their glasses to the prospect. For the first time there
had really seemed to be a chance that it might be true.

Even the political differences between the Volunteer and

Don Cossack armies had been patched up, and the ever-politically-minded soldiers of the Kuban, in spite of certain separatist, and non-co-operative tendencies on the part of both Cossack governments, had on the whole joined up willingly to strengthen the forces which were already struggling to throw off the grip of the Soviet Government on their territories. At Denikin's Headquarters at Ekaterinodar towards the end of July, plans had been nearing completion for a major drive along the whole front.

In conjunction with a general offensive northwards by the Don and Volunteer Armies, it had been intended to carry out a large-scale raid deep behind the enemy's front, to attack the Tambov-Koslov-Orel railway system, and to disorganise the back areas of the 9th and 10th Soviet armies. The original plan was to employ two cavalry corps – the Caucasians under Konovallov, and the Don Cossacks under Mamentov, but unfortunately the Soviet High Command, alarmed at the success of Denikin's recent counter-offensive which had regained so much territory, struck first, early in August.

The Soviet 10th Army under the renegade ex-Imperial General Kluiev starting from the Kursk-Voronezh area, drove southwards against Kharkov, whilst the terrifying ex-N.C.O., Budenny, with his Cavalry Corps, attacked down the line of the Volga from the area around Balashov and Kamyshin to clear the Lower Don area of White Russians. Barely, therefore, had Denikin's planning stage been completed, when the troops required for it became involved in dealing with a fresh danger, and Konovallov, although holding up Budenny, could not be withdrawn for the advance to Koslov.

Although the threat to Kharkov was relieved, the troops were now in no state to take part in any further offensive and Denikin had finally decided to limit the scope of Mamentov's raid to a shallow penetration of the enemy's front towards Koslov. For this amended operation the only remaining troops available were Postovski's 12th Don Cavalry Division, the 13th Don Cavalry Division, the Combined Cossack Division, and one dismounted brigade.

Each division consisted of approximately 2,000 sabres, 1,000 dismounted men, one battery of horse-drawn artillery, and a section of armoured cars. The first phase was launched on August 10th, when Mamentov's troops forded the river Khoper near Uryupinsk, and broke through the front of the 8th and 9th Soviet armies. They then moved rapidly on Tambov which was captured by the advance guard of Postovski's Cossacks.

Railways and munitions were destroyed and then, almost without a halt, Mamentov pushed westwards towards Koslov, detaching one cavalry regiment to deal with any Soviet troops who might threaten his rear from the direction of Balashov, and on August 21st after stiff fighting, Koslov itself was captured, and Mamentov had reached a point only 225 miles from Moscow, where considerable panic set in and the Soviet High Command rapidly despatched their 21st Brigade to stabilise the situation.

Mamentov's troops had covered 110 miles in ten days and in spite of considerable resistance had liberated large areas from the Soviet forces and collected many recruits. His troops, however, had been guilty of extensive looting and had freely executed any Bolshevik commissars and their sympathisers wherever they were found, and by that time the natural tendency of Cossack troops to return home with their booty, added to their well-known disinclination to move any great distance from their own territories, deterred Mamentov from making any further movement northwards. On August 25th he turned westwards and marched sixty miles towards Lebedyan which he occupied on August 28th. Here he concentrated his forces for a sweep southwards towards Voronezh and on August 31st he occupied Elets where the troops wasted two whole days in looting, loading up their ponies with food, drink, furs, jewels and anything else they could carry – even items of furniture.

On September 3rd, however, the advance on Voronezh began, with Postovski's cavalry covering the right flank from the direction of Ismailkovo, and on September 6th, Kastornay was captured, and reconnaissances were pushed eastwards towards Voronezh which was captured on September 11th.

In the Voronezh area Mamentov was joined by a brigade which deserted en masse from the Soviet army and became incorporated from then on in the anti-Bolshevik forces. Troops who only recently had been fighting on one side often found themselves fighting on the other and it was this practice which had a disastrous effect on the White Army during the final stages of the campaign, as conscripts who were enrolled as soon as fresh areas were occupied, had little interest if any at all in the issues at stake, and no knowledge of what they were being called upon to fight for. They were, therefore, seldom reliable, and when the tide of battle turned against them they often cheerfully murdered their officers and joined the other side.

Between September 12th and 15th, further to the east of the Voronezh-Liski railway at Rojestvenski Hawa, Mamentov regrouped his forces in preparation for his return to the Don, and on September 15th, with Postovski guarding his right flank from attack from Liski, he slipped between the Soviet 8th and 13th armies, crossed the River Don on September 17th and completed a march of 450 miles in forty days. He had inflicted severe casualties on four Soviet divisions, destroyed many important points on the railway system, collected a considerable number of recruits – albeit of doubtful loyalty or military value – and had acquired a very considerable quantity of loot. He might have done more but for the homing spirit of the Cossacks throughout the raid, which can be gauged from the fact that, out of the original force of about 10,000 men, only 4,000 were still with their regiments when they returned to their home country. Most of the missing 6,000 had vanished with their loot from Voronezh, though they wandered back later, bringing with them ponies, food, flour and anything which took their fancy from the villages from which they had driven the Bolsheviks.

The raid aroused great enthusiasm, although subsequent courts of inquiry seemed to think Mamentov had failed to carry out his orders. He certainly achieved a striking success, however, at a time when it was badly needed, but as in so many operations, owing to a complete lack of co-operation with other formations and the irresponsible behaviour of the troops, the Whites were robbed of the full fruits of his enterprise.

*

By this time the lines on which the British Mission's new liaison groups were to be organised had been approved, and officers of all kinds had been arriving in Russia for nearly a month. They were a very different type from the reluctant and war-weary men that Holman had allowed to go home.

They had all come out in answer to General Holman's appeal for "the best and nothing but the best", and each one of them not only came well within that category, but also set a new standard of excellence.

I could always get support from Roger Ling, the senior artillery liaison officer at Mission Headquarters and outstanding among the others were Robert Dickie, of the Argylls, Cuthbert Hargreaves of the East Lancashires, and Captains Read (Devons), Prickett (D.L.I.), and Sumpter, Drury and Mackay (Artillery). In addition, Norman Lack, who had left to attend to some private business of his own, turned up again in Novocherkassk and from this moment stayed with me almost to the bitter end as my personal interpreter and assistant, backed up always by his plucky Scottish wife.

At Novorossiisk, R.A.O.C. officers and staff were available now for unloading and sorting all incoming goods, and at the front a group of officers was attached to each separate army of Denikin's command.

Unfortunately we had no soldiers to help with the work of distribution, only officers. We knew that everyone at home heard nothing but the news from the Northern front where British troops were employed and we often wished that we might have a few of them. Nevertheless, we began to feel we could now take a stronger line with the Russians because at the headquarters of the White Army and working in liaison with Denikin, Holman himself – supported by a staff of representatives of all branches of the service – determined that British equipment should at last be properly distributed and used.

The Don Army at this time, the beginning of September, 1919, was composed of 1st Corps, 2nd Corps and 3rd Corps, and the Cavalry Corps under Mamentov. Each of these Corps comprised one or more of the nine infantry divisions which made up the total force at Sidorin's disposal, but there were also detached cavalry brigades working on the flanks of the larger formations, which were either put at the disposal of the corps commander or grouped together for a definite offensive action under one of the best-known leaders such as Mamentov or Sekretiev.

The general line occupied by the Cossack Army was by no means continuous, however, and with the enormous front there was to cover, the operations were principally confined to the infantry formations. These, supported by armoured trains and armoured cars, worked up and down the main railway system, most of which ran north and south, while the intervening tract of country was kept patrolled by bodies of cavalry. Small infantry detachments watched crossings and bridge heads, which were of great importance as the rivers of the district nearly all ran east and west, parallel to the front, and therefore formed very considerable obstacles to an advance. Theirs was not an enviable job, however, as bands of cavalry, both Red and White, roamed across the country between the railway lines. They were likely to turn up at any moment and, though never in very large numbers, always created a considerable panic, whichever side they belonged to, as both sides were dressed exactly alike and you could only tell which side you were fighting by a little strip of white or red cloth stuck in their caps.

In addition to the distance from the railways which had to be covered in supplying rations and munitions, the lack of horses, following the removal of large numbers by the Reds and the enormous wastage through lack of veterinary services, made it impossible to maintain any considerable number of troops far from the rail-heads. The 18-pounder ammunition, in fact, was only carried in loads of twenty rounds in one-horse country carts, for the most part driven by women.

Each corps of the Don Army had a chief of artillery, under whose command were one or more batteries armed with British equipment as well as numerous batteries of Russian guns. For repairs, both for these as well as for rifles and machine guns, they had a make-shift mobile workshop mounted in railway coaches and working at the railhead. At these workshops were supposed to be spare parts, in addition to those carried with the batteries, but I found that most of the spares had been handed over to the workshops, which were often 100 miles away, while all the things which the workshops should have had with them were lying in a store at Novocherkassk – if, in fact, they had ever been sent up from Novorossiisk.

To overcome the hopeless conditions, I detailed artillery instructors to the different corps and, before sending them to the front, divided up all essential spare parts and drums of buffer oil we could lay hands on. (Officers of the other arms attached to units of the Don Army, of course, received detailed instructions from the heads of their departments at Mission Headquarters and were only attached for administrative purposes to my group where they were looked after by Robert Dickie, the senior administrative liaison officer.)

These officers were to go to their respective corps railheads, organise the section of the workshops responsible for repairing British guns, supply them with all available workshop stores and then proceed to corps headquarters with the stores required by the batteries. At corps headquarters they were to report to the Corps Artillery Commander, explain their duties and instructions and then push on to each of the British armed batteries on the front, spending a few days with each, instructing the personnel and overhauling the equipment. At the end of a month they were to report to me.

The artillery school now had several fairly efficient Russian instructors and was better left to itself and, as the Russians absolutely refused to instruct or organise their classes on our system, I decided that my officers were better employed in the forward area. They were perfectly capable of running their own show, of course, so, having given them the lines on which to work, I attached interpreters to them, issued as fair a share of canteen stores and rations as I could squeeze out of the base, and sent them off with a hope that I might come across one or two of them on my next tour of the front.

As to the officers engaged in liaison work, they were to discover what British stores and uniforms had arrived, find out where they were and insist on proper distribution, and above all see that they safely reached the front line units.

The greatest difficulty was transport. I couldn't wait for everyone to fit himself up with a private railway coach, which was the ideal, so I went to Sidorin and Ataman Bogaievski and begged that four or five should be allotted for our use so that our mobility should be ensured. I left Dickie to fight this question out in my absence and, having been temporarily lent a first-class coach of ten compartments, I filled it up with stores of all kinds, and set out for 3rd Corps' Headquarters. Whether it was correct or not, I hung a large Union Jack over the door of the coach as a sign that the British Military Mission was in the offing! I felt it was time someone became aware of us.

CHAPTER TEN

Millerovo had become the advanced army's headquarters since the big move northwards had begun earlier in the summer, and we reached it after a night's journey from Novocherkassk.

Travelling, however, seemed to grow worse with every journey we made. The whole countryside was gradually being laid waste by the see-saw fighting of the past year and the stations and the villages grew shabbier with every visit we made, the windows boarded up where the glass had been broken by the shelling and little gouges dug out of the plaster where flying shrapnel had bitten into it. On some of the houses, the hammer and sickle had been scrawled and the doors daubed with red paint during the last Red occupation, and machine gun bullets had marked the façades. The posters with their slogans – applicable to both Reds and Whites, "War to the finish" and "Death is Better than Slavery" – grew more tattered every time I saw them.

At Millerovo, while waiting an opportunity to see General Tarakanov, who was deputising for Keltchevski, the Chief of Staff, I went to visit a unit which, although it was situated much farther back on the line of communication than ours would have been, appeared to correspond to a casualty clearing station. They had just received more or less complete a British field ambulance equipment for 210 beds, but, as usual, had split it up according to the urgent requirements of smaller units in the forward area.

I had a talk with the hospital staff and obtained information of the localities in which other medical units were stationed, took a list of their principal requirements, and went back to my coach. I ate that evening with Sidorin who gave me more news about the front, and a signed order giving me a free passage throughout the entire army area.

During the evening, Lack appeared. "I've arranged with the Station Commandant that we can be attached to the next north-ward-bound train," he said, so we decided to stop at Chertkovo, which was the railhead for the 2nd Don Corps, as I wanted to inspect the workshops there as well as to see how much equipment and clothing was being hoarded instead of being sent to the front.

We arrived at Chertkovo early in the morning and I got an officer called Mulligan, who was on artillery liaison duties, fixed up on a motor lorry and then went to examine railhead stores.

There were hundreds of mixed sets of clothing and equipment available, but they had been so broken up there seemed little hope of reassembling them again. However, I wired for help and got the work organised. The artillery store contained absolutely nothing!

There were also a few aeroplanes stationed at this place, but they were a pretty mixed lot, including an old Albatross left behind by the Germans, and a Nieuport captured from the Reds, still with its red star painted on it.

I also visited the 7th Bandaging Unit, or mobile dressing station, then on their way to the front. This was a new unit of non-military character, organised and equipped by the "Society of Towns" – a sort of rural council – and consisted of one doctor and four nursing sisters. They had twenty-five carriages and fifty horses and drivers.

"But only 250 bandages," they said. "Although we are working for the army, they refuse to give us any help at all in the way of equipment from the military depots. They say we're supposed to receive all these from our own organisation."

They were desperate to reach the front but the doctor told me that the Station Master at Millerovo had refused to send their train on until he had been given a bottle of surgical spirits.

"To make into vodka," he explained.

We moved on after lunch and reached the headquarters of

the 3rd Corps at Kantimirovka by evening. The 1st and 3rd Divisions were holding the west bank of the Don, and were in touch with the 2nd Corps on their right flank. Their front extended north and south of Pavlovsk but they had been driven back from the ground they had occupied when Holman and I had visited them earlier in the year and were opposed to the 23rd Bolshevik Division, composed principally of Caucasian Cossacks who were a pretty tough lot of fighters.

On the left of the 3rd Division was the 2nd Don Rifle Brigade, who were trying to force the bridgehead over the Don at Liski, where the Reds still held strong high ground commanding all the approaches to the bridge. Further to the left, the 8th Division were trying to outflank Liski and attack it from the east, supported by the 2nd Division further to the north, who were endeavouring to cut the Liski-Voronezh railway line in the direction of Davidovka. Further north still, Mamentov's Cavalry, though desperately short of ammunition, was trying to cut the same railway line, while Skouro and his Caucasians, still farther to the left, were supposed to be falling back in the hope of joining up with him after being driven back from Voronezh by Red reinforcements.

To me it appeared that the combined offensive on Liski was developing far too slowly, and that the Reds were being given too much time to re-group their forces and bring their strength to bear on both flanks of the 3rd Corps. On the left a large gap between the 3rd Corps and Mai-Maievski's Volunteer Army was very insecurely filled by Mamentov's cavalry, and there was still another gap on the right at its junction with the very weak 2nd Corps. If the enemy succeeded in breaking through, the distance to the railway was only short, and the 3rd Corps would stand a very good chance of having its line of communication cut, and probably lose all its equipment.

The staff of the 3rd Corps seemed quite happy about the situation, however, and General Ivanov, the commander, gave me leave to go where I liked so I left an officer and stores with the artillery commander, and went back to my coach hoping to ush on to Pukhova next morning.

We eventually got away, attached to a mournfully slow train, and at Westratovka just north of the newly repaired Kalitva bridge, we bumped into one of the medical units of the 5th Division stationed around Rossosh for reforming and training. It was short of stores and equipment of every kind, of course, but I felt able to be generous as I had received several large sacks full of excellent hospital clothing, socks, medical stores and drugs from England, and the gratitude with which these indispensable things were received by the neglected Russian soldiers amply repaid the expense and trouble caused by their despatch. I never allowed the Russian Staff to touch any of my personal stores.

At Pukhova, the headquarters of the 2nd Don Rifle Brigade was in the village with various batteries of artillery of all calibres, one armed with British 18-pounders. They were supported by Don armoured trains. We rode with General Yenko of the Finland Guards to his reserve company, and were shown off to as many of the troops as possible.

"While British help has been shoved down their throats as propaganda to keep up their fighting spirits," he explained, "the results of it have been infinitesimal in the forward areas."

Their uniforms were dreadfully ragged, and only about ten per cent had at most two or three articles of British uniform in their possession. Their spirit, however, seemed very good and their discipline better than anything I had yet seen. They were formed on a nucleus of the old Finland Guard Regiment, and their officers were keen as mustard and with considerable military knowledge. I was able to send up stores and clothing and preserved fruits for the officers' mess of this regiment, and gave their medical officer three hundred bandages out of my private supply.

I was beginning to feel at last that I was achieving something but my announcement that I intended to see the 17th Battery next day brought raised eyebrows and loud protests.

"Oh no, Sir Major," I was informed. "Shells constantly fall near it."

"What of it?" I asked.

"It is too dangerous."

Knowing what some of the Russians considered dangerous, I decided to take a chance. However, the steady heat of the summer was now finished and autumn had begun almost imperceptibly in dry windless weather and a slight nip in the air in the early mornings. The leaves had begun to disappear and the evening horizons had begun to take on the blue look of winter so that the lights of approaching motor cars and lorries were diffused by the mist. On this particular day, it had become cool and heavy rain had begun to fall and the troops about me exuded a strong smell of damp wool, leather and fur. I decided, therefore, to spend the morning with the armoured trains and leave the trip to the battery until the weather was better.

Most of the armoured trains in this area were lightly covered and consisted of a forward and rear armoured truck with the armoured engine in between them. Their armament was one light field gun and six to twelve machine guns. The heavy armoured trains usually had a British 60-pounder or a 6-inch French Canet or even, in fact, any heavy gun which could be conveniently mounted on them. They ran up to meet the Reds every morning and have an hour or two's long-range shooting match, and they also preceded all infantry attacks and often fought with great dash on their own, though they stood considerable risk of being cut off by roving bands of enemy cavalry. Their moral effect, however, was so great that hostile troops were not inclined to tamper with the railway line if there was any chance of the train appearing.

The lack of artillery on either side made the position of the armoured trains and armoured cars one of considerable strength, and they seemed to be just as frightful to the ordinary Russian infantry and cavalry as British tanks did to the Germans on their first appearance on the Western Front. Armoured cars – some of them made from old tank turrets – were especially mobile on the open steppes, and could round up large bodies of infantry, who had nothing but ill-aimed rifle fire to offer in reply.

The armoured train commander's demands for guns were as usual ridiculously large, but like many of the Russians, Colonel Kanderin imagined he only had to ask and the British Government would provide masses of the most up-to-date war material on the spot like rabbits out of a conjuror's hat. He gave me a pass to go on any armoured train I liked and accompany them into action, so I arranged to go up on one called "Gundorovitz" next day to strafe the Red position south of the river.

During the morning the Army Commander's train arrived with two of my officers, Lloyd Davies, a Sapper, who had come up as Sidorin's guest, and Prickett, a gorgeous Cockney who was no respecter of persons – particularly Russian Generals – and had turned up to see his Stokes mortar battery in action with the Finland Guards. I warned Davies of my experience as Sidorin's guest and suggested they both joined me on my coach. Prickett was foraging for a coach of his own, which had been promised him by the Finland Guard officers from a dump of serviceable ones abandoned in a siding just south of Liski Bridge, and he eventually found one with three good coupés, a full-sized sitting-room with an end window, and an excellent kitchen. It also had the advantage of being small and light and we used it until our final farewell to our railway homes the following March.

Sidorin had gone off in a car to visit the left flank, where the 2nd and 8th Divisions were operating, and as there was no room for him in the car, Lloyd Davies, his guest, was not unexpectedly left to his own resources. I asked him, therefore, to go round with Prickett, who was now attached to the Finland Guard, and was sure to be "in front of" rather than "in" the firing line for the operations of the next few days.

At 2 p.m. the rain stopped so I obtained horses and Lack and I, with a rough map to guide us, went off in search of the 17th Battery then forming part of the 2nd Rifle Division of Artillery. There was a watery sun and puddles covered the ground, and we moved at a walking pace, chilly with the mist across the bare, black unfriendly steppe which seemed to stretch away to eternity, unrelieved and empty, curving into folds and valleys and hills that were all the same drab colour.

We found Battery Headquarters at Liski and met Colonel Podsepukov, the Commander, and the colonel of the 3rd Don Rifles, whose headquarters were in the same village. I promised them a few stores and medical comforts and then went off to look for the battery position.

A somewhat nervous Cossack guide was lent to me but, as Norman Lack was not an experienced horseman, we had to go slowly. The Reds commenced shelling the village as we came out, but the fire was very scattered. Shells fell about seventy or a hundred yards away and houses were set on fire. The panic-stricken residents left as quickly as they could – though nothing fell nearer to me than fifty yards, the smoke of the explosions black against a bright sky.

We passed a battery of 6-inch Russian howitzers in action – one gun was out of order and they had only twenty shells left for some time to come – and eventually found the so-called "dangerous" position of the 17th Battery.

The rain of shells I had been led to expect seemed to have appeared at some other time and the bare steppes were empty of shell bursts. Certainly there were forty or fifty shell holes round about but the officers denied that they had suffered any casualties, and although this was their fourth day in action their entire wagon line and bivouacs were only 150 yards directly to the rear of the gun position. The guns were beautifully clean and working perfectly, the observation post was where it should be, about 600 yards in front, and the battery commander was firing at a Red armoured train just appearing like a slow-moving slug south of Liski Bridge. The men were chiefly pleased with the quantity of British shells they had, though there were no spare springs or buffer oil.

Two aeroplanes were droning above us, dropping bombs on Liski station, but they never came below 5,000 feet which, considering the lack of hostile anti-aircraft fire seemed excessively high. The Reds, however, engaged them with an elevated field gun whose "duds" set us running as they came whistling down to plunge into the ground close by. There was also an artillery strafe going on against our advanced posts in front of the bridge-heads. High explosive was being mostly used as such shrapnel as they had was very unreliable, and the shells were flinging up fountains of black earth and mud.

We returned to the coach in the evening pretty well done in and found several of Yenko's officer's, including the general himself, being entertained by the indefatigable Prickett. He dealt with the dignified senior officers in exactly the same way as he did the young and noisy ones and they were eating out of his hand.

The following morning after breakfast with the Finland Guards, Lack and I started off for Ostragozhsk. Lack, feeling a little sore, was in a country cart this time, together with my kit and several complete sets of medical equipment, and we eventually left him behind.

My Cossack orderly seemed to know the way well, and we passed through the village of Konoritsi where the Lugansk and Gundorovski regiments were stationed. They were holding the south side of the river Don along the railway line with small posts, as there were no crossings between Liski and Korotoyak.

They were bivouacked alongside the road, washing their shirts, cooking their food and combing their lovelocks, one eye on the girls and the peasant women who came with their children to gape at them. The air was full of the smell of wood-smoke and, though the shops were empty, the one café was open.

The two regiments were dismounted Cossacks from the Lugansk area, and had made a great name for themselves during the last expulsion of the Reds from the Don country. Their brigade had with it a battery of British 18-pounders, and I gave the Commanding Officer a chit to draw stores from my coach and a note for Prickett asking him to give the messenger who carried it tea and jam when he arrived. I was just preparing to push on for Ostragozhsk when Lack turned up, so, leaving him to complete my somewhat inadequate instructions in Russian,

I escaped and continued my journey. As soon as I got clear of the village and turned southwards I heard the thudding of the heavy bombardment of all types of artillery on my right, and saw the unfortunate town of Korotoyak being well strafed and burning in several places, the smoke rising in a black and oily column into the clear blue sky.

I had no idea of the military situation and several parties of troops apparently entirely on their own were wandering along the steppes road which I was following. I eyed them warily but nobody seemed very interested in me or was able to enlighten me, so I kept on my way to Ostragozhsk, as I'd had a long day and wanted to get into billets before dark. I also decided that as everybody seemed to be moving away from the front it was possible that the Reds were beginning to drive us back from the north bank of the river.

Lack was quite an hour behind me, so having seen my pony watered and fed, I wandered about Ostragozhsk by myself. It was a typical steppe village with low heavy-shouldered houses, some of them with painted fretwork on the eaves and doorways and gaily-painted shutters, and wide unpaved streets where pigs and chickens wandered. The square smelt of laurel and the autumn wind blew through the village, scattering russet leaves.

My French, as usual, stood me in good stead, and I had just found the 8th Division Headquarters, and been shown a billet by the Camp Commandant himself when Lack arrived and was able to get me into touch with General Guliga, the divisional commander, who had won a great reputation as a cavalry general on the German Front. I went over all the usual ground with regard to the distribution of stores, took a list of requirements, handed over the medical equipment to their doctor, and had half an hour with Guliga's chief of staff to try to find out how things were going on his section of the Front. He was very nonchalant about military matters, however, though as usual hospitality was lavish.

Next morning I was wandering round the town when, suddenly, numbers of horsemen galloped past and there was the sound of bugles and shouting, and men appeared fastening on their equipment.

"The attack on Liski's been postponed for lack of troops," I was told. "Guliga and his 8th Division have been ordered immediately to Pukhova to support the 2nd Don Rifle Brigade to carry it out as soon as possible."

I said goodbye to the general, and before we left, he gave us a meal and summoned his personal orderly, a huge, bearded ruffian.

"Drink the health of the British officers," he ordered.

The orderly must have had an asbestos throat as he put down a huge tumbler of fiery neat vodka – swallowed standing strictly to attention!

We sent a wire to the headquarters of the 2nd Division and set off – Lack in his country cart, myself on my Cossack pony. On the way we passed through one of the German settlements, dating back to the days of Catherine the Great who had introduced them to bring efficient village institutions into her country. It was like any other village but there was a notable improvement in sanitation and neatness and, considering the Germans had first been introduced 150 years before, their institutions had lasted remarkably well.

At Ribensdorf, where 2nd Division Headquarters were now situated, I suggested to General Krasnyanski that a visit to the front line where the soldiers might be doing some actual fighting, would be in order. He acquiesced readily. Two carriages were ordered, each drawn by three white horses, and we were off at a gallop into the broken and charred town of Korotoyak.

Houses were collapsed where shells had landed and there were charred beams, and here and there the body of a cow or a horse lay on the scarred earth. A chicken coop had been scattered and the corpses of its recent inhabitants lay flattened in the grass, surrounded by their own feathers, and a few dazed inhabitants stared blankly at the wreckage of their homes.

This seemed much more like business, and once I was into the town, which only the day before had been blazing under a heavy artillery bombardment, I felt that I had fallen among a really good lot of soldiers with whom I could get on. On the outskirts, firing a few rounds at a village in the enemy's hands north of the river, was my old friend the 3rd (4.5) Howitzer Battery which had trained and equipped at Rostov.

Krasnyanski and I went on to the Headquarters of the 1st Brigade and, as most of Korotoyak was still under observation from the Reds, we decided to abandon our white-horsed vehicles and walk up the main street to the square. Many houses were still burning.

There were a few holes where the shells had fallen and several dead horses still lay about the place, sometimes still in the shafts of their carts. They were beginning to smell and the air was polluted by the odour. The church had been almost entirely destroyed and the White advanced posts were holding ruined houses along the banks. As we passed, heads popped up. Fierce eyes grinned at us beneath the shaggy Cossack caps and teeth gleamed under the ragged fringes of moustaches. A few shouts followed us with waves and catcalls.

A bridge of boats and trestles across the river was on fire, the smoke hanging low over the water in the reeds, and at the far end was a nasty mess of dead men and horses and broken vehicles, where a column had been caught trying to cross. A horse struggled to rise against the harness that held it to the bodies of its companions, while another one, its coat gleaming with water, lay dead in the shallows, its hooves in the air, its belly split open. The smell of decay came on the breeze. More bodies were piled among the splintered carts blocking the end of the bridge and a few dazed men were listlessly backing up more horses in an attempt to pull the wreckage clear. The Reds held the bank about 500 yards away and desultory sniping was going on. As we watched, we were joined by the village priest and two small boys, and to my dismay, the General coolly led us all down into the open.

"We must have a look at the bridge," he said, "and talk to some of the men there."

If this had been on the Western Front we would have been

brought down within five minutes, but after having a good look we walked back and never had a shot fired at us. Back at Regimental Headquarters I met more officers and N.C.O.'s, but not a soul had yet received a British uniform.

"But, good God," I said, "sixty thousand sets have been received by Don Army Headquarters!"

We reached Division Headquarters in the evening and sat down to supper with an excellent band. Three extremely pretty girls were also there, and among these, to my amusement, I saw a girl called Natasha whom I had seen at the 2nd Corps Headquarters and who had borrowed a lift on my coach on my way up the previous week. Like many others she gained employment in the areas where she wanted to go. We danced after dinner, although I was dead beat and was to be called early to go up the railway towards Liski on an armoured train.

The train started before its time rather than after, however, and – I think – at the order of the General I was not called in time to join it. Since I had spent several pretty strenuous days, I wasn't sorry and decided to stay with the staff; and I spent the time in fierce argument, trying to persuade them to distribute what British clothing I could get for them on some rational system. I gave Krasnyanski all the remaining hospital stores, tea, sugar, and tobacco, that I had with me and suggested that he should send an officer back with me to collect more from my coach next day. Instead of an officer, however, he sent Natasha, who drove in the country cart with Lack, to the evident pleasure of both, and she succeeded in wheedling more than a just share of jam and chocolates out of the British officers whom she waylaid when she arrived.

From the information in our possession, it now appeared likely that the Reds would abandon Liski to our troops without opposition but there was an indication of a growing concentration of Red cavalry on our right rear opposite Kazansky. It looked as though they were trying to induce the 3rd Don Corps to lengthen still farther their communications by occupying Liski, so that the main Red counter-offensive across the Don would thus have an additional chance of dashing down

on Kantimirovka or Millerovo and separating Army Headquarters from its principal units.

As the evening wore on, in fact, rumours became rife that
the Reds were, in fact, already well across the Don and driving
straight down on the railway line, and the familiar expression
of "wind up" became very pronounced.

"How long are we staying here?" I heard someone ask un-
easily, and from then on the inquiries flew in all directions.

"Is it true the Reds are within five miles of us?"

"Will this lot remain loyal?"

"Is it true the Kubans have broken away?"

I didn't know what to answer but I did know that the Kuban
Cossacks were having meetings and knew they had been thinking of pulling out of the war for some time.

In the middle of all the alarm, however, a comic element was
introduced by the arrival of a representative of the American
Red Cross in the shape of an American Lieutenant named
Boyle, accompanied by my old friend Abramov, the interpreter and the hero of the episode at Du Chayla's dinner party.

The plight in which these two arrived was pitiful. They had
started optimistically for the front in a baggage wagon, with
no food or stores, and on their three-days' journey had nearly
succumbed to starvation as, instead of the civic receptions and
guards of honour they had anticipated, they had been ignored
and neglected throughout, and they were now desperately
hungry and weary and feeling very sorry for themselves. In
addition Abramov was only too conscious of the rumours of
cut lines of communications which were floating about, and
was reduced to a state of absolute terror.

"Sir Major," he said, "you must save us!"

We all played up to his state of mind, and at an impressive
mock conference, at which we all acted the heavy heroes, we
made a plan of action for the "last stand" of the British
Mission.

We steamed off south next day with the Union Jack flying on
the armoured train beside the Don Army flag, but before leaving, I lectured Abramov sternly.

"It is your duty to stay with the brave American officer," I said. "Since you have so thoughtlessly led him into danger without adequate cause, you must get him out safely."

As a matter of fact the danger was practically non-existent, and everyone arrived safely at Millerovo on September 18th.

CHAPTER ELEVEN

I got away again next morning in good time, taking all I had left in the way of hospital necessaries, tea and cigarettes, as the 1st Division at Novoe Kalitva was the last unit of the 3rd Corps I was to visit. This division was supposed to be the best in the Don Army, and the 1st Brigade was composed of the Cossack Regiment of the late Tsar's Imperial Bodyguard and the Regiment of the Don Ataman's Bodyguard, all picked men and all well-trained and disciplined. To these two regiments came all the survivors of the old guards regiments, but while their esprit de corps and the quality of their officers were very high, they were usually given the toughest work to do.

This was my first view of an organised body of the celebrated Kalmuk Cavalry, who, though Don Cossacks by naturalisation, were actually members of the nomadic tribes who lived on the steppes near the river Sal and the river Manytch. They were of Mongol appearance and Buddhists by religion and they went in for horse breeding. Several of the best-known horse-breeding stations in South Russia were in their country and they fed their children a great deal on mares' milk, so that when the Bolsheviks took away almost their entire horse stock from them, they became very anti-Bolshevik in their sympathies. They were excellent fighters and well-disciplined, but once they got out of hand they were as cruel as any savage. The regiment was only about 400 strong, and their colonel, a youngish man with one of the most extraordinary fierce and self-confident faces I have ever seen, was a European type, though Kalmuk blood showed its presence in his complexion and his narrow slanting eyes.

The Kalmuk Cossacks could always be distinguished by the

yellow band which they wore round their dark blue-topped caps instead of the red band of the ordinary Don Cossacks, while the Siberian Cossacks wore a pink band and those from the Urals a mauve one. In the 1st Division, the two Guard regiments also had distinctive caps, the Life Guard Cossacks having a red-topped one, and the Ataman's Bodyguard royal blue. All Cossacks also wore wide stripes down their riding breeches corresponding in colour to their cap band instead of the narrow red piping of the rest of the Russian Army.

Owing to the shortage of horses, the organisation of regiments was on the principle of three infantry companies and one mounted sotnia armed with lances as well as swords, as the Don Cossack is a lancer in contrast to the Caucasian who is a swordsman only. Machine guns were run on the regimental system, each unit having its own section, and this brigade had several rather useful-looking limbers on which they were carried with special mountings on the seats, so that they could be fired over standing corn or hay during the summer fighting on the steppes. They had received no British uniform whatsoever from the latest supply, and I only saw a dozen or so old khaki drill jackets in the whole company. Lewis guns had been issued to them, however, though with only six spare drums to each weapon and no tools, but they were never a popular weapon with the Russians, who always clamoured for the Vickers.

We visited the observation post of the 2nd 18-pounder Battery and had a view across the river towards Kazinka and Varvarovka. The enemy appeared to be very quiet, and when an attempt was made to cross the river no resistance was met with. It was found impossible to build a bridge, however, so the whole division was rafted across, to the great interest of Lloyd Davies, who wanted to go at once to fetch one of the pontoon bridging trains, which had already arrived at Millerovo, and do the thing in the approved "sapper" style. I handed over all my spare stores, socks and food to the regimental messes, and decided to return to Kantimirovka next day. As there was some good marshy ground close by, however, I went off after snipe in the evening, accompanied by an officer, with two lancers on horseback as beaters. I shot four couple to their intense delight, saw a few hares, and was savaged by mosquitoes as a reward.

I had my usual conference with the divisional staff and commanding officers on supply and distribution of clothing, the maintenance of British equipment, instruction, and the general situation – not only locally, but in Europe generally. Endless political connundrums were asked me, to which I had to give guarded replies. Every indication of German assistance to the Bolsheviks was produced for my information, and I could see that, all through their division, which was the first of Krasnov's model army divisions to be organised under German supervision, there lay a lingering admiration for the system.

I promised to send up another 18-pounder and an officer to overhaul their equipment and bring their spares up-to-date.

While waiting for my coach to arrive at Yvestratovka, I met a new body of troops on trains in sidings at the station. This was the Tulsk Brigade, which had come over en masse from the Bolsheviks to join Mamentov's Cavalry Corps during their raid. They were a well-seasoned and well-equipped body of troops, officered for the most part by members of the old Imperial Russian Army who had been forced into the Bolshevik service for fear of their wives and families being massacred.

"It was the Communists who were responsible for all the wrongs done by the Bolsheviks," they said. "They enforced discipline by execution, but they themselves obey no laws or regulations."

Several highly-skilled German officers had been seen instructing the Red Army, it seemed, and my informants told me more were expected. Over 400 ex-Imperial officers were included in the Tulsk Brigade.

"It's now all up with our families," they said. "Mamentov executed too many Bolshevik commissars and Jewish revolutionaries."

I later heard that the Reds systematically rounded up all their relations, young and old, and had them shot.

I left at midnight and arrived next day at Kantimirovka, where General Ivanov put down his demands for what he considered essentials. I was expected at a few days' notice to produce 15,000 complete sets of uniform, eight motor cars, twenty motor cycles, five Stokes mortar batteries, unlimited Vickers guns, aeroplanes and medical instruments, 1,000 cavalry saddles, twelve batteries of 18-pounders, and numerous British officers' uniforms.

"*Something* will be sent up with the Corps Liaison Officer," I said guardedly and put the onus for explaining the shortages on to that unfortunate individual when he should arrive.

I wanted to get to Novocherkassk at once but, on going to the Station Commandant to arrange for my coach to go south by the first possible train, I saw a much-beflagged engine entering the station, and Zerebkhov, Ataman Bogaievski's A.D.C., jumped down to greet me with "You're just the man we want!"

After shaking hands, he went on. "First of all," he said, "the Prime Minister, Alfuerov, wants back his coach which was lent to you. And secondly, His Excellency the Ataman is going to the front and wants you to go with him."

*

This was wonderful news and I didn't hesitate to transfer my belongings. Bogaievski greeted me cordially.

His first visit was to have been to the 2nd Corps, but as usual everything was changed at the last moment, and the train moved off instead to Yvestratovka, from whence we went off again to see the 1st Division, whose headquarters were now north of the Don at Gorokovka. A Russian battery in action there was entirely equipped with British uniform except for Cossack caps, and stores had been sent up from Kantimirovka for the 18-pounder batteries. We motored back to the train in the evening and left for Podgornya during the night.

Striking eastwards next morning, we took the car across the

Don at Semeiki on a raft poled by ancient bearded villagers, and followed the troops on to Varvarovka, which had been captured the previous evening by the 6th Infantry Brigade. Two field guns, sixteen machine guns and 300 prisoners had also been collected in the village. The prisoners were terrified as they expected – quite rightly, as it happened – to be shot by their captors, and there was much pleading that they had been forcibly enlisted by the Reds and that they had not dared to desert for fear of what would happen to their families. It was the Tulsk Brigade all over again, but this time they were taken out of the town and all shot with machine guns. It wasn't only the Reds who committed atrocities.

This was the type of fighting that characterised the war. Death by actual direct contact in the heat of battle with bullet or shell was uncommon, but the massacre of prisoners and towns-people, starvation – and worse, the scourge of spotted typhus and cholera – were the real enemies.

It was a sickening experience but the hatred engendered by the Civil War precluded any mercy and, as our opinion was never asked, it was wisest to try not to see what happened.

None of the regiments of the 6th Brigade had any stretchers – only large poles joined by sacking – and they were shockingly clothed, many men with no boots. What happened to the British clothing that *did* arrive at the Front, I couldn't think, but rumour had it that the Cossacks sent it home for best and carried on in their rags at the Front!

We could hear fighting going on to the east, so we drove on without escort to Guilusha, where we found the Kalmuk Regiment and the 4th Don Infantry Regiment, who had captured it that morning from the south. The Life Guard Cossacks were providing outposts round the village, with their Headquarters at the priest's house, but our most advanced posts were beginning to fall back after meeting strong opposition about three miles north and east of the village.

Our idea was to return next morning via Pavlovsk, which should have been captured by the 7th Brigade, so we slept in the straw on the floor with our equipment on. A certain amount of sniping began early in the morning, but with the Life Guard Cossacks, I felt as safe as anywhere in Russia. The next morning, we heard fresh news.

"Pavlovsk's still in the enemy's hands," I was told. "Our advance on Juravka's been driven back."

Our troops had withdrawn due south, and if we had continued as intended we should have driven straight into the Bolsheviks' hands. Bogaievski decided as an alternative to return to the railway and see the troops of the 8th Division, but here news awaited us that Liski had at last been captured, so he ordered an immediate move in that direction, and before dark we were steaming across the railway bridge into Liski station. Away on our left the Volunteer Army was still going strong, and their advance guards were already closing in on Kursk, so that the whole of the Don country was now cleared of the Reds, and an advance into the Voronezh and Tambov areas was expected.

Next morning we set out on an armoured train supporting the 2nd Don Rifle Brigade, who were trying to force the crossing of the Koretz river, but one of the battalion commanders had let them down, and the operation was fizzling out, and men were beginning to drift back, their equipment abandoned and dragging their rifles. A cart full of wounded appeared, the men's heads jolting as the wheels struck the ruts and bumps. A few men on horses passed, slouching in their saddles, one or two of them with bloodstained bandages. Their faces were sullen and ugly, as though they blamed headquarters for their failure.

Then, while I watched, a Red armoured train appeared about 600 yards away over the rise. No one had known it was there and it was quite unexpected. Someone called out and pointed and heads were jerked round, then everyone dived for shelter or began to scuttle to safety. The ambulance carts were whipped into a gallop, the occupants screaming for mercy as the jolting jarred their wounds, and the horsemen about us scattered for all they were worth, harness jingling, swords slapping the saddles.

The train came to a stop and the first crack of its gun stopped everyone dead for a second as they paused to see where the shell would land. It threw up earth and stones near our own armoured train, which began to fire back at once. Fortunately, the shooting was bad on both sides and the light armoured train in front of us received most of the damage, and we saw splinters fly off the cars as the shells exploded against it. The engagement was indecisive, however, and both sides eventually withdrew to safety without a great deal of damage being done.

On our return to Liski, Bogaievski took me on one side. "You must speak to the crowd at the railway station," he said. "About Britain. You must explain your reasons for wishing to see Russia restored to peace."

This was the first time that the anti-Bolshevik forces had occupied Liski and I had a most attentive audience, standing on carts and boxes, shaggy bearded faces against the old-fashioned fretwork eaves of the station buildings. Broad-beamed peasant women came in from the ploughing with ancient instruments such as were never seen in Europe, and stood around watching, surrounded by their ragged children. Men in flat, peaked caps and peasant blouses stood on the fringes of the crowd, some of them less amiable than the women and clearly wondering what they could get out of the visit.

We left in the afternoon and set off south again by car to get in touch with General Konavallov's Cavalry Corps, who were across the Don again and advancing towards Kalach. The road was in a frightful condition as rain had fallen during the night but we eventually lurched and slid into Bichek, where we inspected miserably-equipped and weary-looking troops of the 2nd Corps. Konavallov had pushed on early, however, and was reported to be making his headquarters for the night in a small village about half way to Kalach, which he hoped to capture next day.

The Ataman decided to try and catch him up before night-fall, and so we drove straight across the steppes in a powerful Packard car. The track was so cut up, it was obvious that

cavalry had used it that morning, and we met several parties
of horsemen wandering aimlessly about, none of whom seemed
very interested in us. Those whom we stopped were unable to
give us any of the information we required. We halted and
there was one of those interminable discussions about whether
we were on the right road or not that always seemed to be part
of every journey by car.

The weather was deteriorating and there was rain and mist
in the air now and I didn't particularly look forward to a
night on the steppes, particularly as we had no proof that a
large group of cavalry which had passed ahead of us was
friendly.

The argument grew louder, and we all climbed from the car
and tried to peer into the growing darkness, to make out the
tracks. We were just beginning to feel bewilderment and sheer
weariness, when a body of horsemen suddenly loomed up in
the mist in front of us, directly along the track we were following.

"Quiet!"

As everyone stopped talking, you could almost cut the
silence with a knife, and we saw the shape of horses moving
towards us, large in the poor light, rifles and shaggy caps quite
clear. They seemed huge in the mist and I was just wondering
what would be the best move if they proved to be Reds when
they halted.

Three soldiers detached themselves from the main body and
approached us. The centre horseman wore a flat peaked cap at
a jaunty angle and to our great relief this proved to be Konavallov himself. The rest of the group was his personal escort.

"We came out to meet you," Konavallov told the Ataman.
"We thought you would need a guard for the rest of the way.
There are Red cavalrymen about."

I decided that we'd probably seen quite a few of them but
that by the grace of God those we'd stopped to ask the way
had been friendly.

Konavallov agreed. "They were probably Red deserters,"
he said. "We beat a group of them yesterday and they're

probably making their way back to their own stanitzas, on the look-out for loot. They're unlikely to give you any trouble."

I wasn't so sure. If they'd known we had the Ataman with us, any one of the larger parties we'd seen might well have decided he would be worth taking prisoner.

"There's a force of about 1,000 Bolshevik cavalry been reported advancing from Boguchar," Konavallov went on. "We expect them to make contact with us any time before full dark, so the sooner we get within our line of picquets the better."

He gave directions and turned his horse, and the other horsemen wheeled round behind him. We followed in the car, bouncing along the uneven track in their rear. There were still another two miles to go to safety and we finally lost sight of them as they cut across country but eventually we roared into the village where Konavallov had his headquarters about an hour behind Konavallov's group, and sat down to a supper of omelettes, soup, bread, butter and wine served by an attractive Turkish girl called Ayesha.

The rain had started to fall just before we arrived and it was coming down heavily now. As we finished eating, we heard the thud of a gun and heads jerked up to listen. There were more thuds, and then the steady thumping of regular firing followed by the tap-tap of machine gun and rifle fire close by.

No one seemed to take any notice at first but I noticed that orderlies began to come in with reports from Konavallov's cavalry group commanders. My neighbour leaned over to me. "The Reds are reported in and around Juravka," he said.

Apparently, the Red cavalry they'd been expecting had been reinforced by other units and was now a powerful formation and was beginning to look dangerous. Other elements of Reds, although actually still withdrawing due north from Nijni Mamon, were moving across our communications and were strong enough to be a threat.

The firing increased, growing in fits and starts and it seemed to me now to be nearer. Then I noticed a couple of officers whispering and became aware of a tense atmosphere growing about the headquarters. My neighbour reassured me that all was well.

"We're pulling in our squadrons to concentrate," he said. "There's nothing to worry about."

The behaviour of some of Konavallov's officers didn't seem to agree with what he said. They were still whispering and I caught the word "Bolshevik" several times.

Ayesha, the Turkish girl, was still going about her duties with an unchanged expression, but I kept seeing her eyes flicker towards Konavallov. It was quite clear there was something in the air and even as I wondered what they were all talking about, I saw another group of officers begin talking quietly together and caught a few anxious glances in the direction of the Ataman. It dawned on me that the situation was probably more dangerous than we had believed it to be and that the Reds were seriously threatening our communications as well as our present position.

"We'll be in a tight corner if we're attacked during the night or early morning by any of the Red cavalry in the neighbourhood," Zherebkhov said, and since I had no wish to be caught from any lack of precautions, I insisted not only on mounting a Lewis gun in the Packard and making the chauffeur start up the engine every two hours, but also saw that the horses and a suitable escort were kept saddled up in the yard of our billet. I knew how hopelessly casual the Russians were, and although orders had been given for even more elaborate precautions than these, none of them had been carried out.

The activity increased rather than diminished as it grew dark, little flurries and then great crescendos of firing coming over the still air as the Cossacks grew jumpy and blazed away at anybody – friend or foe – who came near. Throughout all this the Ataman appeared unmoved, and Ayesha amused us with stories of her life as a Red Crescent nurse. She had worked with Mohammedan Cossacks from the Caucasus and with the Bolsheviks who had forced her into their service.

About 11 p.m. we all lay down on the floor, but before going to sleep the Ataman said to me with his slow quiet smile,

"Bon soir, mon Major, je pense que demain matin nous allons voir un très joli petit combat de cavalerie."

*

Not long after dawn, renewed firing and the sound of horses in the village indicated that an attack was to be made on a large column of Reds who were engaged with some of our cavalry not far away. The streets were full of men leaving billets and forming up, their boots and clothes splashed with the mud that the rain had left. They were already clattering off to form up in regiments in the open space outside the village, and in a short time long columns of them were jingling up the rising ground about a mile away. Their scouts were already under long-range machine gun fire, judging by the sounds from the far side of the village, and occasionally we could see one of them turning or riding back and forth along the brow of a hill to indicate where the enemy lay. I rather hoped that we should see a good example of cavalry fighting but as it happened, it turned out to be a pretty tame affair.

The Cossack squadrons jingled away across the steppes and then, breasting a rise, the Red cavalry appeared, followed by guns and a column of carts. Our own guns and carts moved forward towards them, making that peculiar swish-swishing noise of wheels through grass and, before they knew where they were, the Reds found they had Cossacks on two sides of them and scattered firing started. The officer in command of the Cossacks was on a hillock behind which a battery was posted. A couple of hundred yards away, two Cossack squadrons were covering it. The enemy had let themselves be caught in a hollow about two miles away.

The Red artillery opened fire, and the Cossacks wavered as the shells burst among them. A horse fell with kicking legs, then, as the officers set about them with the flat of their swords, driving them forward, they began to take position and we saw their sickle-like sabres flash.

A squadron nearby swept past us, their gear jingling, their leather creaking, their horses snorting, and, with their officers

yelling and urging them along, they joined the general forward movement. They drew their swords all together on a
shouted order and the pace of the horses changed to a canter,
then they swept onwards to join the other formations, brandishing their weapons and yelling, every man straining forward
on his mount and eager. As they pounded forward and reached
the Reds, the sabres slashed and a couple of men toppled from
the saddles. One of them sat up, holding his head, then the
Cossacks were sweeping past, swinging round the rear of the
Red cavalry, and the Reds began to throw in their hands
before the two formations were properly locked together.
Flags were thrown down and weapons followed. A few more
men toppled from the saddle before the excitement died down,
then the Cossack squadrons drew rein and took up formation
behind and alongside the Reds, shouting and barging their
mounts against those of their captives to herd them into line,
and the whole mass began to move slowly in our direction.

The Reds surrendered about 1,100 men, several light guns
and a lot of transport.

*

I was back at my Headquarters at Novocherkassk late the next
evening, highly delighted with the result of the trip. I wanted
to push off again to the 1st Corps on the right flank but I was
very short of stores and spare parts, so I decided to go straight
on down to Novorossiisk to re-fit and then spend a week in
Novocherkassk before starting off again.

In Novorossiisk I found a splendid lot of canteen stores,
rations, clothing – in fact, everything that could be scrounged
from the base. Chief of all my prizes were several rolls of
khaki cloth which had been sent for repairs to our own uniforms. This I handed over to the Military School of Tailoring
for manufacture into uniform for the Russian officers.

Meanwhile Dickie, digging out stores, had got the "Q"
Department in good order and had started off his Liaison
Officers for their first visits to the corps headquarters to which
they were to be attached.

I wasted no time in calling on the Ataman to thank him for my trip and he invited me to accompany him to a big fête at Starocherkassk to celebrate the anniversary of the Battle of Azov. We travelled on a river steamer which had been acquired for him, but it was a frightful old wreck. The ceremony consisted of the usual impressive memorial service in the open air, followed by an inspection of troops, and a dinner in the town hall of the old capital of the Don Cossacks. As the rainy season had not yet really begun, Starocherkassk was quite accessible from all sides, though during the winter it became an island surrounded by miles of floods through which the actual course of the Don river was unrecognisable.

On my return, the Ataman told me that he had appointed Alex Smaguin to be attached to me for liaison duties.

CHAPTER TWELVE

I went round at once to see the Smaguins. I had grown very attached to them during my brief visits to Novocherkassk. Alex was a likeable man, despite his faults, and his wife Moussia was a great beauty with an outstanding personality and superb courage, and through the hectic three months which lay ahead of us, although I was to meet her on less than a dozen occasions, I became very attracted to her.

We realised at once that we were both dedicated to the cause of the White Russian Armies and, in the coming weeks, she helped me constantly in my support of the Don Cossacks and in the end I found myself assisting her and a few of her friends to escape. In the last brief period we were together in Novocherkassk, she worked for me as a highly competent intelligence officer, and, through her Russian contacts, just as Norman Lack and his wife were doing, she picked up scraps of conversation and much invaluable information regarding the separatist intrigues which were now beginning to develop in the Cossack command. All of this helped me in preparing plans to cover all possible eventualities, and by this time it was becoming obvious that there might be some. At the same time she proved an invaluable guide in my contacts with the refugees who were dependent on me and was of inestimable value in preparing their orderly evacuation.

Yet, overshadowing these more prosaic activities, she could also, at a second's notice, react like a flash to the spirit of the moment and radiate all that lay in her vast potential – of which she was well aware! – to inspire laughter, confidence and affection. In addition, she acted as a tactful and sympathetic go-between with all sections of the refugees, helping to soothe their nerves and bustle them into preparing for the final evacuation.

We all tried hard to look on the bright side and to avoid facing this fact of evacuation but things had changed enormously since the summer and more and more we were having to accept now the possibility of defeat.

Without doubt this possibility was brought about often by the sheer inability of the White Russians to organise themselves, and of the generals to act in concert with each other to co-ordinate their attacks, by the inevitable corruption, laziness and indifference of many officers and officials and by the curious Russian inability to react swiftly to events or to take even the simplest precautions against disaster. The "cordon sanitaire" which Churchill had visualised across Europe against the advance of Communism was obviously beginning to crumble but I tried hard not to condemn the Russians for their shortcomings. While acknowledging their existence, I endeavoured always to adopt the attitude of a sympathetic friend trying with them to overcome the appalling difficulties with which we were undoubtedly faced.

When I appeared, the Smaguins welcomed me with open arms and at their house I bumped once more into Madame Rechitovski, the Abramovs, the Tchebyshovs, who were now both working with the Senate, and Helen Routchenko, who with her husband had lived at Revenki about sixty miles north of Novocherkassk but had come into the capital for greater security. They were all a little sad because one of our friends, Helen Abramov, had died of typhus.

Our time together was short because, almost immediately I had to leave again, bound for Surovikina, but during the week I was in Novocherkassk, Lack had been busy and his great value was that he interpreted with his brain as well as with his mouth and picked up innuendos which no Russian interpreter could – or would – ever have passed on to me. Moussia talked with the generals often, and passed on what she heard, as did Alex when he was sober enough, but Lack had still further advantages. Having come from Petrograd with his wife, he was well-known to the refugees, who often gave parties for later arrivals of refugees they'd known in the North, and he could pick up all sorts of gossip because he wasn't a soldier, as also could his wife.

The evening we arrived at Surovikina, it began to snow for the first time. For some time there had been a cold drizzle on and off, which was neither rain nor snow but something in between, and now the wind got up, the trees bending under the pressure of the gale. The wind tugged at clothes, crawled up the back and froze the fingers, then the snow began to fall, the wet feathery flakes whirling down out of the darkness to lie thickly on the ground, white against the iron-black of the buildings. The air grew colder and noses were tucked into up-turned collars, and the place looked beautiful under its mantle of white, full of houses with frosted panes and warm yellow lights. Beyond them the hills lay in bold blacks and purples.

By the next day it had started to rain again, but there was a feeling of excitement in the air, particularly among the British, at this first snow. It was dirty now, and filling the gutters with slush, but we had noticed how the sound of the bells from the church had been muffled by the falling flakes and somehow we were looking forward to seeing the famed Russian winter.

We wished to inspect a medical unit established in the village, because one of the officers with me, Roche, was tremendously keen on the question of immediate and permanent segregation of typhus patients. He received a rude shock, however, when he saw the utter absence of any efficient measures for this purpose. Arranging for patients to go into the hospital trains wrapped up only in sterilised blankets while their infected clothing was systematically de-loused and prepared for re-issue, seemed simple enough to us after what we'd seen in France, but it was still an administrative feat utterly beyond the Russian medical department. It was made additionally difficult, too, because all clothes, or blankets or stores of any kind, once they had been in a soldier's use for any short period were thenceforward looked upon as his personal pro-perty, and could not be wrung from him. Roche, however, insisted on visiting the sterilising and de-lousing appliances and they disclosed an appalling state of affairs.

A cellar was used as a "sulphur box" for de-lousing clothes, but judging by the endeavours to waste time and change direction made by the Russian medical officer, this apparatus was not in use. By devious routes, we were taken to a dilapidated boiler on wheels.

"*This* has always been used till *quite* recently," we were told. "It's only idle now because the man who understands it has gone sick."

It was perfectly serviceable, in actual fact, despite its dilapidation, but had obviously never been used for months and, despite protests from all sides, Roche persisted in his advance on the "sulphur box". Again we were delayed and offered an alternative.

"It's the sulphur box I wish to see," Roche insisted.

"But we have shown you the sulphur box," the Russian said.

"That wasn't a sulphur box."

"Wasn't it?"

"No."

"It's very efficient."

"It's not a sulphur box."

Eventually someone whispered to the Russian doctor and he turned to Roche. "The man who keeps the keys has to be found," he said. "He seems to have disappeared. We have sent someone to look for him."

By the time we were allowed to reach it, they'd managed to start a sulphur fire in the cellar, which would have killed every louse within a four-mile radius, and had already practically asphyxiated the staff who were supposed to be in charge of it. They had clearly never operated it before.

The only bright spot in all the apathy and inefficiency was one with which I was becoming more acquainted and which threw a very strong light on one of the most vexed questions regarding social conditions in Russia. That was the keenness, efficiency, and persistence in demanding help and advice, displayed by the Jewish doctors, of which there were always one or two in each medical unit. This was the only capacity in which the Jews were allowed to serve, and comparing their methods with that of the orthodox Russians, it was easy to see the reason for the prominent position they had reached in every area and community where they had established themselves. A more complete contrast it was hard to imagine.

"It'd be simpler to let the Jews run Russia," Roche said. "They seem to be the only people competent to run *anything*."

It was their competence and energy, in fact, backed by their resentment against generations of ill-treatment and intolerance, which brought them so conspicuously to the front of the Bolshevik movement.

*

Next day we pushed off on horseback and reached Manoelen where 1st Corps Headquarters were established. General Alexeiev, the Corps Commander, was at the front, but we saw his deputy, General Markov and the usual vexed question of artillery was discussed. He only had two batteries armed with British 18-pounders and one with 4.5 howitzer.

From Manoelen, we went on in a car next day with General Markov himself and his A.D.C. Markov, who always wore a white fur cap, was much older than most of the Russian generals and had a very quick temper, but he also had a peculiar dry humour of his own and must have been a very efficient soldier of the old school.

We arrived very late at night at Ust Medvyeditsa, the beams of the car lights yellow in the mist and jerking violently as it laboured over the rutted road. Ust Medvyeditsa was now the headquarters of the 6th Division and, as we had been working steadily northwards all the time since we had left the railway, I was not surprised to see plenty of snow about. This, with the mud caused by the rain which had followed the first snowfall, had left the roads in an appalling condition – great deep hollows where everything came to a stop so that whole strings of vehicles of all kinds came to a halt. A car with spinning wheels, its officer occupants still sitting snugly inside, was the first to come to a stop, and while mud-smeared soldiers laboured to release it, a cart behind also halted. Soon there was a huge jam of vehicles, all bogged down in the knee-deep mud, men cursing as they struggled to get them going again, drivers flogging their horses, and sergeants lurching and sliding from one end to the other of the quagmire in an attempt to get some order into the chaos.

It was now November, five months since I had paid my first visit to the Don Valley in the broiling heat and found everybody full of optimism over the victorious advance of the Cossacks. Faces were graver now and there was none of the joyous expectancy of those days. Times had changed and instead of the hoped-for advance on Moscow, the White armies were suddenly in retreat everywhere.

Most disquieting news was coming back now.

"There has been a general retirement of the Volunteer Army from the Kursk salient," we were told. "It's causing the withdrawal of Skouro's cavalry. They suffered heavy losses in the Voronezh fighting. The whole of the 3rd Don Corps has pulled back, too. They're holding a line running from the railway from Podgornya to Valuiki."

The mission of the 1st Corps appeared to be to hold the approaches to the Ust Medvyeditsa bridgehead and to keep in touch with Wrangel's left flank. But Wrangel also was in trouble on the Volga Front where the Bolshevik river gunboats were playing a very important part in his discomfiture, and the volatile temperament of his Caucasian cavalrymen was beginning to show signs of unsuitability for the continuous dogged resistance which the numerical superiority of the Reds imposed upon them.

We motored out to Krasni village to visit the 4th Plastoune Brigade, and, considering the state of the tracks, I was surprised that our heavily-loaded car ever got us there. With every bump and rut, the chassis and springs groaned, and every minute I expected one of the tyres to blow. But we drove straight on and stopped at the first body of troops we saw, which happened to be a reserve company moving up to the front. A battery of British 18-pounders was firing spasmodically at long range and, as I saw the hesitation and the pauses in the firing and the obvious consternation round the guns, I went to see what was wrong. Owing to the lack of sufficient buffer oil or to faulty springs, the guns had to be pushed back by hand after every shot for the last few inches of their recoil into the cradle. Despite their problems they seemed to be making very heavy work of the firing, and I couldn't see quite why the guns were elevated to such extreme range.

"Why not wait until the enemy come nearer so as to shorten the range," I suggested to the Battery Commander. "Or, better still, push your guns closer up behind your own infantry trenches."

In reply, I got a somewhat startling answer.

"I can't get any closer to the infantry," he said. "There are trenches 500 yards farther on and unless I open fire as soon as our infantry can see the enemy advancing they will leave their trenches and run away."

This was rather a dilemma, I agreed, so I asked to accompany him to the observation post to see how the guns were firing. We moved *past* the infantry trenches and came to the O.P. 300 yards in front of them, and in a No Man's Land. It was a high mound about seventy yards square and on it and around it were congregated a party which ought to have drawn the fire of all the Red artillery in Asia – two battery O.P. officers, the brigadier and twenty mounted Cossacks, two large fires burning and about ten or twelve horse-holders and orderlies. We all stood on the top of the mound with our glasses and had a magnificent view of the country before us, and we were left quite untroubled.

About 6,000 yards away were the Bolsheviks, mostly cavalry, quietly wandering into a village in small parties, groups of horsemen with flags and an occasional gun or cart dark against the snow. A couple of patrols were advancing in our direction, and one of our forward posts was firing with machine guns and rifles at them at a range which could not have been less than 3,000 yards. They appeared to cause few casualties. Meanwhile an 18-pounder and a 4.5 howitzer were dropping about one round every three or four minutes into the village and its approaches. I saw a house collapse with a shower of tiles and a cascade of wooden planks, and a puff of dust and smoke through the windows. Figures ran in all directions and I saw pigs and chickens bolting down the street, then a column of smoke began to rise where a fire had started among the wooden buildings and I saw the flickering red of flames.

The shots were very effective and the Reds scattered, then I saw a section of their guns which had entered the village coming into action in a farmyard – *in full view*! They were not molested by our own gunners, however, and after waiting nearly half an hour for what I had expected in five minutes, and quite ready to dive for cover as the Red shells landed on the mound, I finally saw the flashes of the guns and heard the reports. But what they were firing at goodness only knew and the shells fell about 1,000 yards short of us on to an inoffensive piece of steppe, flinging up clods of earth and mud. They fired about forty rounds without any apparent change of line or range. Only about fifteen shells exploded.

I was fairly itching to see a little counter-battery work and even at that range I thought we could have shifted them, but suddenly all attention was diverted to the main attack which appeared in the form of about 400 Red infantry in three lines who appeared from our left front, emerging from a fold in the ground about 4,000 yards away. They carried large red banners and were urged forward by officers waving swords which flashed in the sunshine. They didn't seem very eager to forge ahead, however, and here and there an officer spurred his horse forward and set about some reluctant man with the flat of his weapon. The lines came closer, straggling and ballooning a little here and there, and we could hear the shouts of the officers, then fire was opened on them and the 4.5 howitzer got well on to them with instantaneous fuse within a few minutes. The 18-pounder battery commander was too far to the left, but once they had found the range, the first half-dozen shells pinned the advancing line of infantry down and they all fell flat to the ground. Three more salvoes sent them back hell-for-leather in the direction from which they had come, a horde of running figures heading full-tilt for shelter. Behind them they left scatterings of equipment, flags, an occasional casualty and infuriated shouting officers, and one aimlessly-wandering riderless horse.

At the sight of the enemy retreating, great excitement was shown by a sporting-looking little officer nearby clad completely in British uniform down to the last detail of a greasy-collared Burberry, button gaiters, and a soft-topped khaki cap worn in such a way as to put the earliest of "Gawd Blimies" to eternal shame. He made incessant requests for action to the brigadier and, on receiving approval, whistled through his teeth and fingers to collect every available mounted man. Climbing on to his pony he galloped off, followed by his men, in the direction of the enemy, waving his sword, kicking up clods of earth and clouds of powdered snow and pursued by the cheers of the onlookers.

"The battle is over," the General said gaily, clapping his hands. "The Reds are retiring and the cavalry are about to pursue. We will go back to Brigade Headquarters and have some tea!"

We were enjoying an excellent meal when, from the incessant running to and fro round the telephone, I gathered something had gone wrong. I could hear artillery cracking away on the ridge just above us and when I asked what was happening, I was told that the enemy had been reinforced, that my friend in the greasy Burberry had been forced to fall back and that there was a danger now of our left flank being separated from the cavalry who were about five miles out in that direction.

This resulted in a roar of laughter all round.

I had expected to see some action taken, but I was told, "Oh, that's all right. Even if they *do* break through, there's only one more hour of daylight and they'll all go back to the village for the night!"

I supposed it *was* all right so I doubtfully finished my tea, and we all packed into the car and somehow got back to the Divisional Headquarters in pitch darkness.

*

Disturbing rumours still came in from the far left of the Don Army about a heavy Bolshevik offensive which had developed in the areas where the Volunteer Army joined the Don Army near Valuiki. The famous Bolshevik cavalry commander, Budenny, was making steady headway south and, should he cut in between the Volunteer Army and the Cossacks, the situation would be dangerous.

We had heard a lot about Budenny and had seen pictures of him. He was a tall well-set-up man with a coarse face and a moustache like a horse's tail. He had been a cavalryman since 1903 in the Tsarist army and had served with distinction in the Russo-Japanese War and the World War. He was a product of the St. Petersburg Riding School, a magnificent horseman and utterly without mercy, and he was a man to be afraid of, a fact which was obvious in the faces of the men around me.

I was not to see Budenny's force in action as it happened, because a wire informed me that Holman was expected any day at Novocherkassk, so I decided to hurry back and we arrived late at Baskouskya in the afternoon and changed horses in time to reach Raspopinskya by nightfall.

The last seven miles was over a forsaken bit of ground on the south bank of the Don where Red cavalry had crossed on several raids, plundering what they could before escaping back across the river. We saw shabby villages, mud-coloured and thatched, the only sign of brightness the white walls and green dome of the Orthodox churches, and came eventually to a small stream, not yet frozen over, a clear pebble-bottomed trickle black against the snow as it meandered through tufts of withered grass. The steppes were ominously silent and we saw no signs whatever of our own cavalry patrols who were supposed to be in that area. Fortunately neither did we meet any Bolsheviks.

Next day we got back to 1st Corps Headquarters at Manoelen

and lunched with General Alexeiev. He was very reserved and appeared unwilling to make any definite arrangements with regard to the future. From this I gathered that he had more information than I had, and this subsequently proved true, as the 1st Corps evacuated the north bank of the Don within the next ten days. Knowing that I was in a hurry, he lent me a car to get back to Surovikina that night, but we were dogged with broken springs and burst tyres and had to spend the night at a small hamlet.

We all crowded into the same room where logs blazed in the stove and the tightly-sealed windows and doors held all the heat inside. Men came and went during the night, their uniforms wet with snow that lay heavy in the folds of their coats, and the Station Master came out of the mist, waving his hands, to tell us that the Reds were drawing nearer and the track was jammed solid with motionless rolling stock. Despite all the alarms, however, we had a comfortable night but, unfortunately, I had my 12-bore gun stolen, and worse still, missed the through train to Likhaia so that my return to Novocherkassk was delayed by a whole day.

Since I had left, the 1st Don Flying Squadron's train had arrived in Novocherkassk from the direction of Tsaritsyn, and the pilots reported that Kolchak's army was retreating eastwards along the Trans-Siberian railway.

The British who had been supporting him were already withdrawing their first contingents and vanishing eastwards through the snow, the long-suffering soldiers wondering what all their hardships had been about. Kolchak, in fact, had started his retreat as early as July and when the British troops had been withdrawn it had been the beginning of the end. His troops were now short of food, fuel, clothing and ammunition, typhus was rampant, and already along the railway east, the pumps and points were freezing solid. The Siberian armies were becoming as demoralised as the civilians who depended on them.

"His troops are in danger of decimation," one airman said. "And *we*'re making preparations for the evacuation of Tsaritsyn."

"The morale of Wrangel's Caucasian Army's declining rapidly," another officer told me. "They've had severe losses and heavy fighting, and the Bolsheviks have sent more troops against them, which have been released by Kolchak's retreat."

It sounded ominous, but worse was to come because the Kuban Cossacks were showing a distinct inclination to throw in their hands at any moment and go home, and Wrangel had handed over his command to Pokrovski, and was taking command of a Volunteer Army group on the Kharkov Front from Mai-Maievski whose drunken orgies had finally brought about his downfall. Important messages had been neglected by him and he had been recalled from his command by Denikin.

It was a grave situation, and the airmen had moved westwards to Surovikina, as they did not fancy their chances if the railway were cut between them and their only line of retreat to the Don country. I hadn't much time to talk to them, nor could I help them in any way, so I arranged with the Station Commandant for a passage on the west-bound train that evening. I scented a pretty busy time when I arrived at Novocherkassk.

Everything seemed fairly normal at my headquarters when I arrived, however, but the town appeared to be very full of people. There had been a great influx of refugees from the Voronezh, Kursk and Kiev areas, many of them people of high social position who had fled at a moment's notice and had travelled down almost starving and with no personal belongings. They had lived in horse trucks when they had not been able to beg a seat on one of the few staff trains which happened to move up or down the line. Some of these wagons had been converted into crude living-rooms, some even with windows cut in the sides and with the sliding doors replaced. All kinds of gear was piled on the roofs, and the refugee coaches were surrounded by peasants selling food or bartering with chickens at the windows where the refugees hung out, offering jewels and furs and anything they possessed for the wheaten pancakes and hard-boiled eggs and stringy meat. The trains were packed with people and were hotbeds where the typhus spread like wildfire once it broke out.

Occasionally hospital trains appeared, bearing the ruins of
White regiments and the stench that accompanied them was
appalling. They never had enough of anything, and the shortage of bandages and disinfectant caused the wounds to fill with
maggots so that they stank of sickness and putrefaction.
The low murmur of wounded men could always be heard, and
you could see them at the windows, moving feebly, while
groups of orderlies lifted down the bodies of those who had
died in the night.

Great masses of people were arriving now in sleighs, carriages and carts and gathering in the waiting-room where big
pot-bellied stoves, almost red-hot, were surrounded by the
husks of chewed sunflower seeds. As all the windows were
tight-closed there was a dreadful fug on, which, though com-
forting to the half-frozen refugees, was a great breeder of
disease.

A few people had arrived in the coaches of the British Mission whose officers had been only too glad to put stores, clothing, and accommodation at their disposal. Many of them had
been kept for weeks as hostages in the prisons of the "Extraordinary Commissions for Combating Counter-Revolution",
which was composed of the most villainous collection of
"agents provocateurs", blackmailers and murderers that the
Bolshevik Commissars could find to do their work for them.
Many of the refugees were already on friendly terms with the
British officers and, going round to the Central Hotel the day
after my return to get news from Prickett and the machine
gun instructors who lived there, I found a party going on,
presided over by Mrs. Lack, the only English woman in the
city.

The guests on this occasion were Svietlana and Irene
Mouraviev, two extraordinarily pretty girls. They had escaped
with their mother from Kiev, and they were both quite de-
lightful and spoke perfect English. They were all out to make
up for the appalling experience they had just come through,
and, with Christmas drawing near, we were all in accord with
what we considered a very good idea.

CHAPTER THIRTEEN

In view of the suddenly deteriorating situation I was more firmly convinced than ever that the great thing was for every available officer to be in the forward area helping to restore morale, and now that the cold weather was beginning, to see that no single article of clothing was retained in railhead stores that could be put on to the back of a fighting soldier.

Consequently, as it was just a month to our English Christmas Day – the Russian Christmas would be thirteen days later – I tried to arrange for all instructors and liaison officers to join the fighting units and stay a fortnight with them. They were then all to return to Novocherkassk a few days before Christmas, which we would then celebrate together in English style, later returning to the front to be with the Russians in time for their own festivities.

Things were going from bad to worse at the front, however, and Denikin's strategy, whose faults had been so frequently pointed out to him, was bearing evil fruit, and many pigeons we had expected to turn up eventually were at last coming home to roost. All those recruits who had been swept so abruptly into the White Army were proving quite useless now, and were busy changing sides as fast as they could. Regiments were mere skeletons and many of the officers had neither the skill nor the courage to do much about it. In addition, the shaky finances, the indifference of the Allies and the over-stretching of resources; the laziness, the carelessness and the contempt of the officers were all having their effect, as the hard-pressed rankers at last began to take matters into their own hands. Finally, owing to lack of organisation, inefficient control of the railways and maladministration in the newly-conquered districts, Denikin had found himself utterly unable to hold the vast front he had created against everyone's advice from the Dnieper to the Volga, or to produce those better conditions of life which his propaganda had constantly promised in exchange for Bolshevik tyranny.

Denikin was a thoughtful, resolute and well-balanced man himself, who was courageous and honest, but he was not a good speaker and had never been able to take hold of the imagination of the troops. In addition he had no commanding presence, and he lacked that indefinable something which captures the imagination and stirs the heart: he owed his success only to hard work. He was also morbidly sensitive against aristocrats, courtiers and officers of the ex-Imperial Guard, and took care to protect his dignity against slights by them which were often purely imaginary. Many of the men who surrounded him didn't like fighting, and these men, dressed in absurd uniforms, all spurred and laced, took great pains to avoid work. But though Denikin was strong-willed and inflexible himself, he showed an inexplicable lack of resolution with them. While a real soldier himself, he did not seem to dare to ask anything of his subordinates.

In addition, typhus as well as hard fighting was beginning to cause heavy casualties among his troops now, and petty jealousies and intrigues were beginning to occupy the minds of too many of his leaders. Moreover, the general conduct of the troops – officers as well as men – in the back areas, where too many of them remained, was rapidly alienating the sympathies of the peasant and working classes, who were assiduously backed by the tireless German and Bolshevik propaganda, and there was an increasing suspicion that Denikin and Romanovski, his Chief of Staff, though not actually fighting for a restored monarchy, would in the end re-establish many of the abuses and despotic institutions which had caused the downfall of the old regime.

Worst of all, was the news – again exaggerated and distorted by the anti-allied agents – of the turn which political events in England had taken. The final blow was the report of Lloyd George's speech at the Guildhall in London on Novem-

ber 9th, which, summed up, told the struggling Russian
Loyalists that they had failed to do what was expected of them,
and could now stew in their own juice!

*

Things had suddenly changed!

I was faced with many awkward questions and curious
glances. The well-educated refugees and senior commanders
remained friendly to me and accepted my somewhat lame explanation of "political interests over which soldiers had no
control", but from many of the younger officers and more
irresponsible civilians I got many angry looks and muttered
insults which, after an evening vodka, they took precious little
pains to conceal.

It was all very hurtful and humiliating, and the thing which
cut me most when trying to reconcile myself to the rapidly
lowering barometer of British prestige, was that, despite all our
efforts to explain in letters home how very much more than a
family quarrel between Russians was at issue, the ground was
deliberately pulled from under our feet by politicians whose
knowledge of the subject did not go far enough to know that
Kharkov was a town and not a general; and that the Sea of
Azov was ice-bound during most of the winter; and who had
even cheerfully described the blood-thirsty Trotsky as "a
saviour of democracy".

While I was struggling to appease our critics, Holman
suddenly appeared out of the blue, followed by two special
trains of the picked airmen of 47 Squadron. He declared that
he was going on to Valuiki, which was the threatened joining
point of the Don and Volunteer armies, and upon which a
strong Bolshevik cavalry corps under Budenny was advancing
in an endeavour to capture the line running south. Budenny's
plan was to drive the Volunteer Army westwards to the
Crimea, and the Don Army eastwards into the heart of their
own steppes from which he knew well they would be reluctant
to withdraw south. As a final and most crushing blow of all, he
hoped to send a strong cavalry raid due south to seize the rail-

way line between Taganrog and Rostov to cut off all the stores,
aeroplanes and tanks in Taganrog.

Against this offensive, all the reserves Denikin could lay his
hands on were to be used, and Holman in person was to direct
a series of bombing and machine-gunning raids, to be carried
out by the crack British pilots of 47 Squadron. Tanks were also
hurrying up as fast as the rapidly disintegrating railway
system would let them, and it was hoped that if only the heart
could be taken out of the aggressive Bolshevik cavalry commander, his advance would be checked, and some counter-
attraction on the Baltic, Polish or Far-Eastern Front might
draw off the attention of the Red Armies, while the bitter suffering of winter in the starving Russian towns would bring about
sufficient anti-war feeling to cause considerable embarrassment
to the Soviet Government.

The town was white with snow now and passing carts and
cars were plastered with it. There were fires burning at the
corners of the streets near the great frozen piles of cleared
snow, and icicles hung in festoons from every building. Windows were frosted up, only small circles showing where someone inside had cleared them. The dirty streets had been emptied
of snow but the ruts and potholes left over from the summer
had frozen solid and filled with water, which left a skating rink
for horses and men, and the public horse-drawn sleighs, as they
passed, clattered over the lumpy ice, their occupants huddled
under the moulting fur robes and bounced from side to side by
the uneven surface. Figures trudging past were black against
the whiteness, their heads down, their collars up, bulky in their
winter clothing, and over all was the heavy leaden colour of
the sky which seemed so low and so weighty it seemed to rest
on top of the houses.

Although Holman was clearly occupied with plans, he still
managed at a picturesque ceremony in the Ataman's Palace to
invest the faithful Bogaievski with a K.C.M.G. I was glad the
Ataman had received this distinction because, when things were
no longer auspicious, he showed what a stout-hearted soldier
he was, and how loyal to the Allies he remained.

F.D.   O

Holman left soon after the ceremony and in Taganrog shortly afterwards I heard rumours that he was up in the Valuiki area personally bombing the Bolsheviks. I also heard some very disquieting news on my own account, to the effect that senior staff officers had just arrived from England to take command of the liaison groups, and that, at any moment, I might have to hand over my Don Army Group to one of them. The Ataman wrote to Holman at once asking that I might retain my position, as we had always got on so well together, but events moved so quickly in the next few weeks I had no time to bother much more about it until the arrival of my successor about a month later settled the matter.

Among other things with which I occupied myself at Taganrog was the supply of naval guns for the Don armoured trains, and Captain Fremantle, R.N., Senior Naval Liaison Officer, told me that 6-inch Armstrongs were already on their way from Novorossiisk, whilst others which were being put on special mountings in Taganrog ought to be ready in a fortnight. Meanwhile he was sending two naval officers and about ten men up to Novocherkassk to explain their mysteries to the Armoured Train Battalion.

We were all a little on edge about this time because there had been a little trouble among the personnel of the Tank Corps at Taganrog. As with many other British formations still employed after the Armistice on distant fronts, a spirit of restlessness and a desire for demobilisation had led to insubordination. Fortunately this was not serious but everyone was a little concerned as troops in Russia were often affected by the Communist propaganda and there had been one case in the north of Russian troops murdering their British officers.

However, when I had left for Taganrog there had been little or no indication of the storm which was brewing just over the horizon or of the rapid deterioration which events were shortly to take. A certain amount of anxiety was still felt for Holman who appeared to be spending more of his time on the wrong side of the Bolshevik lines than his exalted rank demanded, but we knew he was in good hands with 47 Squadron and, on my return to Novocherkassk, I found several pleasant surprises to counteract the increasing gloom of the news.

First of all was the arrival of a naval officer, Durnford, and a group of ratings, and secondly there was a large supply of parcels from home with winter clothing. For me there was a set of wooden stirrups which I had found invaluable for keeping away frost-bite in France, a sheepskin *shuba* or heavy coat covered with khaki cloth, and a grey *carracul* Cossack cap to match the collar. These last were a present from the Ataman, who had often told me I never wore enough clothes. They were made of British greatcoat material and certainly arrived at the psychological moment because winter was upon us now with a vengeance and the cold had become bitter.

The streets were covered now with thick black ice, and it hurt to breathe and the fur hats we wore were thick with rime, the stiffened bristles tickling our faces. Every window was screened with a crust of frozen snow now and it was so cold the Cossacks had taken to wrapping cloth round their stirrup irons to avoid getting frostbite in their feet. Droshkies had been replaced by sledges, the bells strangely gay in view of the gloomy news, while the streets were covered with caked snow which was lying piled up at the corners. The damp cold of October and November had given way to the real Russian winter, and despite the invigorating atmosphere and the still cheerful optimism of most of the Don Army staff, there was a noticeable decline in morale of the lower ranks and of the apathetic population as a whole.

It was easy to see by the dejected and rather subdued tone of conversation at any gathering of Russians that they were beginning to wonder what was going to happen next. You rarely heard "*Na Moskvu*" these days and all talk of reaching the capital by Christmas had ceased.

"If only Tsaritsyn had not fallen," I heard. "If only the Allies had sent real troops."

Unfortunately, with the mobile warfare, no one really knew what was happening and as always where lack of information of any kind is predominant, speculation took a pessimistic turn. And there was certainly plenty of cause for pessimism because, by this time, fuel for railway engines was so short there was barely enough to enable such trains to operate as were considered essential for evacuating military and civilian personnel and stores from the forward areas. The chances of a civilian being able to travel had now almost vanished because there were no normal passenger trains, and in many cases, for lack of an engine to pull them, lines of railway carriages which had been the homes of many people for a very long time were simply left in the sidings. It was with this situation in view that I succeeded in getting two or three coaches earmarked for members of my group and certain refugees in Novocherkassk, and had them guarded by Cossacks at the orders of the Don Government.

There were far too few police about, of course, and far too many troops who appeared to have leave from the front and seemed to spend their time cursing the Allies and breaking open the wine shops. As usual, all the best were sticking it out in the fighting line, but so far as the Don Army was concerned the fall of Tsaritsyn on the right flank and of Kharkov on the left had caused a general withdrawal on Novocherkassk and Rostov. Moreover, a new force of Red cavalry had now crossed the Don on the front held by the 2nd Corps, and the defenders were rapidly falling back on the Tsaritsyn-Likhaia railway and the line of the river Donets through Kamenskya and Lugansk.

This was practically the same line as that held by the Cossack Army when I had first arrived in May. It was then a very strong one, but now things were different. With the cold the rivers had become sluggish and slabs of ice had formed along the banks, before breaking away and swirling into the current; making navigation difficult and banging against the pillars of the bridges. They had congealed again as they had come to a stop and more ice had built up around them, while the river itself had filmed over and the ice had stretched farther into midstream, until the water was completely covered. It had now set hard and thickened over until it was strong enough to bear the weight of a man, a horse, a gun. The advantages of a river front had thus been neutralised and it was now possible to cross anywhere, so that there seemed no likelihood of being able to hold it any more easily than any other position.

Wrangel's counter-stroke on our left, despite its backing by General Holman personally with his tanks and bombers, appeared to have fizzled out completely. Wrangel was a magnificent commander who had led a very mixed lot of troops in the Caucasian Army brilliantly, but the main elements of these troops were Cossacks from the Kuban who were already considering political separatism and were beginning to pack in the fighting. Budenny, in fact, seemed to be achieving his object of separating the Volunteer Army – with the exception of its right-hand corps – from the Don Cossacks. The army was withdrawing now in a south-westerly direction on the Crimea, and the right-hand corps was falling back in the direction of Rostov, the only place where it could evacuate its railway material, staff and hospital trains across the Don.

To add to its difficulties, all the lines running from the forward areas had rapidly become crowded with rolling stock and blocked with broken-down engines. The stations and sidings were full of abandoned, snow-plastered trains, their engines burned out, the carriage doors hanging open. Even the movement of troops was coming to a stop and thousands of passengers from the abandoned trains trudged southwards, discouraged and desperate, glancing nervously back as they listened for the crack of Red rifles behind them.

Overnight, it seemed, the whole front had collapsed in chaos and it was obviously our duty to evacuate all the material at Taganrog connected with tank, aeroplane and machine gun depots, as well as the machinery of Denikin's government, all of which would have to cross the Don by the single narrow bridge at Bataisk a mile south of Rostov Junction.

CHAPTER FOURTEEN

There was a great deal of gloom on December 1st when I prepared to start up the line again to the 3rd Corps at Likhaia, to pick up my liaison officer and get back before the English Christmas Day.

As usual, before leaving I went to see the Ataman to get the latest news. He looked grave.

"Owing to differences of opinion among the commanders and the critical situation on the front," he said at once without preamble, "I have assumed command of all Cossack armies in the field."

This command had previously been held by Sidorin, while the Ataman was only the titular Commander-in-Chief, but Denikin had urged him to take over command as there was general dissatisfaction, not to mention suspicion, at Sidorin's conduct. Denikin was contemplating moving his seat of government to Ekaterinodar so as to clear the forward railway systems as far as possible for the sole use of the troops and refugees who were beginning to flock southwards in ever increasing numbers, and though Sidorin still held command of the field troops, he was now subordinate to the Ataman in all affairs. Bogaievski was very popular with all ranks, and the change in leadership was greeted with great satisfaction, except for Sidorin's own particular gang – headed of course by the fat and genial Du Chayla – who were by this time seriously contemplating the possibility of making a separate peace with the Reds on terms which they considered favourable to their ambition of an independent military republic of Don Cossacks.

Denikin's plans and his pledges to restore a United Russia under a government elected by the people had never appealed to the Don Separatists. Though opposed to Bolshevism, they were equally determined never again to come under a central Russian government which might be as reactionary in its land policy as the old Tsarist one had been. And the Cossack reluctance to leave their own country in the hands of invaders while they continued the struggle elsewhere was becoming more evident every day. While a considerable force stuck together, prepared to cross the Don and even the Manych to the south if need be, there were also large numbers of troops who deliberately drifted away into their villages, deserting their regiments, hoping to get on the right side of the advancing Bolshevik armies as they overran the country of the Don. The woods were full of these men, some of them armed for their own safety and determined to keep their freedom.

Worse still, among the loyal section of the army and taking their cue from those of their leaders who were more occupied with political intrigues than with military achievement, was the party who still waited to see which way the cat would jump. These, though nominally devoted adherents to Denikin's cause, were even at this very time receiving overtures from the Red government and were soon actually discussing the terms under which they were prepared to betray their friends in return for a promise of an amnesty, and autonomy for the particular corner of South Russia in which they hoped to spend their lives in self-complacent security.

*

It was late in the afternoon on December 23rd that a message arrived at my house from Moussia Smaguin.

"Because it is your Christmas," she wrote, "because you are far away from your homes, your parents and your friends, and because you have come so far to help us, Alex and I hope you will dine with us on Christmas Night and bring one or two of your friends with you. Svietlana will bring her balalaika and sing for us."

I had planned to have our own Christmas party at my house on that night, but as some of our officers had not yet got back to Novocherkassk, I postponed it until the 27th, which also happened to be my birthday, and joyfully accepted the Smaguins' invitation.

Meanwhile the evacuation of Novocherkassk now seemed not only inevitable but imminent. Headquarters was a waste of torn paper and full of smoking fires as documents were destroyed. Every now and then a horseman appeared in a hurry, dragging his mount to a standstill with slithering feet, or a car shot past, wildly driven and containing two or three grim-faced officers, their clothes plastered with snow. The refugees were preparing for yet another move and were packing their few pathetic belongings into bundles and battered suitcases.

I set about preparing my own plans which by this time I expected would have to be put into effect at the latest by January 2nd. Personally I thought that, for political reasons, the Russian command would be anxious to avoid any of the British officers getting too deeply involved in their final operations, but I also knew that many of the Russians, both civil and military, were watching every move we made, and were just waiting for the opportunity to complain about us leaving them to their fate. I had decided, therefore, that two officers, Dickie and Read, should join me in being the last to leave the city with the rearguard under the command of General Janov.

The remaining officers, with the Smaguins, the Mouravievs, and some of the younger and more active personnel connected with the Liaison Group were to be ready to move at six hours' notice in Mission coaches as soon as the situation became critical. To all others for whom I felt any personal responsibility I offered the most urgent advice to leave Novocherkassk at the first possible moment, to get themselves through Rostov and across the Don at Bataisk, and thence to Ekaterinodar or even Novorossiisk. They would be helped by the Mission as far as possible.

I intended to make it quite clear to the younger element that, with the exception of interpreters, Russian liaison officers and their dependants, they were at liberty to make their own arrangements if they wished and that I would help them as far

as I was able, but that they could not count on Mission
coaches, all of which would be earmarked for Mission officers
and for those who were remaining to the last with me. It was,
of course, impossible to lay down any firm procedure, but
I thought that these plans were better than no plans, and
would improve the chances for everybody, and though in the
end the first party to leave telescoped with the second, they
worked.

For the moment, however, I had only those coaches which
were being kept for me, but with the assistance of Norman
Lack and authorisations from Sidorin and the Ataman, I was
able to collect two more, in which to get the most difficult
cases away as soon as there was a southbound train to which
they could be attached. I was never able to whistle up a special
engine or a coach at any moment and it simply developed into
scrounging individual coaches – in one case an engine, complete with driver – and helping individuals as best I could.
The co-operation of the railway employees and the engine
drivers cost us much rum and many roubles.

By the middle of December all hope of my getting up to the
front again had gone, and of all the British liaison officers only
the machine gunners and one who was with the 3rd Corps
artillery were unaccounted for. Three officers, in fact, did not
turn up until the 27th, as they had become involved in the disorderly withdrawal on the Kamenskya-Lugansk line, had lost
all their transport, and had had to burn their coaches at Likhaia
Station.

Sidorin had already fallen back with his headquarters to
Persianovka, a pleasant little village only ten miles north of
Novocherkassk, consisting mainly of small wooden country
cottages owned by townspeople as their summer homes.
Beaten units were already beginning to drift through the town,
first the train loads of wounded, jolting and wretched, the
straw bloody from their injuries; then the horsemen, slouched,
head down, their shoulders covered with sacks, old coats,
shawls, anything they could find to keep them warm; then the
wretched infantry trudging silently through the snow, their

faces grey with fatigue; and finally the refugees, silent, exhausted, most of them out on their feet and half-starved,
pushing carts, carrying bundles or children, or riding in huddled groups on wagons pulled by exhausted and stumbling
horses.

All northbound traffic on the railway from Novocherkassk
had been entirely suspended by this time so as to leave the rails
free for the move south, but all along the route trains had come
to a standstill, one after the other, their sides snow-plastered
and coated with ice, their windows frozen up.

As news from the forward areas increased in gravity, I went
to General Popov who was supposed to be organising the
defence of the town, and offered the services of myself and five
or six other officers as soon as my evacuation plans had been
put into effect, placing ourselves under his orders either to
join a fighting unit or for any other duties connected with the
defence of the town.

I could get no definite reply from him, however, as a particularly oriental type of resignation, and leave-it-to-fate attitude appeared to have fallen on the Russian commanders. They
seemed surprisingly indifferent to the condition of their troops
or the state of the front. The old lazy indifferent attitude of the
Russian Imperial higher command showed in their casualness
and the way they managed to live in comparative comfort in
their headquarters or in their trains while the troops starved or
froze around them, or in the way they rode in cars and carriages while the wounded walked.

There appeared to be no sign of any policy, nor any effort to
develop one. Lack did his best to discover something positive
from his Russian contacts, but without success, and in despair
I went to Janov, the commander of the escort squadron of the
Ataman's bodyguard regiment of Cossacks, and asked him to
take us along with him. As a British officer I wasn't a bit
afraid of what might happen. Always I felt that even if things
didn't go according to plan, I'd be rescued. I was quite wrong,
of course, and as I learned later, the British government was as
quick to repudiate its servants as any other.

I understood that the Ataman would probably stay on till the last possible moment and leave the capital with the rearguard, but all I could get in the way of satisfaction from Janov was an invitation for myself and any other officer I liked to bring with me to join his regiment as soon as fighting looked like starting in the town, and go along with him as far as I liked.

For the moment, however, my chief problems were the salvaging of what I could of such technical artillery stores as remained in the Hootenok depot. Against the snow, black figures were already hurrying backwards and forwards, loading equipment into carts and lorries and wagons. They seemed to be handling the job most efficiently, so I started to organise the safe evacuation of my second group, who were a pretty helpless – as well as a pretty hopeless – lot of civilians. There were elderly men and women among this group, most of them people who had never had to do much – or even think much – for themselves, and they seemed uncertain how to behave in this new crisis which had been thrust on them.

Whenever I saw them, they plucked at my sleeve with such questions as "What shall we do?" "Where shall we go?" "Who's going to look after us?" It was impossible to be angry with them. One was not even entitled to be. They were in such a pathetic condition and quite unable – because of the circumstances that existed – to help themselves even if they'd been able by temperament to do so and I tried in all humility to do what I could for them.

To help me with them, I was lucky enough to have Lack and his wife, who was a tower of strength in calming the panic and instilling confidence. One or two had threatened to kill themselves if the Reds came and she had to persuade them that it was our intention not to leave any of them behind, keeping their spirits up and providing an excellent medium through whom I could contact and control the stream of apprehensive Russians who crowded round her in the hope of getting a seat in one of the Mission coaches. Stout-hearted and clear-headed, she insisted that she and her small daughter would leave only when the last group were on their way. I decided Lack should go with her, as he was a poor horseman and would be of far more use helping her to deal with the railway travellers than suffering misery riding over the snowbound steppes with Janov's cavalry. One of the Russians, Pashkov, who had been educated at Cambridge, would remain with us to do all our interpreting work.

With the approach of Christmas Day, the cold intensified and the clouds grew black as soot and the falls of snow were more frequent. The sun looked like a cold orange over the dove-grey colours of the snow, and there was a haze in the north where a storm was spreading but, though the streets were kept reasonably clear, the pavements were buried in snowdrifts. Rumours that a breakthrough by Budenny's cavalry in the Valuiki area was threatening both the Don and the Volunteer army increased public apprehension, but so far as I was concerned Sidorin and his staff maintained a stony silence on the news.

By this time I was beginning to be certain that many members of the High Command were seriously debating disengaging themselves from the White Army, and the absence of any news from Mission Headquarters encouraged me in the idea that I was going to have a somewhat sticky situation on my hands.

However, my rather woolly plans had been made, the personnel concerned briefed, and my snow-covered railway coaches on the sidings visited to see that they had not been stolen, and we got ready for the Smaguins' party.

General Pavlov, whom I had met before, was there; together with Svietlana Mouraviev and her balalaika, and Helen Routchenko – whose husband had just died of typhus so that she was looking sad in her deep mourning black. She had disregarded the strict rules for Russian widows by coming out so soon, but she felt it her duty to do so.

"This is no time for rules," she insisted. "And I know my husband would have wished it."

Moussia came forward to greet me, looking quite radiant. She was obviously conscious of the inspiration which had led her to organise this very special party of her own, and, as she stood there smiling, I had to go all Russian and kiss her hands.

The first greetings over and Dickie sharply rebuked by Alex for not appearing in his kilt, we were all ushered into the dining-room and sat down to dinner accompanied by the drinking of innumerable toasts; then, with an air of intense expectation, we moved into the sitting-room from which we had up to then been barred. There, upon the table with the twinkling flames of its candles sparkling on the tinsel frost and cotton wool snow with which it was decorated, was a real English Christmas tree. And tied to the branches with pink ribbon bows were presents for each of us. Mine from Moussia was a miniature white bearskin mat, and from Alex there was a bottle of vodka with a drinking mug engraved with his initials. I was so touched by the gesture I could only sit down silently beside Moussia and mumble my inadequate thanks.

By this time I was more than a little in love with her – if one could be in love in circumstances of the kind we lived in. We were dedicated to the same cause, and I might often have made more of our feelings for each other if I had not always been so desperately busy or if I had not been governed by feelings of loyalty to her husband.

It was a very peculiar relationship, and I never realised how close we were until later when I looked back on it. I had never really paid her very much attention, because I was too oc-cupied with my work to notice her as a woman until just before this Christmas party. My meetings with her had always been marvellous reliefs from the tensions in the past but this party suddenly brought her very close to me.

After Pavlov left, to take over the command of the cavalry force which was to cover the defence of Novocherkassk, Alex, sitting beside Helen whom he very much admired, began tell-ing us stories of when he was an officer of the Empress of Russia's Guard Regiment of Lancers. He had been attached to the haemophilic Tsarevitch and had accompanied him on duty. The boy had always had a soldier or a sailor to make sure he didn't fall or injure himself in any way that might cause him to bleed to death; but every one, officers and men alike, were always watching out for his safety. He had also known the imperial family intimately and gone to parties with the four murdered grand duchesses.

It was a moment for reminiscences, and I found to my surprise that Moussia had been at school at Eastbourne where she had played hockey on the field adjoining that of my own school, and she remembered how we used to kick a football over on to their pitch so as to get a chance to talk to them. Svietlana, whose father had been Minister in the Russian Embassy in Madrid, was sitting quietly on cushions as she strummed a few chords on her balalaika and sang snatches of Russian songs in a soft contralto voice. With her mother and her sister Irene, she had spent several weeks in a Bolshevik prison in Kiev as hostages until rescued by Denikin's troops. Helen Routchenko's house at Revenki had been commandeered as headquarters by the local Commissars during the previous occupation and she and her husband had been forced to entertain a collection of brutal illiterates who had ruined their home and humiliated them by forcing them to do menial tasks for them. Everybody seemed to have suffered some enormous personal tragedy, and, with the exception of the British, everybody seemed to have lost near relatives in the appalling disaster which had overtaken Russia.

What a strange party it was! At that moment the Reds were barely thirty miles away and our defeated and disheartened Cossacks were retiring in considerable disorder just to the north. Yet we British officers were being entertained for Christmas in our own English way, by these few surviving representatives of the best of the Old Imperial Russian regime, in a way they could ill afford. I was deeply moved by the tenseness of the situation.

As time went on and one by one the candles spluttered out, the conversation became more personal. Svietlana's balalaika was silent now and soon only five candles remained alight. For some minutes nobody spoke. I had the feeling of waiting for something of vital importance to happen and I sensed that Moussia was feeling it as acutely as I was. The Bolsheviks were at that time advancing and we were living in an extraordinary situation.

As the candles died one by one, the voices dropped lower and lower and sentences became disjointed. Alex, sitting next to Helen Routchenko in the far corner of the room, was almost invisible in the shadows. Moussia was next to me, on a large sofa beside the fire but screened from its light. Two candles spluttered and went out, then a third. Svietliana sang a couple of bars of a Cossack folk song and the few sad minor chords of the accompaniment seemed to be blown off the strings of her balalaika by a soft wind rather than plucked by human fingers.

I could sense the strength of Moussia's dominant personality beside me. She was quivering under the influence of those emotions which the extraordinary poignancy of the moment had strung up to the highest point of tension.

The fourth candle went out and, with a sudden flash of memory, I compared the extinguished lights to the "gone for ever" minutes before the zero hour of a great attack on the Western Front. But here was no carefully synchronised clock, no minute of sixty seconds, neither more nor less. Here was now just a sixteenth of an inch of wax and a spluttering wick still remaining between us and something for which no operation orders had been written, no definite objective allotted, no indication ever given that it was anything at all. Nobody spoke but I believe that all eyes like mine were fixed on that last candle . . . going . . . going . . .

One final flicker, and for a moment there was that complete blackness which succeeds the extinction of a strong light before the eyes can become accustomed to the weaker flicker of a fire, which was all that now remained. Then it was over . . . over in reality, but leaving a memory which no time can efface, because during those few seconds when all eyes were blinded, I felt the presence of a soft radiant form bending across me like a flash of lightning in its quickness.

Two soft lips rested on mine for one exalted second in which I knew that the passion which they imparted was so intense that they dared not linger, and a hand rested lightly on mine and remained there, and through its touch raced the torrent of unexpressed and inexpressible sympathy which the preceding moment had unfettered.

Four or five seconds from start to finish, and a few more while we all waited in the red glow of the firelight, each one waiting for the other to speak, and then Moussia rose and suggested more candles and some wine to drink a health. It was all over, the spell broken as fresh lights were lit. Farewell toasts were drunk, and, struggling into our *shubas* and snowboots, we gathered on the doorstep for a last goodnight. I stood alone for a while with Moussia. The evening had been rather an emotional interlude that was a climax to all sorts of strains. Throughout our friendship, there had been a much stronger communication of love or even more than I realised, but the circumstances had never allowed it to develop.

We finally, reluctantly, pulled ourselves away and stumbled back to our house along the white frozen street, with a full moon shining cold and clear, and making the night like day. In the distance there were the sounds of a few shots, probably fired by a hilarious Cossack at a stray dog – then it was no longer Christmas night, 1919, and we remembered that Novocherkassk, the capital of the Don Cossacks, was in danger of capture.

I spent next day at Hootenok making final arrangements for the loading of all spare stores and getting the railway trucks shunted from the siding on to the main line. I also issued everything in the way of clothing and medical comforts to such units of the army as I could get in touch with as they retired through Novocherkassk, and urged the Russians to empty all their own stores of everything they could not evacuate. Then I started making ready for my own dinner party on the 27th.

This went off all right, thanks to the efforts of the Army Commander's band which he lent me. All the old group were there and I'd seldom seen Alex in better form. He insisted on

First divisional guns in open country

The Russian battery commander leaving his two horse carriage

Women making hay on the steppe

Don Cossack villagers

trying to fight the band-master, and Norman Lack fell backwards through a window into a heap of snow. Svietlana
Mouraviev's lovely sister Irene fed her French bulldog with
chocolates till it was sick and General Janov, despite his wife's
entreaties to be taken home with a headache – which nobody
believed – danced the *lisgintka* with such vigour he fell on his
back and couldn't get up.

We ended up with *Auld Lang Syne* in the traditional manner,
and I felt, as we crossed hands, that the last few hours at Novocherkassk were rapidly approaching, and this really was the
end of my association with the Cossacks to whom I had become so devoted.

*

By this time, the railways were chaotic and every train was full
to overflowing with refugees, many of them, unfortunately,
able-bodied men. On some of the trains that were moving
slowly through the yards, the occupants were more soldiers
than refugees, packed solidly inside and out, the men clinging
to roofs and buffers and hanging out of the windows. A lot of
them were drunk with the drunkenness of despair. These
trains often belonged to regiments and the troops were living
off the population, requisitioning more than they needed and
selling the surplus. One regiment had two hundred carriages
reserved for its baggage alone, while the stations were swarming with refugees, mostly women and children, often ill or
starving, desperate to go south. The units were often mixed
and nearly every regiment had trains blocking the line. Their
sick and wounded were in a pitiable state, however, and many
hospitals were already without medicine, nurses or doctors,
and starving, infected patients staggered about in quest of
food. The all-important cavalry were finally exhausted and
broken communications and lack of discipline rendered staff
work impossible.

While we struggled with our own evacuation, a rumour
came from the south-west that Mission headquarters had
evacuated Taganrog. I couldn't believe this to be true as I

should have been informed, and only a few days previously I had received an order on no account to move my own headquarters without reporting my new location to the Mission. This order had been brought about, I subsequently discovered, by the panicky movement south of other liaison groups which had been driven back with the armies and had more or less ceased to function.

My chief apprehension was for Holman who, I knew, had not returned to Taganrog. The evacuation of that place during his absence was sure not only to hamper his plans but also to leave him in ignorance of what was going on in his rear. On the other hand, I felt that if it *were* true, I was now entirely on my own and could take whatever action I thought fit to extricate my personnel and stores and re-form south of the Don as soon as Sidorin's headquarters settled down again.

In fact, I heard nothing more of Mission headquarters for nearly two weeks, by which time they were established at Ekaterinodar where Denikin had moved his own headquarters, but as the Russian Christmas Day drew near it was obvious that there was going to be little chance of any of us passing it in Novocherkassk, and on the night of January 2nd, on receiving the evening report from headquarters, I decided that what was left of my people must go the following day.

I warned the officers at dinner, and all night long the remaining kit and reserve stores, with the exception of the light travelling baggage which the last of us were keeping behind, was taken down by sledge and country cart to the Mission coaches in the sidings, the drivers forcing their way through the crowds of people heading out of the town and all the small vehicles and barrows carrying the belongings of the peasants.

The sidings were chaotic. Guards posted along the track chafed their hands and stamped their feet in the frozen snow while men with crowbars worked over the points, and the clang of metal on metal rang in the air. Engines sighed and clanked and occasionally a train moved off, watched enviously by those who had no place on it, moving slowly through the crowded station and yards, a vast snake of coaches behind one overloaded engine. More rarely, a big train passed through on an open line, perhaps a general's echelon, its windows frozen, the glass opaque with frost, or a hospital train with red crosses visible on the side.

Lack's duties of arranging trains commenced, and next morning, with hoar frost glistening on the trees in the avenue in the centre of the city, I sent a messenger round to call on the remaining Russian families with a curt injunction to be ready to embark at the station at 5 p.m. They had all been warned to have their things ready for a move at six hours' notice, so, by giving them eight hours, I allowed them ample margin. The officers now had nothing to do but help the groups to which they were detailed, and the refugees were pretty lucky to have so many to look after them.

I went round to the Smaguins' house myself. Signs of packing showed everywhere but the bundles they were preparing seemed pathetically small, and most of what they packed were not so much essentials as treasures. Like most of the refugees, when they had headed south they had not thought of hardship, and they had brought with them sentimental things rather than warm clothes, and they were now packing such articles as family ikons and things like that. Moussia appeared, barefooted, her hair down and thoroughly mutinous. She had a good Russian temper that could explode in a moment.

"There's no hurry," she said briskly. "Surely you're not getting frightened? Alex has gone to Rostov to see his father and mother-in-law off, and won't be back till tomorrow, and I can't go without him."

I had no time for this type of argument. "I'll call with three droshkies at 4 p.m. to take you and your baggage, packed or unpacked," I said and went straight off and paid a round of visits to the rest to see that all was going well.

It was, except that one coach with artillery stores, in which Lack and his wife and two other officers were to travel, was blocked on the line between Hootenok and Novocherkassk and was not likely to get into the station in time to go that night. For the rest, however, thanks to the excellent work of

Dickie and Lack and to the distribution of a good deal of rum and paper roubles and the frequent use of the name of the "British Mission", all the other coaches were attached to reliable trains belonging either to government or army staffs, or to the army commander's special which was due to leave before midnight. The recently-arrived naval officer, John Durnford, and the sailors were in their two horse boxes and had made themselves responsible for escort, porterage, cooking and the general cheering up of the refugees, who were now about to depart for an unknown future, with little hope of better conditions than they were leaving behind them.

The sailors were magnificent. They had arrived in Russia in the middle of the débâcle and hadn't the foggiest idea what was happening around them. But they weren't in the slightest perturbed, though I noticed that they seemed to be travelling light.

"What happened to your guns?" I asked.

They grinned. "Oh, that's all right," they said. "We tipped them off the line to let the traffic through."

At 5 p.m. I called again for Moussia and to my astonishment she was ready. She was grumbling, but not bad-temperedly.

"You've all got the wind up," she said. "I don't know what all the fuss is all about."

Her Cossack maid, who was staying behind, tearfully brought us some tea, and Moussia gave me a beautiful pink enamelled penholder, by Fabergé.

"To remember me by," she said simply.

We drove silently over the snow to the station, the snow swishing and squeaking beneath the wheels. Only once did she speak and then all she said was, "Promise me on your word of honour that you will find Alex when he returns from Rostov and look after him."

"Yes," I said. "I promise."

She sighed. "He is so stupid," she said. "He will get lost and killed if nobody is here to take care of him."

By 7 p.m. all the coaches were full. The Routchenko children and their mother had been brought to the station and we were all standing in the snow between the railway lines, eating chocolates and making the usual silly disjointed conversation which takes place when people in a crowded space are waiting for a train to go off. "Seeing off" at a station was a thing I had always hated and had made a point of avoiding during the war, but in Russia people seemed to have been watching trains off for years and to have waved farewell to half the country.

I decided to get the goodbyes over and slip away, but it was harder than I thought. When the moment came, the Russian temperament broke through all the bounds of reticence. What we had done had been a collective effort but the expressions of gratitude were given to *me*, as though I alone were responsible for the whole business, and it made it a very hard task for me to carry it all off calmly as I went through the packed and dimly-lighted coaches for a last word and handshake.

Some of the elder women prayed for me and blessed me.

"We who are old, weak and uninteresting have not been forgotten in favour of the young and beautiful," they said and what I was endeavouring to pass off flippantly as an au revoir became a tragic and nerve-racking affair. The old ladies wept on me and I began to wish they could be gone. I was young enough to be embarrassed by emotion and was still eager to have a crack at the enemy with the rearguard.

Eventually I slipped away for a few words with Durnford and the rest of the officers who were leaving, to whom I gave instructions for the disposal of stores, and for the re-forming of the group at the new army headquarters at Sossika, south of the Don. Then with Lack, I made for the Station Master's office. I had hardly turned away when I heard the roar of steam, and as it stopped, a sharp hiss like a sigh, and the first slow clank of the wheels over the points. I turned and watched the train move slowly away, grubby-looking and plastered with snow, faces pressed against the glass where small patches had been rubbed clear in the frost that covered them, hands waving, handkerchiefs fluttering.

I saw Moussia's tearful face and her call, "Goodbye! Take care of yourself!" Then it began to curve away as it came to a bend in the tracks, and the last I heard of the refugees was Moussia calling out to me to remind me of the promise about Alex, and I was left staring at the blank bare end of the last coach as it edged through the crowded rolling stock and vanished from sight.

That night, Russia's Christmas Eve, I moved all my kit out of the house where we had lived and we concentrated at the Central Hotel.

CHAPTER FIFTEEN

The following morning Clarke and Fitzgerald, two missing officers, arrived from the front, minus all their kit, and we had to consider how to fit them into the over-crowded coach in which Lack and his wife were due to start that evening. The town had grown panicky by this time, and Bolshevik leaflets were appearing, threatening British officers with torture or death if captured, or informing the inhabitants that Kolchak was in retreat to Irkutsk and that the White armies everywhere were being forced back. They were brief and to the point but they had a ring of truth about them that was frightening, and people in threadbare coats began to shuffle from lamp post to lamp post to read the official notices, and look at the flags on the war maps in shop windows.

Looting was beginning already and windows of empty houses were being broken and doors smashed in, furniture destroyed, boxes forced open, and materials and household articles scattered about the roadways. Fires also kept breaking out all over the place and the streets were jammed with people leaving for the south. Outside headquarters they were loading telegraph apparatus on to snow-plastered motor lorries and people were begging the soldiers to take them with them. But no one had any time for anything except their own affairs and the appeals were ignored.

The weather was still bitter and the Russians muffled themselves up in anything that came to hand, some of them swathing themselves with straw under their shirts. The railway south was blocked, we heard, the water freezing in the pumps at the stations, and one hour of anguish succeeded another as long strings of wagons wound along the streets threading in and out of footsore travellers carrying their possessions.

Even the troops had caught the alarm now and were sneaking off to safety and General Karpov, of the Infantry School, the Town Commandant, endeavoured to repress it with strong measures. Cavalrymen were on the streets and he hanged a Cossack captain on a tree just outside our hotel as a warning to deserters.

I spent the whole day with Lack trying to get the last wretched coach on to the main line in Novocherkassk station, but the railwaymen were mutinous and difficult. Their promises had never meant much because supplies had always been sold and ammunition had always failed to reach its destination. Many of them were Reds, too, and were doing all they could to hamper things. Occasionally we had to threaten, but it didn't help much and we had to use troops occasionally to move the coaches ourselves, watched all the time by the sullen railway workers, many of whom were only waiting for the Bolsheviks to arrive.

It was with a sigh of relief that I saw the delayed Mission coach eventually fastened to a Rostov-bound train and, having said goodbye to Lack and his wife and the two officers who were going with them, I turned up the hill from the station for the last time with a great sense of relief that I no longer had any responsibility about stores or refugees. They had all gone south and once across the bridge at Bataisk, forty miles away, they were safe.

The Reds were still two days' march from Novocherkassk.

*

I knew the Russian staff were too busy for me to worry them that night, so with Dickie and another officer, a red-faced sturdy Devon man, Read, I made arrangements for a start at half an hour's notice, packed three country carts with our kits and forage for our horses, and put our orderlies on watch turn and turn about in the courtyard of the hotel, to see that nothing was stolen or commandeered. It was still freezing cold, the hoar frost like a thick fur over everything, and I was afraid that someone would take advantage of the attempts of the guards to keep warm.

At 3 a.m. I was awakened by a somewhat agitated interpreter, accompanied by a staff officer from the Palace.

"The Ataman!" he said. "He's not staying with Janov's rearguard! He's leaving at 5 a.m. and he's very anxious that you and all your remaining officers should make use of his special train and go with him!"

I still didn't like the idea of quitting but it seemed a way of providing transport for Clarke and Fitzgerald and they were accordingly dug out and told to go.

Pashkov also came to advise me to leave. "You'd better disappear while there's still a chance," he said. "Many of the troops and townspeople will turn Bolshevik the moment the Ataman leaves."

I decided to stay on, however, and Dickie and Read agreed. Our party was now reduced to the original small group, and all we had to do now was keep in touch with Janov and try to go out and have a crack at the Reds on the Russian Christmas Day when the last big counter-attack to save the town was to be made. It was only then that I thought of the season and I thought what a funny way to celebrate the birth of Christ it would be.

All day long, stragglers of the 2nd Division had been pouring through the town, and the only troops who were ready to fight or could do any good were in the Cavalry Corps, now under Pavlov, who were delaying the enemy's advance near Persianovka, ten miles away.

Alex Smaguin returned on the Russian Christmas Eve, and he and Pavlov, who for some strange reason seemed to have left his command, dined with us at the Central Hotel. By this time nearly everybody, including most of the servants, had left – with the exception of two flashily-dressed maids who didn't attempt to hide their delight at the imminent arrival of the Bolsheviks. The great echoing building with its bullet-splashed entrance was empty, its carpets muddied where heavy boots had tramped across them. It was becoming shabby and dusty already and there was an overturned plant in the hall. We had great difficulty in getting any food and even had to forage for it ourselves in the kitchen. Out in the town, where the white-decked roofs of the Cathedral were black against the leaden sky, there was a little sporadic shooting where Red sympathisers had appeared, and agitators were haranguing the people in the working-class areas. It was dangerous to go out and a few people had been shot, and everyone stayed off the streets if possible.

We were all pretty exhausted by this time and expected a strenuous time next day, so we turned in early. But sleep was hard to get because of the constant running up and down the passages by the few remaining occupants of the hotel, and the banging of doors and boxes, which were being removed to places of security. At 3 a.m. I got up and went down to check our transport, in case some of the now thoroughly desperate inhabitants or a looting party of Cossack stragglers had made off with them, and the Russian Christmas Day broke fine and bright with the noise of the guns coming quite clearly over the still air from the direction of Persianovka.

Sidorin had told me he was going out to take direct charge of the battle and, as he had asked me to go with him, we went over to headquarters which was now established in the deserted Palace. Our horses were saddled up and our kits packed, as I was pretty sure that we should not spend another night in Novocherkassk. A disorderly column of transport of all sorts was pouring through the town mixed with refugees and armed and unarmed soldiers. The station was jammed now with panic-stricken people and wildly-driven military cars kept tearing past. Demoralised and disordered troops, the men in rags and reluctant to obey their officers, kept appearing, followed by terror-stricken traders and peasants, old men, women and tiny children riding on shaggy ponies, and carrying their feather beds, pots and pans. They seemed to know we were leaving and didn't hesitate to show their disgust. The station was an inferno of noise and we kept seeing outbreaks of violence in the distance and flames.

Yet despite everything, other soldiers and large numbers of the inhabitants still walked casually with that maddening Russian nonchalance about the streets near the Cathedral which was thronged with the devout for Christmas Day.

All the morning we waited outside Sidorin's office, but he made no move, then Pashkov overheard a sinister conversation which threw considerable light on many subsequent events. A group of Cossack senior officers were discussing the situation in subdued but angry voices and some of what they said came to Pashkov's ears.

"What is the good?" they were saying. "Why leave our country and our possessions to fight for Denikin and the landlords? What will *they* do for us if they do win, except take our land from us again and go back to the old ways of the Monarchists? The Reds would make peace with us and leave us alone, so what good to us are Denikin and the English?"

It was now nearly 3 p.m. and I gave up all hopes of getting out to the scene of action, so I decided to ride towards Hootenok where heavy firing could now be plainly heard. Crossing the square towards the hotel, even the machine guns seemed to be tap-tapping away close by, so that I judged them to be at the end of the long street leading past the barracks.

Collecting my horse and giving orders for everybody to saddle up and proceed with the transport to join Janov's cavalry, I started for the edge of the town, the horse's hoofs padding on the crisp snow. Suddenly an excited Cossack captain galloped down the street. As he pulled his foam-covered horse to a stop, it went down on its knees, exhausted.

"It is all over!" he yelled. "The counter-attack's failed! The Reds will soon be in the town!"

People started to run immediately, shouting the news, and the crowd scattered at top speed, the cab drivers lashing their old hacks to a gallop. I found I was surprisingly indifferent to the news and rode to the top of the hill looking over the plain towards Persianovka, which was covered with small bodies of troops black against the snow and groups of guns retiring in great disorder, their horses lashed to a frenzy and pursued by parties of what I imagined were Red cavalry. They were well covered, however, by machine guns and light field guns which were in action close to where I stood on the edge of the town, barking away at the enemy and covering the ridge with smoke, so that the Reds, probably because they knew the town was already theirs, seemed very reluctant to push too hard. This was clearly the final scene in Novocherkassk, and, feeling depressed, I turned my horse and rode off to find Janov to see if he was going to counter-attack before it became too dark.

No such thought! Of 120 men who should have been standing by, not more than sixty could be found and these were straggling casually on to the parade ground opposite headquarters. At the front door were three or four cars, into which Sidorin with most of his staff were hurriedly climbing. Seeing Agaiev there, I asked him what was happening.

He smiled his usual enigmatic smile and waved his hand eloquently towards the south.

"We're going away!" he said.

"What about us?" I demanded.

"I don't know," he said.

Sidorin carefully dodged us and got into his car, and off they went before I had time even to thank them for their "solicitude".

*

I stood watching, standing in the snow, staring after them as the cars drew away, the tracks made by their wheels dwindling into the distance. Everything seemed incredibly silent as they vanished, then a single shot in the distance, where some agitator or some drunken soldier fired a rifle, brought me to my senses.

I had had the whole of my plan cut and dried long before, as I had guessed somehow that they wouldn't bother their heads about us. Collecting my party outside the Palace, I arranged that we should stick to Janov's cavalry as previously settled and that we should not be separated from our baggage at any price.

And then I remembered . . .

"Promise me on your word of honour that you'll look after Alex?"

I had promised Moussia to do what I could for her husband, but I hadn't the slightest idea now where Alex was. He'd told me the previous night that he'd stay with us and that he had a country carriage for himself and his kit, but I had heard stories of a riotous party that morning and I set off hurriedly back to his quarters where I found him – as I fully expected – slightly drunk and totally unprepared to start, though as usual, thoroughly, tiresomely, maddeningly genial!

"It'll be all right," he kept saying. "There's plenty of time."

He was infuriatingly off-hand and I was not very polite, because the pro-Bolsheviks in the town were growing bolder by this time and were sniping more and more at stragglers. Corpses lay in the streets, huddled in pools of blood, and the leavings of the refugees both military and civil were now being looted quite openly. Every now and then you would see a man slip away round a corner, carrying an expensive picture or an article of furniture, quite indifferent to the misery of the long lines of people heading southwards.

It was growing dark by now and when I had left Janov, he had been on the point of starting. So, with more force than ceremony, Alex and his kit and an old white-headed general who was with him were urged along in their carriage by Pashkov and myself, and we joined up with the others, who were anxiously awaiting us, just as Janov's column moved off.

*

Slowly we rode down the long mile out of the town and across the little river which ran at its foot and out into the steppes. They were blanketed with snow, and the temperature was somewhere about ten degrees below freezing. The Russians' faces were expressionless in the light that came from the snow. The evening haze was caught weakly among the undergrowth, purple-coloured through the weeds rustling in the breeze that had risen during the night and now licked the hummocky ridges of the plains. Ahead of us the immeasurable line of hills stretched ominously, eerily empty, and underfoot the snow was trampled to slush along the road.

Shells were falling in the centre of the town itself by now and fires were going merrily. Small bodies of horsemen approached us and disappeared again in the growing dusk with no sign that they were friend or foe, and two armoured trains steamed slowly through the station towards Rostov, the smoke from their engines hanging darkly against the sky.

On reaching the open ground outside Novocherkassk, Janov formed up the 200 Cossacks who were still with him, drawing them up in lines, the men's faces grey and strained in the poor light, the horses snorting and pawing at the ground. When everything was silent except for the jingling of bits and the clink of equipment and creak of leather, he proceeded to harangue them. He seemed very excited and wasted a great deal of time presenting decorations to two or three soldiers. I quite failed to see the point of the ceremony. As far as I knew there were now no other Don troops in the vicinity and parties of three or four cavalrymen who could be seen about half a mile away were probably Bolshevik scouts. Janov paid no attention to them, however, and when his little performance was over, he simply marched off southwards towards the crossings of the Don. He seemed quite uninterested in anything about him.

My party travelled in the gap between his advanced guard and the main body. The moon was up now, the snow dazzling white and hard enough for the horses to tread on without sinking, except where the track had been churned up. The light gave the snow a pale blue corpse-like hue and the flat bare steppes, covered with frozen pools, seemed endless, so that the column looked like a gigantic snake crawling across a desert. A nagging breeze plucked at our clothes but ahead of us was only the cold serenity of the hills, bare of trees and empty of life.

To the best of our belief the Red cavalry patrols were occupying the outskirts of Novocherkassk by now and, while our own cavalry corps was supposed to be holding them up, if they had left as quickly as the other troops I had seen that day, there was certainly nothing now between us and the enemy. Yet Janov took no steps to adopt a fighting or protective formation and the column wound unguarded across the endless snow that was broken only here and there by dark patches of pine forest, the men with their heads down and huddled in the saddles, indifferent to what happened to them. There were no scouts out on the flanks or ahead so that they could have been caught, in their misery, by any raiding party of Bolshevik cavalry. It was bitterly cold and frost settled on eyelashes and brows and every now and then we had to walk to bring back the circulation. We wore mufflers over mouths and noses to stop them freezing and icicles formed on them from our breath.

We were heading for Starocherkassk where we hoped to cross the river Don on the ice. It had been just 6 p.m. when we left Novocherkassk but it was past midnight when we arrived at the river crossing, beyond which Janov hoped to find billets in the first village, where an advance party had preceded us. Thanks to the *shuba* and sheepskin cap which the Ataman had given me, to my wooden stirrups which I'd copied from a set I'd seen used in France by General Sir Henry Rawlinson, Commander of the Fourth Army, and a Jaeger scarf wound round my neck outside my high fur collar and twice round my body, I had kept quite warm, though the cap I wore was covered with grey rime.

Alongside me, Read was in acute misery. His horse had slipped and fallen in a mixture of ice, mud and water which had been churned up at the edge of a shallow stream by the endless column of transport and by the horsemen who had passed by during the last twenty-four hours. He had been thrown down and within five minutes of getting up his clothes were frozen as stiff as a board and he was suffering the most extreme discomfort. We gave him what we could but it was a marvel he didn't catch pneumonia.

The ice on the Don must have been pretty thick, as fires had been lit at intervals to show us where the smooth track lay, and only a day or two before six-inch howitzers had been dragged across it. The horses were strung out in a long column in the darkness, just visible against the light colour of the ice, moving in little groups and huddles and long indifferent strings. There was no talking, just the scrape and shuffle of hooves and an occasional hoarse shout from a horseman to one of the dark figures standing with his mount alongside a fire.

We reached the trees at the other side in safety, but the village where we'd hoped to rest was full of refugees with not an inch of floor space anywhere, and no sign of our advanced party. Either they or we had gone to the wrong place.

We disconsolately set off for the next village five miles farther on, and here we found what we so badly needed in the shape of rest and a chance to feed our horses, overhaul our transport and make plans for the next move. The place looked beautiful, with starlight on the snow and heavy warm-looking houses with frosted panes, outlined in bold black and white, the stars brilliant in a clear atmosphere that made the night unearthly.

Every now and then in the hut where we lay down, illuminated by a wick in a saucer of oil, the door was flung open and men came in, bringing clouds of steam, crossing themselves before an ikon on the walls, taking off fur caps and grunting as they pulled icicles from their whiskers. Janov's men spent a wretched night, however. There wasn't room for all of them and many of them were outside without fires, huddled back-to-back trying to keep warm, the horses restless as they nibbled the sparse grass that had been uncovered for them.

It was 4 a.m. when I rolled up on a bundle of straw. I had arranged to be awakened at eight but when I went round to Janov's headquarters I found he and his officers had been drinking and were quite unwilling to move.

"Mid-day," they kept saying. "Mid-day will be soon enough."

I could find no trace of our village on the map but it appeared to be four miles east of Olginskya. The Russians were

Armoured train with naval gun

Armoured train

Refugees waiting for a train

Dickie and Lack

The author (*left*) with Major Hargreave

still sitting or lying about the room round the remains of their meal, some asleep, some still talking, and there was evidence of plenty of wine and vodka having been drunk.

Stiff and cold and grey-faced with weariness, I finally decided I had done all I could do by way of sticking to the unpredictable Cossacks. We were south of the river now and the Reds would certainly flock into Novocherkassk to loot and rest before re-organising to sweep southwards to force Denikin back from the Don and Manytch river lines. Owing to the ice these were now really very little use but my officers, my stores and Mission Headquarters were, I hoped, safely over the bridge at Bataisk by this time and I wanted to find out what was to happen next, and what Bogaievski and Sidorin were going to do. I also had to make arrangements for reforming the group at whatever headquarters they might decide to use and take and distribute all the stores which had been saved from Hootenok.

Accordingly, I took my leave of Janov and Alex, who said he would stay with the cavalry.

"I'll go with them across-country to Sossika," he said. "They expect to find Army Headquarters there."

For a while, everyone stood around in an indeterminate huddle, uncertain what to do and uncertain how to say good-bye, stamping their feet and surrounded by the scraping of the horses' hooves and the breath hanging heavily on the frozen air. Dickie, Read and I moved off about 11 a.m., and made as straight as we could for Bataisk. I thought we had very little time to spare, as my idea was to get ourselves and our horses on to any of the Mission or staff trains that might still be hung up there, or proceed by road as far south as it was necessary, to reach Sidorin's new Headquarters.

Our horses were pretty exhausted, however, as, with our heavy clothes, saddlebags, etc., they had had a lot of extra weight to carry, though the snow was not very hard and lay in lumps along the track. Off the track, they sank almost up to their knees.

It was essential now to get to Bataisk before dark, as a

search for railway coaches in the confusion which I knew we should find on every siding at this large station, would be no easy job. In Olginskya we cut across the line of march of several units of the 8th Division and of some cavalry of the 1st Division, but they had no idea what was happening and were utterly indifferent to us as they plodded onwards, crouched in the saddles, the horses' heads hanging with weariness, every man surrounded by his own little cloud of pale smoke where his breath and the breath of his horse hung in the air. Icicles hung from shaggy caps and moustaches and formed round the noses of the horses. They had crossed the river the previous night, but nobody seemed to know if they were remaining at Olginskya or not, or what troops were behind them.

CHAPTER SIXTEEN

Dusk was just falling again when I saw columns of black smoke on the skyline, and I knew that Bataisk was in sight. Pashkov's horse was done to the world but by urging our mounts on for a quarter of a mile and then dismounting and leading for three-quarters of a mile, we managed to get them along somehow and arrived about 4 p.m. It had been a nerve-racking trip because, in addition to the conditions, we had never known when we would run into Budenny's cavalry.

Dickie had gone ahead, travelling in a country cart, and was on the look-out for us, and I was greeted with unexpected good news from all sides. The refugee coaches had already safely disappeared south, with the exception of Lack's which was due to go that night. Two trucks of stores, mostly beds and other things of no great importance, and a flat car with a done-in Ford car, had been lost at Nakhitchevan, where large quantities of rolling-stock had been abandoned and Lack himself had had great difficulty in escaping. But he had finally managed it and everything else was safe.

Several Mission coaches, Bogaievski's coach, and Sidorin's coach were all in the station on their trains and waiting with steam up. Refugees waiting on the platforms went alongside the coaches, begging for places on them and holding up their children, their eyes desperate. But to the men hanging on to footboards, waiting for the signal to go, there was too much human misery about them for them to be able to concern themselves with individuals.

I was told to go along at once to the Ataman's coach, while my horses and kit were loaded and attached to a Mission train which was shortly to start for Tikhoryetsk where we were all to concentrate for further orders.

Owing to Holman's continued absence, nothing definite could be settled, but General Cotton, Chief Artillery Adviser, lent me twenty more horses, with which I intended to mount as many officers as I could and form an emergency troop for any purpose – such as rescue – that might crop up. Not only were several of the tanks and their British officers unaccounted for, but rumour had it that Sumpter, Frecheville and his interpreter – all members of my group – and other British officers were still missing somewhere north of Rostov, and considerable anxiety was felt for them because, by this time, the Reds were swarming all over the countryside up there.

However, it all came to nothing in the end, and the station of Bataisk gradually disgorged all its traffic southwards to Tikhoryetsk, except for the train containing Sidorin, which remained at Sossika, where he had established his new head-quarters.

A heavily loaded engine moved away in fitful stops and starts, its wheels spinning. Then as they began to grip, the train moved slowly, then faster and faster with a wild clatter of wheels, so that the track trembled as it thundered past, scatter-ing cinders and staining the snow. One train followed another, watched by sullen-eyed railwaymen and the wretched refugees who stood hopelessly staring after them.

There had been a slight thaw and the roads were a foot deep in melting snow and slush, when I went to await the return of the coach which Lack had used, and which I meant to use my-self. Almost immediately I was greeted with the information that the long-expected British colonel had arrived to assume command of my Don Army Group and wished to take it over at once.

Fortunately for me, I knew him and he was thoroughly aware of the disappointment I felt. There seemed to be so much that I was giving up. Despite the confusion, we had stayed till the end, evacuated over fifty refugees in our own coaches, and got away every single artillery store of value, and my officers were already collected at Sossika trying to get in touch with their Russian units and picking up the threads of their old work. As a unit we had never ceased to function throughout the evacuation of Novocherkassk and Rostov.

Unknown to me, Holman had returned from Ekaterinodar where he had gone on his return from his activities with the Volunteer Army. During his absence, as I had heard earlier, Mission headquarters at Taganrog had packed up on its own, leaving quantities of equipment and brand-new aeroplanes behind, and the whole outfit had rushed to get over Rostov bridge before the line was cut. I was furious because they had left me out in the blue without information or instructions.

*

Rostov had been a shambles. Wrangel, who had been cheered at the opera house not long before, had finally resigned his command in disgust and was heading south. He was besieged by people begging him to take them with him, while others wanted to know why he was giving up his command and were complaining of headquarters' indifference. Rumours of sedition had reached him, yet even at this moment of peril Denikin had continued to busy himself only with issuing political programmes full of catch phrases which had done nothing to combat the growing tangle in Rostov.

The war maps in the shop windows which earlier had shown the summer successes, had now shown only how the Red armies were ringing towns like Omsk and Kharkov. There had been a monumental traffic jam in the railway yards, with stalled trains, many of them scarred by shellfire, extending for miles back along the steppes, and the station staff had been overwhelmed and indifferent anyway to the chaos, and had even been demanding increased wages for their work.

Trains packed to the windows had overflowed the junction, as they did at every station all the way to the coast, while their passengers had tried to bribe the station masters and engine drivers to get them moving before the Reds came. And every time one showed signs of moving, the rush of people towards it had broken limbs and crushed the children and the elderly underfoot as barriers broke and doors were torn off in the melee.

People had fought to get aboard and thrust their bundles into the broken windows, and within seconds, every inch of space had been occupied, inside and out, every buffer, roof and footboard crowded with them. The posters showing Red atrocities which were supposed to encourage recruiting had only increased terror and made matters worse. Many of the trains had been full of troops, many of them drunk and in-different to their officers, and as staff trains had passed through, grim-faced officers were seen at their windows.

In quiet areas the soldiers had even begun now to join those who were robbing the civilians, using their weapons to force them to hand over their treasures or their surplus clothing, and on station platforms the bodies of children suffocated in the crush to board trains had been laid on barrows for everyone to see, in the hope that it would stop the panic.

The centre of the city had been full of moving people, two huge human currents moving in opposite directions through the slushy snow. Among the shops – still left as they had been decorated for Christmas – people had been looking for any-thing to make a strip of red to purchase immunity when the Reds arrived. Finally, half-starved, infected, typhus patients from the hospital had appeared on the station begging for places on the trains south.

It had been snowing and it was said the Reds had got into a position on the hills to the north and were firing on the town. How true this was, we never found out, but the passage through Rostov seemed to have been a frightful affair and Holman was so infuriated at the way some of the officers from Taganrog had joined in the scramble, he said he was going to organise a book in the R.T.O.'s office on the station which would have to be signed by every British officer passing through, together with his reasons for being there.

The town had been so chaotic, it was said, that the military commander had hanged both men and women and left their bodies dangling from the lamp posts as a means of restoring order.

All the shops had been shuttered and there had been no food for the desperate refugees, who had finally started to cross the river by the ice before ice-breakers arrived to bar the passage to the Reds. It had been tried once but the ice had frozen again as fast as it was broken.

A great many lives had been lost because there had been no organisation and Holman's hope of bringing some order to the situation came to nothing, because the battle on the white plains to the north had been finally lost and on the night of January 8th, the Reds charged into Rostov. Budenny's men were now flushed with victory and their leaders lorded it in the house of a man called Paramanov, a wealthy merchant, which not long before had been the headquarters of the White generals. An orgy of looting and murder went on in the town and only this had given the Whites a chance to dig themselves in at Bataisk on a strong position on a line of hills, south of the Don with the river just below them and a great area of marshy ground on the Bolsheviks' side. Although the river was frozen, the marshes remained impassable and, despite eight frontal attacks that were launched by the Reds, the position held.

Holman, still furious that British officers had added to the confusion, came up the line to Tikhoryetsk where various fragments of the Mission were congregating at the station on their way south. With the exception of my own Don Group, everything was in turmoil in the Rostov-Bataisk area and he tried to organise some control. But things had become impossible by this time and I personally was having to rely on officers finding their way to me on their own initiative and nothing more. I simply cannot understand how we managed to gather together again, but we did. Since my group was likely to be taken from me in the near future, I was in a sour frame of mind and bitterly watched the other groups concentrating on Tikhoryetsk and Ekaterinodar. The re-organisation of the front now looked like requiring an entirely new arrangement of British assistance to conform with it, and I felt sure I was going to miss all the excitement.

By this time, the Caucasian Army, now commanded by Pokrovski, had fallen back from Tsaritsyn along the Tikhoryetsk railway but still held positions along the line of the river Manytch. Joining them on their left were the 1st, 2nd, and 3rd Don Corps based on the transverse railway from Torgovya to Bataisk, with Pavlov's Cavalry Corps in reserve for the whole section of their front up to Bataisk. Next to them was Borbovitch's Guard Cavalry Brigade of the Volunteer Army, holding Bataisk itself and the country to the shore of the Sea of Azov, while the south bank of the Don River was held by Kutyepov's Corps of the Volunteer Army, including the famous Markov and Alexeiev Regiments. The whole force, excluding the Kuban Cossacks of Pokrovski's Command, were under the orders of Sidorin and as the front gradually stiffened he pushed them forward to Kushchevska, where they remained till the recapture – and loss two days later – of Rostov about a month later.

Before I left Tikhoryetsk, Holman took me on one side.

"I think it will be best to withdraw the British officers from the Don Army altogether," he said.

I tried to persuade him that we were still wanted, and he eventually agreed to let the group carry on, so I returned to Sossika on January 20th, and spent a few days handing over to my successor all the information I could.

Things were actually beginning to look unexpectedly brighter for Denikin's Army now, as the Reds had suffered two successive defeats in their efforts to cross the Don and Manytch Rivers – each time at the hands of Pavlov's Don Cavalry Corps, assisted by Toporkov's Caucasians. They had lost several guns, at Bataisk and at Vieseli, but, unfortunately, these successes were more than counter-balanced by the behaviour of the Kuban Cossacks, who were now leaning definitely to a "stop the war" policy. Pokrovski had nothing like the influence over them which Wrangel had had, and their politicians were harp-

ing again on the hope of autonomy in return for their ceasing
to resist.

Gradually their forces were drifting away to their villages,
disappearing in ones and twos and groups during the night, or
simply turning away in front of the despairing eyes of their
officers and shuffling off sometimes as a complete squad, company or even regiment, sick of the fighting and the mismanagement and the overwhelming strength of the Reds.
There was nothing anyone could do to stop them. Meanwhile
a fresh Red offensive launched simultaneously on both flanks
of Sidorin's Army Group succeeded in driving the Caucasian
detachments back on Torgovya and exposing the flank of the
1st Don Corps.

When I started off again for the front, the cold had become
intense and the efficiency of the few railway locomotives was
down to its lowest ebb, so that the journey was an exercise in
patience as the trains crept forward only a few miles at a time,
each one jammed hard up against the one in front in case some
well-bribed station master should shunt another train in
between. The drivers were often inexperienced and our train
crawled along at barely ten miles an hour, dragging an over-
load of at least eighty coaches, stopping and starting, halting
to let the train in front get clear, then starting again with great
snorts from the engine and the shrieking of steam as the wheels
spun on the track in an effort to get the vast load going again.
Every time it stopped we got down to stretch our legs or even
brew tea, knowing perfectly well we couldn't be left behind
because each fresh start was so long-drawn-out it was always
possible to climb aboard before the train got going properly.

The jolting caused by the straining engine resulted in hardly
any of our food remaining long enough on the table for us
to have a chance to eat it but it lessened after we had threatened the driver with violence for breaking our last remaining
cup.

We passed wrecked trains and burned stations, signs of
earlier fighting or of raiding cavalry. Conditions were already
becoming nightmarish with typhus everywhere. Every station

and public building displayed the red lettered notices insisting on the precautions against the disease and pointing out the need to wash oneself and one's clothes but, as there was no fuel to heat water, this was difficult and washing arrangements for the crowds of refugees on the railway were negligible. Nobody changed their clothing because most of the refugees *had* no change of clothing and they were so packed into the compartments it would have been quite valueless. There was no medical service and lice swarmed in the woodwork of the neglected rolling stock, and in the tattered uniforms and the sheepskin coats of the peasants. The disease had spread like wildfire and whole truckloads of people perished unattended or froze to death because they were too weak to help themselves. Their bodies, frozen stiff like logs, were dumped alongside the track, stripped of boots and clothing which only passed on the disease to the healthy who removed them.

At Bataisk, I went straight to Borbovitch's Cavalry Brigade Headquarters and had my first definite news of the two officers who were missing north of Rostov.

Sumpter, who had been en route for Kiev when the front had collapsed, had attached himself to Borbovitch and helped run a mounted Lewis gun section with great skill. He had now left for the base and was safe. He was killed later in Asia Minor.

Of Frecheville, however, only the worst could be learnt. A week before my evacuation of Novocherkassk I had sent him off to the base to get money and stores, but I had heard that, while passing through Rostov he and his interpreter had been diverted by a staff officer from Headquarters to join one of Kutyepov's Volunteer Regiments and assist in siting trenches and preparing defences for an attempt to save the city. From this point information of his movements was varied and vague, but we knew that the Russians he had joined had left him and his interpreter in the village they had occupied without information of their movements and he had been captured by the advancing Reds, who had murdered him. His body had been tied to a saddle and dragged round the streets. Later a raid was

carried out across the ice of the Don into Rostov and a Bolshevik Commissar was captured by the Volunteer Army
wearing Frecheville's tunic. I was told he was beaten to death
with steel ramrods, a not abnormal fate for prisoners in this
civil war.

*

While there appeared to be no immediate chance of getting
down the Torgovya line owing to the shortage of engines, I
took the chance offered me by the Commander of the armoured
train, "Ataman Orlov" to visit the extreme left flank at Azov,
which was held by Volunteer Army troops and a detachment
of local anti-Bolshevik sportsmen who called themselves the
Black Sea Horse. The southern bank of the Don between
Bataisk and Azov was not held, and if the Reds had enough
troops they could always cross the ice and raid down south.
To compete with this eventuality the armoured train with two
field guns and twelve machine guns was patrolling between the
two termini, visiting each one about every three days.

The units at Azov seemed pretty efficient, but most of their
British guns had been sent back to Umanskya for overhaul and
I only stayed there one night. When I got back to Bataisk, an
engine was due to go down the transverse line towards
Metchetinskaya, which was an advance base for the Don Army,
so I arranged to be attached to it, and set off at once. I was able,
therefore, to visit in quick succession the headquarters of the
3rd Don Corps, the 2nd Don Corps, which now consisted of
nothing but a few shattered remnants of the 4th and 7th Divisions and only mustered about 1,000 men, and finally my old
friends, the 1st Don Corps, which had dwindled to about 700
men of the 6th Division and a few groups of cavalry who were
trying to keep in touch with the Kuban elements on their
right flank. On each section of the front there were now only
enough men to watch important crossings from the north side
of the Manytch River, and continuous raids were going on
from both sides, a few men stealing across at night against
some small outpost huddling in a hut to keep warm, or a wild

charge of horsemen, scattering the snow to cut down a few running figures before destroying their position and then vanishing back among the trees.

I handed over all spare gun parts to such battery commanders as we could get in touch with, and a quantity of clothing and medical stores to headquarters, but the position looked very dubious by now, especially on the 1st Don Corps front, because of the wavering resistance of the Kuban Army. The day I left 1st Corps Headquarters, in fact, General Markov, my old gunner friend, told me he was becoming very pessimistic, and on arriving at Torgovya junction a few hours after the news of a heavy Red attack up the line we found the place in utter panic.

There was considerable agitation about the place as we arrived and people were moving about with a marked uneasiness which could easily be stirred into far more at the slightest wrong word. No one who has not been involved in a civil war or a vast military disaster such as we were experiencing can conceive the appalling demoralisation. It was visible in the behaviour, speech and expression of everyone I saw, as though it were a spreading epidemic of lack of confidence.

A few officers talked quietly. "What's happening next?" one of them asked. "They say the refugees are arriving by their thousands."

The crowd surged up and down the platform as fear communicated itself from one to another and people began to hurry towards their carts, pushing things aboard quickly, looking over their shoulders nervously as they did so. Someone slapped a fractious child and, as it screamed, the noise broke across the general sounds of mingled wretchedness.

"The Reds are coming," someone said, and there was a general surge towards the road again. Then, as they realised it was a false alarm, back the crowd went to the station, the refugees without seats begging the people on the trains to make room for them. The soldiers had to harden themselves to the tragedy, however. Human life had become so cheap and death

was so common no one was any longer able to feel any emotion
at the horror.

Russian officers watched their men with worried eyes, wondering if they were ready to turn on them, and discussed quietly
in agonised tones whether the Reds had reached their destination ahead of them, remembering how officers captured by
them were sometimes turned naked into the snow to freeze or
were despatched with hammers to save ammunition.

As usual, there was no definite information, nobody was
exercising any proper command, and everybody was accusing
everyone else of letting them down. Sounds of firing were
easily audible to the north, and several parties of stragglers from
the Kuban regiments in the area were in the frame of mind
when a wine-shop was a very attractive bait. We could hear
shooting in the town, also, and we knew that once the wine
was passed round, the Bolsheviks would grow bolder, disgruntled soldiers would join them, and eventually the whole
place would become a shambles.

I had my coaches attached to a train due to leave any moment for Tikhoryetsk, but seven hours finally elapsed before
we left, as the train was found to be made up of wagons required for other purposes. After having seen the train broken
up three times to remove these coaches and one that was too
decrepit to move at all, Lack, who had made his way back to
join me after seeing his wife and daughter safely on the way to
Novorossiisk, finally boarded the engine in a fury.

There was a noisy argument, a few threats and a little obvious
fingering of a revolver holster, and eventually the driver was
persuaded to get a move on. All this while our horses remained
saddled in a box next to our car, as things looked very tricky
and continued to do so for some hours. We eventually reached
Tikhoryetsk about thirty-six hours later.

Denikin had already arrived and a good deal of excitement
was being displayed over the expected appearance of Mr. –
later Sir – John Mackinder, who had been sent out from
England as British High Commissioner, and had been instructed to form his own opinion of the situation. He had the

fullest freedom apparently to act as he thought fit to improve it, provided he did not send for British troops to do any actual fighting.

A close conference between Mackinder, Holman, Denikin, Svegintsev and Keyes was held in the railway station and resulted in the written Mackinder Guarantee, which was published in all British and Russian Orders. This agreement was to the effect that, so long as the "Armed Forces of South Russia" would fight it out, pull themselves together and endeavour to drive back the Reds from the Kuban, so long would the British Government be responsible for evacuating their non-combatants, sick and wounded, and offer all the help possible, short of actually bringing troops from Constantinople to take part in the fighting.

It was translated in many ways by its various readers, but it was by no means agreeable to the British Government. There is even a story told that hardly had it been received in London than a cable came back – too late to catch Mackinder who had returned to Constantinople – ignoring the plenary powers with which he had been despatched and entirely repudiating his actions. Fortunately, there were several strong men on the spot who, taking all responsibilities on their shoulders, saw that the agreement was carried out to the last letter, and thereby avoided what would have surely been a dark blot on the already moth-eaten escutcheon of British prestige in the Near and Middle East.

CHAPTER SEVENTEEN

I remained in Tikhoryetsk only long enough to hear the results of the conference from Holman, then I hurried back by the first possible train to Sossika – or Kushchevska, wherever Sidorin might be. Imagine my surprise on returning to Headquarters, when I found my successor had gone back to Ekaterinodar for another job, and I had got my old group back again. It seemed almost too good to be true. Even the disasters seemed less deep with the knowledge that I could help to do something to retrieve the situation.

On the eve of my departure, I had received a batch of letters from the Base reporting the safe arrival of the refugees from Novocherkassk. They had apparently been treated with a considerable lack of courtesy by some of the officials there and it seemed they had begun to form a very adverse opinion of the British Mission. They were now reduced to the direst circumstances. They had no money to obtain food, no accommodation in the overcrowded town, no certainty of their future destination, and only a few scraps of baggage and belongings.

Typhus was raging everywhere by this time and there was practically no medical service. The epidemic had spread terribly by now and, for lack of hospitals and lack of drugs, the sufferers were packed together in private houses, stations and railway carriages. Half the army and the local population was contaminated with the disease now and the sick who were left behind could only expect death. Men collapsed and died in the streets and warehouses full of dead were found. As trains carrying the sick arrived, the call was "Anybody who is alive, get out" and a few haggard ghosts would stumble out. The vans often contained thirty to forty bodies, officers and men lying together.

Desolation and anguish gripped the countryside and dead horses, and abandoned wagons, guns and equipment blocked the roads. Thousands of wounded died untended when hospitals had to be evacuated and they were hurried to the railway on improvised stretchers, only to succumb to cold or lack of care.

The lines were blocked everywhere. At first when a train stopped through faulty mechanism or lack of fuel, its passengers waited for relief, staying with their trunks and belongings, but finally hunger forced them out on to the track hoping to get on to the next halted train ahead of their own. Everyone seemed to be starving, but the local inhabitants, for their own sakes, hid their supplies. Desertions from the army were now in the thousands, and officers lost all sense of responsibility in the need to escape, and the troops straggled to the sea without any adequate rearguard, pressed all the time by the Reds.

The Mission tried to bring a little order, disinfecting stations and vehicles and turning shops and cinemas into new hospitals, but in one station we heard that several ambulance trains had been found, which had been there for days waiting a chance to move on.

Amazingly enough, during this time, there were many Russian officers who were still busily engaged in exchanging and selling loot, and those employed on equipment work had enormous sums of money. There had even been an outbreak of debauchery and gambling and some highly placed officers were involved. All this, while wounded officers were hanging themselves, and refugees – mostly officers' families – were dying of cold and hunger in the trains into which they had packed.

The army was utterly exhausted. Skeleton regiments trudged southwards, their feet wrapped in cloth and sacks, artillerymen dragging their rusted guns, the exhausted men falling from their horses to freeze to death before they woke. They were accompanied by freed Red prisoners who were in as bad a state as themselves, all moving along in a deep silence, even the sound of their feet muffled by the snow. Horses had also developed a foot disease and the gunners were being forced to discard guns and equipment, and risings were breaking out everywhere. Green Guards under Nestor Mahkno were sacking the towns and looting the trains and commissariat depots, and disorder was at its height. To the north, the Red Army, advancing on the heels of the Whites, was capturing whole strings of trains every day, all of them full of women and children, starving and ill. Any officers who were found, wounded or otherwise, were murdered and the rest were flung out and told to walk.

Amid the wreckage, dejected people were trying to bury their dead in the frozen ground or were simply leaving their bodies alongside the track to join the vast winding snake of humanity, indifferent to anyone worse off than themselves in their efforts to put as much distance as possible between themselves and the Reds. A few, taking their chance, still lived among the wreckage of trains which had broken down and been pitched over the embankment to allow others to go through, burning the fittings to cook their meals or keep warm.

In the towns, the authorities had forfeited all respect, because the price of bread was still rising and there was no coal. The railways were practically at a standstill and there were sick everywhere, and in the middle of all the disorder I received news that Alex Smaguin had eventually arrived at Sossika, but that he was more dead than alive and was down with pneumonia, and suspected typhus. He was not expected to live, so I sent a wire to Moussia, who had already returned north as far as Ekaterinodar, and within two days she was up at Sossika with him, nursing him in the coach he shared with the other refugees.

The risk of infection was enormous, of course, because there were no doctors in the place and no medicine, but she remained devotedly alongside him, indifferent to the bodies that were lifted out every day and laid by the track. Eventually, when the coach in which he was living had to move forward with part of Sidorin's staff, we all moved up together, reaching Kushchevska about February 15th.

Here all was bustle and excitement as an attempt was to be made to recapture Rostov, and troops were moving through the town. Squadrons of cavalry, ill-equipped still but no longer the wretched men we'd seen in the north, were jingling past, and trainloads of infantry were leaving for the front. I gathered that we were going up to Bataisk, and expected to see the attack. Sidorin took me in his coach, leaving mine at headquarters, but on arrival at Bataisk we were told that Rostov had already been captured, held for two days, then evacuated again. The news was heartbreaking.

Sidorin and Keltchevski were suddenly even more reticent about their plans than usual, but they said they were going to Metchetinskaya to see Pavlov's cavalry, which had just made a desperate march across the steppes and driven back another strong Bolshevik cavalry raid. During their operations, however, they had spent three nights in the open in the worst blizzard of the year, and reported a loss of forty per cent of their strength with frostbite and exposure. Their men were now a straggling, unco-ordinated host, wrapped in any old rags they could find. Casualties among the horses had been heavy and the dismounted survivors were limping and shuffling and dragging their weapons and were quite useless as fighting troops. In Odessa, skeleton battalions of cadets from the local high schools had been marched against the Bolsheviks.

We spent a couple of hours with them, during which Sidorin distributed large numbers of Don War Crosses. We also saw units of the Don Flying Corps, who looked like losing their workshops, as the junction at Torgovya was now unsafe owing to the continued advance by the Reds.

There were several old friends with the cavalry. In spite of his misfortunes, Pavlov was in great form, his face burnt purple with sun, wind and snow. Sekretiev was there, too, and one or two officers I had previously met with Agaiev. We wasted no time at Bataisk on the return journey but went straight through to Kushchevska, where I gathered that things were going from bad to worse. Formations had been sadly reduced by casualties by this time, by the desertion of conscripted men, the defection of the majority of the Kuban Cossack formations, and a growing atmosphere of distaste for Denikin's command by the Don Cossacks. The Don Army was being steadily driven back along its whole front, and the Volunteer Army, in face of an enemy with enormous numerical superiority, was forced to follow suit.

The same wretched scenes were being enacted all over again – the sluggish stream of humanity, the squadrons of cavalry reduced to a few sabres, gunners dragging dismantled guns on sledges, officers without men and men without officers – and always, always the wretched refugees who huddled together hopelessly on the stations. Among them, tame as pet dogs, were abandoned horses, wandering about searching for non-existent fodder, nibbling at wooden palisades and collapsing in the snow-filled ditches to die.

By the end of February there was a feeling of despair all round. It seemed that the end was very close and, though I was now unable to get almost any information at all about the true situation, I gathered that Torgovya had actually fallen, and that the Reds were advancing on Tikhoryetsk both from the north-east and the east. We were never allowed to rest and never in the same place for more than a day or two.

Whenever we tried to get anywhere, the train either stopped through lack of steam or came hard up against the train in front, and progress was slow and halting. When we stopped, a few things were unpacked, then there would be an alarm or an urgent rush to get going again and everything would be pushed back and we would rattle off once more. We never seemed to be able to get proper meals because the emergencies always seemed to arrive at mealtimes and we always seemed to end up swallowing only a few hasty mouthfuls as the train left.

Sidorin moved his headquarters to Staro Minskya and thence again to Timochevsk, so as to avoid using the eastward bend of the railway for his lines of communication. The move left the railway clear for the retirement of elements of the Volunteer Army, and such few remnants of the Caucasian Army as were keeping up the fight, and it had an ominous look about it.

Everywhere people were on the move, coming down from the north, thirty or forty to each truck. These they had adapted for their own use so that they were never of any value again to the railway. Many of them would have been better off to have stayed put, because the Reds didn't seem to worry about the people in the towns, only the people on the trains, knowing very well that it was among these they would find the aristocrats and merchants and the ex-Imperial officers they loathed so much.

Every morning they emerged from the trains, their limbs paralysed after a night in an unheated compartment, wretched, and weary, and terrified that their train would break down.

The pumps at all the halts were frozen now and out of action and the passengers constantly had to form chains to fill the boilers with snow. When an engine stalled for lack of water, there was always the danger of it freezing solid, so that the pipes burst, and everyone always piled in to help fill the tank with snow, struggling to get steam up again before it froze or burned out, knowing how much their lives depended on their efforts. When they failed, they joined the famished people staggering southwards, carrying potato sacks or knapsacks made from horse blankets which contained all their possessions, some of them even in modish fur coats and carrying pathetic hat-boxes or reticules or pushing perambulators.

As trains were abandoned, the local people looted everything to get at what treasures they might find. Reports came in of miles of wrecked rolling stock set on fire and still smouldering.

47 Squadron, R.A.F. was at Kushchevska, having been sent up especially to support Sidorin's front with bombing raids and to reconnoitre the hostile movements across the ice at Taganrog.

"We're going back to base at any moment, though," they said. "Orders have come through from Constantinople that all British officers are to be withdrawn from the front."

Try as I could, I failed to get any further information out of Sidorin, and a short ride into a *stanitza* near the station only increased my belief that the situation was now disastrous. I tried to get into conversation with groups of Kuban peasants and soldiers who were hanging about, but they looked sulky and wore shifty looks, and seemed utterly untrustworthy and ready to explode into mutiny at any moment. They eyed their officers sullenly, and refused to obey instructions, collecting in groups despite orders and handling their weapons in a way that suggested they wouldn't hesitate to use them. The wildest rumours were going round: Denikin had handed over his command to Wrangel and had left Russian soil; an attempt was to be made to resist in the Crimea; the British were bringing in crack troops to make sure the evacuation was carried out properly; Kolchak's campaign in Siberia had collapsed in chaos with high officers dabbling in politics, and plots and counter-plots and bad blood between Russians and British.

That very evening orders arrived for the R.A.F. to leave at once, and I wrote a long report for Holman to be delivered by them. In it, I asked leave to stay on for the present, promising to rejoin the moment things became really critical, and suggesting that it was of the utmost importance for us not to desert the now-disheartened Cossacks all at once. I also gave orders for my group, some of whom were still at Sossika, to concentrate immediately at Timochevsk, and to issue all clothing, stores or equipment they could locate to any unit of Sidorin's Army Group, whether Volunteer Army or Cossack, which happened to be near them and looked like doing any more fighting.

All except Watson, who was now my interpreter, had left without a hitch, and I walked over to the Army Commander's siding to make a further effort to get news from Agaiev. To my surprise I found his train had gone, too. The Station Commandant shrugged.

"It has gone south, Sir Major," he said. "And it is not coming back!" It was Novocherkassk all over again!

Not a soul in the station could give me any information about the Army Commander, so I sent a wire to Timochevsk, where I imagined he had gone, telling the officers there to get an explanation of my being left out in the blue, or for them all to return at once to Ekaterinodar and report to Holman. I subsequently discovered that this wire was never sent by the Military Telegraph staff, although they swore they had.

Rumours of more disasters in the north came in thick and fast with every train from Bataisk. Throughout the last few days the situation had become quite indescribable and we were jammed between military trains and trains of refugees and sick, which, unable to get away because of the chaos and the impossibility of shunting, remained anchored to the track by long stalactites of discoloured ice from lavatories and kitchens. The British officers regarded the whole thing fatalistically, knowing how hopeless the Russians were in adversity and how useless it would be to ask for action, and they tossed coins to see whose trains should go first – *when they could go.*

We heard appalling stories. An ambulance train with forty or more carriages of dead bodies had been seen with not one living soul aboard. One carriage was devoted to Sisters of Charity and doctors – all dead – and men were pushing the bodies on to hand carts as though they were coals and throwing them into sandpits.

Certainly the bodies of soldiers and civilians, men and women who had died of wounds or typhus, were being thrown out of the trains at the end of the station platforms, where they were at once stripped of any clothes worth taking. These awful heaps, grey-white and stiff and stacked like piles of timber for the engines, increased in size as each train passed through and disgorged its dead. Every time a train stopped, shuffling, weeping figures climbed down, passing down the body of some loved one, reluctant to leave it but knowing there was nothing they could do. The railway officials cleared them from the side of the track as soon as the train departed and dumped them unceremoniously with the others until a cart came in the evening to carry off the naked load, shovelling them aboard to be buried in a hole hacked in the frozen ground about half a mile away.

Meanwhile, Moussia was slowly nursing Alex back to life,

putting up a terrific fight against tremendous difficulties. She sat up all night in the stuffy, overheated coupé which she shared with him, and only during the day, when there were other officers and doctors to keep an eye on him, would she come over to my coach, which I would then evacuate for her to have a sleep, hot bath and tea, before she returned to her duties.

On my return from my fruitless search for Sidorin, I found her there as usual, but she had just heard some more sinister rumours of the capture of Bataisk by the Reds.

"It isn't hard to get here from Bataisk," she said nervously. "We've got to get Alex away."

"Wait," I told her. "Don't do anything until you're certain what's happened or you might be in a worse position than you are now."

"But what *has* happened?" she said despairingly. "If only we knew!"

I could give her no information, however, and there were no engines in the station, and as far as we knew, nothing but the armoured trains between us and the Reds. So when she went back to Alex, I set to work to mobilise my kit, my horse and Cossack escort, seized two country carts for her and Alex, and made all preparations for a cross-country ride to Umanskya at half an hour's notice.

At 5.0 a.m. next morning Sidorin's train returned from the south as mysteriously as it had gone, and when I went round after breakfast to see him, he behaved as though he'd never been away. I had Watson with me, and with his assistance I fairly let drive at him.

"As a representative of the British Mission at your headquarters, Sir," I said, "it's impossible for me to perform my duties unless I'm given information of your intentions and the movements of your troops." I also drew his attention to the last day at Novocherkassk and to the fate of Frecheville. "I have no desire to figure in a repetition of either of those episodes," I ended.

For a moment he was very angry – "I am an army commander of 50,000 men, and my goings and comings are not for

you to query or criticise!" He was furious, his brows down in a
sulky frown, but when half an hour afterwards I sent round an
invitation to him and Keltchevski to dine with me in my coach
and let bygones be bygones, they both accepted immediately!

A rapid inspection of the store cupboard produced the last
remaining delicacies. Turtle soup, cod's roe, asparagus from a
square tin and peaches from a round one, the last two bottles
of bubbly, and as the pièce-de-résistance of the evening,
Moussia to do hostess.

What an odd dinner-party! Moussia between the two
generals, Watson on one side of me to interpret, and Agaiev
on the other. Not the normal formation for entertaining such
exalted guests, but the one which I thought the situation demanded.

Moussia was in magnificent form, and very soon we were all
the best of friends. Sidorin, in drinking my health, referred to
our "fierce battle" in the morning quite jovially, while Keltchevski was taking full advantage of the proximity of Moussia.
About ten o'clock Agaiev gave me the tip that Sidorin wanted
to talk to me privately, so he and Watson and I went and sat
side by side on the bed in my coupé.

"This morning," Sidorin said, "I was asked by telegram to
guarantee your personal safety if you remain at my Headquarters. I answered, I am quite unable to do so. In fact I
cannot guarantee my own for twenty-four hours. The entire
army is breaking up, and at any moment I and my staff may
have to leave the train and escape into the Caucasian hills to
live like bandits! How can I guarantee *your* safety?"

At the back of my mind immediately was anxiety for the
safety of Alex and Moussia and I was also thinking ahead to the
possibility of a surprise raid by the Bolsheviks cutting the line,
or the Kuban Cossacks turning against us. What Sidorin had
said, unfortunately, was only too true, as I well knew, but it
seemed worse when I got it point blank from the fountain-
head.

Actually, it didn't require much intelligence to see disaster
all about us in the station – in the chaos that existed, the

hordes of refugees, the overcrowded sidings, the wrecked trains which we knew lay alongside the track both in front and behind, and, worst of all, the complete absence of news. I could see myself being left behind but, despite this, I still don't think that I really appreciated the danger we were all in and continued to find the whole situation exhilarating.

I promised to look after my own safety provided Sidorin didn't leave me on a deserted station again with no news and, as I considered that the time was coming when it would certainly be safer on horseback, I said I would stay with him until I received an order from Holman to report back.

We shook hands and the generals left, and for a few minutes I was treated to a short paean of praise from Moussia, who had discovered in Keltchevski a paragon among men. To Keltchevski, it seemed, her slightest wish was already law and it was he who would now arrange everything for her and Alex.

"He said I'd only to ask," she told me, a little spitefully, "and it would be done. He said he'd arrange everything and that I'd no longer any need to worry."

"I hope you're right," I said grimly, knowing Keltchevski and remembering my own abandonment on Christmas Day.

"I can trust him," she insisted. "Even if the British Mission can't arrange things, *he*'ll be able to. Alex will be all right now."

We didn't part on the best of terms. Highly as I regarded Moussia, I was very angry with her because her attitude was bordering on ingratitude.

About 2 a.m. I was awakened by the movement of my coach and, getting up to find what it was all about, discovered we were being shunted on to the Army Commander's train itself. It looked as though a move was being contemplated.

My first instinct was to make sure that Moussia's coach had been attached, too, then I remembered that it was now all in the hands of Keltchevski, and decided to leave it to him.

Nothing happened. We didn't move and I wondered how Moussia was faring. I looked out of the window. The station yard was stark in the snow, the buildings black against the whiteness and festooned with rust-coloured icicles. Thick frost covered everything like a fungus, and I could see a few black figures moving about. There was a roar of steam and I felt satisfied that at least something was happening at last.

Then, a few moments later, I saw a dark figure stumbling over the rails towards my coach, shouting my name. It was Alex's Cossack orderly and he produced a message written on half a sheet of paper in an agitated scrawl.

"For God's sake, help me. The Reds are coming, and the General's train is leaving in an hour. We are to be left behind to be murdered by the Bolsheviks. Moussia."

CHAPTER EIGHTEEN

So much for Keltchevski, I thought, and when a minute or two later poor Moussia herself stumbled through the snow to the coach and implored me to see Sidorin and arrange for them to be taken along, too, I couldn't help rather meanly suggesting that a nocturnal visit to her conquest at dinner would surely do the necessary.

However, I collected her out of the snow and revived her with brandy and biscuits. Her hands were frozen and she had started to weep, quietly and with a desperation that came from too many disappointments and too much strain.

"He says now we can't be taken along," she sobbed. "He says it's nothing to do with him."

"I thought he promised," I said.

"He says things have changed since then."

"I'll bet they have."

I made her comfortable and wrote to the Commandant of Sidorin's train, asking what was being done about Alex, and sent it along by my interpreter.

For a long time Moussia and I remained alone in the darkened coach. She had behaved badly after my party but it only seemed now to prove how human she was and now she was desperately eager to put things right. We had little to say, aware only of the darkness and the silence and the cold and the bitterness and the treachery outside. It seemed like a different world beyond the doors of the coach.

After a while, the sound of the interpreter returning brought us back to earth with a jolt. By the grace of God, my message had worked. The coupling up of all the remaining coaches would soon be carried out, and by dawn, with Moussia's faith in the British Mission restored, we should be steaming safely southwards.

I said good night to him and he went off to his own coach. Moussia made no move to go. Penitent now, and with the last traces of her tears brushed away, I could see her lovely face radiant with gratitude and happiness. Silence now fell on both of us. There seemed so little left to say.

My thoughts went back to her Christmas party at Novocherkassk. Now, as then, we had reached the final moments of a past existence which was indisputably ended, and were faced with a future which was forbidding and obscure. That crisis had been passed; now we were faced by another one. What form would it take, and how would we each be involved? But tonight things were different. The barriers which then had separated us were down, and we knew it.

Before long Moussia was peacefully asleep beside me. For me, time stood still, but it was well past midnight when the slight movement of the coach together with the clanging sounds of the couplings brought us both back to realities.

Her coach was only a short distance down the siding from mine. Muffled up to our ears we walked towards it together. At the foot of the steps leading up to it, I took her in my arms and held her very close.

"Goodbye," she said and then "Thank you for everything – for everything." She repeated the words softly. And then before turning to go she whispered in a tone of misery and bitterness, "Why, oh why, did it have to happen to us like this?" Without glancing backwards she mounted the steps and disappeared into her coach.

As I trudged disconsolately back to my own coach, I felt that for both of us the end of the road was very close at hand.

Shortly after dawn we were steaming slowly en route for Timochevsk where Sidorin was to establish his next Headquarters.

It was the last day in February when we arrived, and I heard news that an officer with a sealed letter for me from Mission Headquarters had been looking for me. He had never reached me, so I thought the best thing to do was to go straight down to Ekaterinodar and report to Holman. On arrival, I received orders to withdraw the whole group from the Don Army and despatch them to the base, but I was allowed to go back myself and stay on a few days with Sidorin after they were clear. I was then to take my leave from him as gracefully as I could and report at Ekaterinodar.

I went in search at once of the coach in which Moussia and Alex should have been riding but found to my delight that it had already been attached to a southward-bound train, and was en route for Novorossiisk. I was sad not to have had a chance to say good-bye to Moussia but it was a great relief to think that they were now safe and certain to get on to a ship embarking refugees as soon as they arrived at the port.

I was not to know until later that their train had been ambushed by Green Guards near Krymsk and several coaches set on fire. Moussia succeeded in dragging the invalid Alex away from the railway line, and had hidden with him and other refugees in bushes until one of Denikin's armoured trains rescued them.

*

I spent two days in Ekaterinodar and was surprised to find that the Tchebyshovs and Helen Routchenko had arrived back from the base and were staying there with friends.

"You'd be wise to clear out as soon as possible," I advised them. "It won't be long before the Reds arrive."

They looked nervous and a little startled, as though this were something they hadn't expected.

"But what about the British?" they asked.

"We're going too," I had to admit, and the news was enough to start them hastily gathering their possessions together.

*

It was a beastly job going back to Sidorin with my orders, but it had to be done. Everyone in his headquarters seemed busy stuffing paper into boxes or throwing them on to fires. Kelt-chevski gave me a sidelong glance but, probably remembering Moussia, refused to meet my eyes.

Surprisingly, of the lot, Sidorin behaved the best and what I had expected to be an ordeal was made much easier by his manner. He gave me that boyish smile of his that could be so charming and which I'd always found hard to resist and made me feel it was no fault of mine.

"Well," he ended. "What will happen now?"

There was no blame and no recrimination, and I found I had liked him more than I'd realised. I had often felt I couldn't trust him, but I had always appreciated his position and could see why he and his friends felt they should not go on fighting to restore the old landlords.

"We have seen a lot of each other," he said gravely. "I think perhaps you will not forget me. In fact I will give you something so that you do not."

And he unbuckled the magnificent curved and jewelled sword from his waist and handed it to me. "It is yours," he said.

I didn't know what to say. I was devoted to the Cossacks and had done my best to smooth over the difficulties between Sidorin and the British Mission and Denikin's army.

"Take it," he urged. "Try to use it to remember Russia."

*

I saw the whole of the remainder of the group away from Timochevsk the same day, but I stayed on for three more days myself, hoping against hope for better news from the north. None came, so I said goodbye to the Don Army Head-quarters and returned to Ekaterinodar, arranging for my coach to be put at once on the main Novorossiisk line.

Only about twenty British officers now remained in the town, to prevent pro-Bolshevik risings and to help protect Denikin, whose position was becoming daily more precarious. I saw Helen Routchenko safely away in one of the Mission coaches, and did all I could to help any remaining refugees of my own personal acquaintance. For a moment there was a flicker of hope that a corps of Terek Cossacks under Ulegai, to whom all remaining war stores in Ekaterinodar were to be immediately issued, might help to stop the Reds advancing. Ulegai was a vigorous, honest, ambitious man but he was also a little unbalanced and touchy and looked for obstacles, though when he made up his mind to do something he did it brilliantly. Unfortunately his troops were of a very doubtful quality, and only two incidents during those last few days at Ekaterinodar impressed me much.

One was meeting Yenko of the Finland Guard Regiment, who were just outside the town – still optimistic and full of spirit. He seemed genuinely glad to see me, and at once said that he'd heard of my trouble with Sidorin. "Still – " he shrugged " – we shall be sure to find you still in Ekaterinodar with the remnants of the British Mission – the last of all to go."

The other concerned Dikov, a staff officer to General Abramov of the 1st Don Guards Division whom I had met when visiting them earlier in the autumn. He was a good soldier and a pleasant companion but he had recently suffered a terrible shock by finding his own brother in one of the heaps of naked frozen bodies on the station at Kushchevska. He now brought a request from himself and the only two other known survivors of his old cavalry regiment – the 8th Hussars. The regiment had had a liaison with our own 8th Hussars, and had made a habit of exchanging Christmas cards and other greetings.

"I want you to take our regimental ikon," he said. "It is hidden in Ekaterinodar. We wish you to convey it to the officers of the British 8th Hussars in memory of the old loyal Russian Regiment."

I agreed, but on arriving at the rendezvous to receive it, nobody turned up and I heard no more of it. Dikov subsequently died of typhus in Prinkipo.

By this time, considerable difficulty was being experienced in keeping the population in order. Disgruntled troops had broken into the wine-shops which had been pointed out to them by the pro-Bolsheviks in the town, and every now and then some sporadic violence would break out, and we would see running figures and hear scattered shooting. Most other shops were empty, their windows still bearing the tattered remains of the posters which had been put up in the high days of the summer, showing the aims and advances of the White armies and the weak attempts at propaganda.

The slogan *Na Moskvu* seemed pathetic now as it stared at us from the torn sheets.

Such shops as still remained open now refused to accept local paper money, and there had been many executions to stop the looting which the Caucasian roughs and demoralised soldiers were only too ready to begin. Men had been hanged from the trees or shot just outside the town and the remaining British officers and other ranks marched through the streets each day because their presence was supposed to have a sobering effect. By the end of the first week in March, however, it was obvious from the hordes of starving stragglers who were coming through that all resistance was rapidly crumbling, and all headquarters of units, including Sidorin's, seemed to be back in Ekaterinodar. As they moved south the railway battalions were tearing up the track and the points behind them. We were warned to be ready for a quick move.

*

It was to be the last day in Ekaterinodar, and for the last time the great Union Jack hung out of the window of the almost deserted headquarters of the British Mission.

We were all assembled in our coaches. Denikin's and Bogaievski's trains left for Krymsk in the morning and we were to leave at night. All day long the streams of refugees, mostly Kalmuks, were pouring through the outskirts of the town, which they were forbidden to enter for fear of exhausting the already rapidly diminishing supplies.

Their fate was to be tragic and in the final collapse of the White Armies, knowing they were marked out for their anti-

Bolshevik sympathies, they headed south in great columns, taking their families with them in small tented carts. They were met by the Reds, and massacred.

*

I was crossing the railway bridge, pushing through the crowds of people all shuffling and hurrying past in their hopeless attempt to get south, when I saw a face I knew. At first I couldn't believe my eyes but there was no doubt about the identity of the owner. It was Angus Campbell, who, since his departure for the south six months before suffering from typhus, I had imagined to be recuperating comfortably in his Scottish home. He looked quite fit again now and had apparently made his way out again to Russia as a civilian in the hopes of being some further use to the people whose cause he had so loyally taken up. He was at that moment trying to take one of our interpreters, Victor Blockine, and his brother back to Scotland. I had only a few minutes' chat with him, as he was off at once, and I had no further news of him till he reached Prinkipo on one of the refugee ships.

By this time it was almost impossible to get reliable news from the front, but the Don Cossacks had been driven south of Timochevsk, and while their main force was withdrawing on Ekaterinodar, scattered detachments on the left flank were trying to cross the frozen marshes of the Kuban river farther west. Mixed with these were the remnants of Kutyepov's Corps of the Volunteer Army. First Stavropol and then Kavkaskya and Armavir had been captured by the Reds and great numbers of people murdered, and the oil supply so badly needed for the railways was now permanently cut off. Contrary to expectation, Ulegai's Terek Corps had done nothing, and the Kuban Cossacks had finally thrown in their hand. It was the final disaster. There was nothing left.

*

About 6 p.m. on March 12th, we steamed out of Ekaterinodar for the last time, and arrived next morning at Krymsk, which was to be the next rallying point for the final defence of the hills surrounding Novorossiisk. Trenches were being dug and a few disorganised troops were being placed in position, not much more than a few sullen men thawing out frozen weapons. We were greeted with still worse news. The whole country south of the railway down to the Georgian frontier was full of parties of Green Guards – deserters from both armies, Georgian adventurers and local bandits – who were sniping at the railway and had occupied Gelendjick, investing Novorossiisk from the south so closely as to raid the outskirts of the town and loot the stores under the noses of the British Mission and the local Russian defenders.

They had plenty of opportunity. At one point the line was obstructed for fifteen miles by the debris of rolling stock and piles of merchandise. There was no one to guard this wealth, and everyone was taking what he wanted. Trucks full of ammunition which should long ago have been up with the fighting troops had been overturned and the wreckage was still smouldering. More bands of Green Guards were raiding the trains ahead, riding alongside the track and shooting at the coaches. Once a train came to a standstill, it was all up with it, and they poured over it, murdering and robbing, even tearing the clothes from the backs of the passengers and flinging them out into the snow to freeze to death. They were growing bolder with every day, and even attacking moving trains, derailing them for the loot they contained, and broken burned coaches and box cars lay with their wheels in the air by the side of the embankment. The surviving passengers continued their journey on foot, joining the long columns of people trudging southwards through the snow.

News of all this undoubtedly had an adverse effect on the morale of the retiring Cossack and Volunteer Army groups, all of whom were converging on Novorossiisk under continuous pressure from the Red cavalry corps. In addition, crowds of refugees were already trying to enter the town and were swallowing up the supplies as fast as they were landed on the quays and hampering the movements of the troops. The lobby of every hotel was full, with people sleeping on the floor, and food was running out and the town mobs were attacking the shops, and even molesting the refugees.

It was obvious now that nothing could save Denikin and his forces and it only remained to take all possible steps to cover the evacuation of his refugees, stores and troops behind the defence of Novorossiisk, on which the British had expended considerable trouble. The Royal Navy had been called in to help.

On March 19th, the Reds captured Krymsk, and as all further resistance outside Novorossiisk had ceased, our coaches were shunted down to the quayside and conferences were held at the Mission Headquarters to decide on the immediate plan of evacuation.

CHAPTER NINETEEN

Novorossiisk, when the great avalanche of refugees and wrecked regiments descended on it, had become a great camp of wretched starving people, terrifying the local population. Denikin had been powerless and had even risked capture daily as his train slowly made its way through a sea of men, horses and vehicles. During the long retreat over 200,000 men, women and children had perished from typhus and exposure, whole trainloads, including the crews, being killed by fever or cold.

Now, all these great hordes of people, some of whom had trudged for miles through the snow, had poured into Novorossiisk, stumbling and weak and too disheartened to make any attempt to protect themselves. Those who tried to do anything were surrounded by a sea of wounded, sick and refugees.

It was freezingly cold, the fierce high wind of the coast piercing the clothes of the starving scarecrows. Ships were covered with ice and the gale swept through the pitiful shelters of the refugees, sometimes even blowing the wagons off the tracks. Bodies lay in all sorts of corners, while the hospitals were besieged by sick, frozen and hungry people for whom nothing could be done, so that those stricken with typhus remained just where they happened to fall. One Russian colonel lay for a fortnight in the cupboard where he crept when he was taken ill.

The typhus was reaping a dreadful harvest by now and people who had lived in great houses now existed in squalid cellars without the simplest sanitary arrangements – while the indifferent frequented the appalling cafés which had sprung up to take the last of their money from them.

Everyone was in despair because they knew that when the British left there would be nothing to protect them from the sabres of Budenny's cavalry. In the bay, the British and French warships, *Empress of India* and *Waldeck-Rousseau*, were hurling shells towards the roads where the Red cavalry was approaching and the concussion of the guns thudded across the town, beating against the ears and rattling the windows in the houses.

The whole foreshore was packed with people, carts and animals – whole families on their knees praying for help, while the criminals of the underworld came out and in the confusion preyed on the elderly and defenceless. Demoralisation had set in completely.

Every street with its boarded shop windows was full of carts, perambulators and hand carts as merchants tried to get their goods to the wharf in the hope of starting their businesses again elsewhere. Troops were throwing away their shoulder straps and officers were tearing off their epaulettes because the Reds had an obsession about these symbols of privilege and liked to indulge in the pleasant habit of nailing them to the wearer's shoulders when captured, while others shot themselves in despair, whilst fat merchants offered suitcases full of paper roubles for the chance of a passage. Young girls were desperately trying to get themselves married to Englishmen – not for love but to get out of the country as British subjects – and several actually did, making arrangements to part as soon as they were in safety. Distraught fathers offered money to British soldiers to marry their daughters, and young girls – some of high birth – prostituted themselves to earn enough money to pay the passage for themselves and their families to ruthless and money-grabbing barge captains and owners of small vessels. Invariably, even as they earned the money, the prices went up as others also clamoured for places, and some of the girls committed suicide.

It was a sick, desperate, terrified city with mobs of people surging to every point where they thought there might be hope of safety, or evacuation. Amid horses, camels, wagons and supplies, they raised their hands to the shipmasters, knowing their only alternative to evacuation was death when the Bolshevik cavalry arrived. They even tried to fight their way aboard ships, and when they failed simply succumbed to cold and despair in a numb blank-eyed silence as they huddled over their belongings, all hope gone, all desire to live long since vanished.

On the evening that we arrived in Novorossiisk, I heard that General Sir Tom Bridges, in whose division I had served in France, had arrived from Constantinople. He was a strong character who, during the retreat from Mons in 1914 had rallied exhausted troops with a penny whistle and a toy drum bought in a Belgian village shop, and he told me that we were to extricate ourselves as gracefully as we could, and that a small remnant of the Mission only would go to the Crimea where General Wrangel, who was now in command, was hoping to reorganise all the personnel and stores that could be evacuated from Novorossiisk.

Denikin had lost all control over his scattered forces, and had forfeited the support of both military and civil elements. He had, in fact, almost been taken prisoner himself outside Novorossiisk when his train had nearly run into Red troops. Certainly he had failed, but he was a brave man, and all who knew him held him in the highest esteem both for his singleness of purpose and for the straightforward, even if unsuccessful, method of trying to carry it out. He had already left, accused by those who had not supported him of all sorts of things from desertion to cowardice.

Holman was working day and night to keep the British promise to help those who had worked and fought with us, but he was shortly leaving to make his report at Constantinople and a battalion of Scots Fusiliers had arrived from the Bosphorus to safeguard British personnel, while a strong naval force was lying off the harbour for the same purpose. The administration of the town was in the hands of a Russian military governor and the commandant of the fort, but they were at loggerheads, so that little was done, and an English colonel was among those who feverishly tried to draw up plans for fortifications and for the evacuation.

Most of the refugees were making frantic efforts to get on to the transport *Brauenfels*, so I got busy at once and made sure the Smaguins and the Routchenkos were supplied with all the stores, spare clothes and bedding I could lay my hands on, and were safely stowed away on board in good time. All my other friends had apparently gone a few weeks before. The Rechitovskis were at Yalta and the Mouravievs were en route for Italy. Lack and his wife had also left and were now probably in England. The Ataman's wife and daughter were reported to have arrived in Cyprus and the Abramovs and others from Novocherkassk were at Constantinople.

There were a few tearful goodbyes and the exchange of addresses. Moussia embraced me with her eyes streaming, stammering her thanks and apologies and I had a lump in my throat again with all the promises to seek them out when we were all in safety.

The approaches to the town were being guarded now only by a few volunteers who were prepared to die to allow the evacuation to take place. There wasn't much time left.

"Later," Moussia promised as Alex weakly shook my hand. "Later! We'll all come together later and have another party, just as we did in Novocherkassk."

"I'll be here to see you off," I said. "Don't worry."

By this time many of the steamers and passenger-carrying ships had gone and only a few transports remained in the harbour, but the water was filled with cruisers, battleships and destroyers, most of them British, their guns trained on the route to the town. The bitter wind was still blowing, freezing the trucks in which the refugees were travelling and icing up the roads along which they were trudging to the harbour. On the wharves were rows of field guns and piles of ammunition, and soldiers were pushing them into the dark water of the bay. Large numbers of new tanks and aeroplanes had also been pushed into the sea, together with mountains of equipment.

The refugees were in the last stage of state of panic by this time. The Reds were shelling the harbour and the mobs were swarming along the waterside in thousands, squatting round bonfires of rubbish taken from the houses. Surprisingly few showed any initiative, however, though one of them had tried to swim to a French destroyer. He had been lifted on board and ceremoniously put back on the quayside. British soldiers were having to force them back as they pushed forward, to allow the last of the Mission trains to get through.

We could still hear scattered rifle fire and the sound of naval guns, and Bolshevik sympathisers were sniping from the rooftops. In places Red infantry had infiltrated into the town, and were going in for murder, rape and every kind of bestiality, while explosions rocked the town as Whites set fire to petrol tanks, and the wind blew an immense pall of smoke across the bay. The waterfront was black with people, begging to be allowed on board the ships. Some of the Kalmuk Cossacks still had their horses and the little tented carts in which they had travelled, and in the water all sorts of rubbish floated – trunks, clothes, furniture, even corpses. Conditions were appalling. The refugees were still starving and the sick and the dead lay where they had collapsed. Masses of them had even tried to rush the evacuation office and British troops had had to disperse them at bayonet point. Women were offering jewels, everything they possessed – even themselves – for the chance of a passage. But they hadn't a ghost of a chance. The rule was only White troops, their dependants and the families of men who had worked with the British were to be allowed on board.

During the night, ships' searchlights played on the route into town and there were the dull thuds of bombardments still echoing in the hills. The Greens were growing increasingly bold by this time and were pushing into the centre of the town, while the local Bolsheviks were murdering people on every side and had already cut up on the roads outside several parties of Kalmuk Cossacks who were endeavouring to get to the port.

The town had no fuel whatever by now, and the station and sheds and huge warehouses smelling of coal and rats were full of homeless people exhausted and dying from fatigue and privations. Every train took away a fresh load of sick and dead who had been picked up in the streets. The peninsula seemed to be full of dying people and the debris of White regiments. It was the nearest thing to purgatory one could ever expect to see.

If the other towns and cities to the north had been disasters, Novorossiisk was the worst of the lot as the wreckage of a whole nation funnelled down to the sea and the only remaining seaport in the area. It came into the town from all sides, the flotsam from the defeats at Kharkov and Rostov and Novocherkassk and Tikhoryetsk and everywhere else where the Whites had been flung back. Pity was an emotion no one could any longer feel. Things had gone beyond compassion and the people had stumbled on without thoughts or feelings, watching their friends and relations fall and leaving them, eating secret scraps of food and looking at the clothes of the men and women in front and thinking "If you were dead, those would be mine."

The strong survived, as they always did, because they were ruthless and didn't mind what they did to survive, but the weak died in thousands upon thousands. Some of them had started their pilgrimage south from places as far north as Moscow and Petrograd and had travelled six hundred or even a thousand miles, at first in comfort, then in less comfort, halting occasionally for a short period of what passed for normality, then, as the Reds drew closer again, moving on once more, first in trains, then in carts, and finally on foot until their numbers, despite the hordes in the town, had been thinned to a mere fraction of those who had first set off.

I had hoped to go aboard the *Brauenfels* for one last meeting with Alex and Moussia before they left, as I had promised, but, next day, while going from Mission Headquarters to my coach, which was on the railway line running alongside the quay, I suddenly felt weak and exhausted. I couldn't account for it at all as, though the times were pretty strenuous, they were not very different from any of the other experiences of the last few months. I felt heavy and tired and it had suddenly become difficult to place one foot in front of the other as I walked.

As I went down the steep hill to the harbour I saw Keyes climbing up towards me. I'd been anxious to see him and hear his views on all that had happened. Since his assumption of the duties of High Commissioner, which had fallen upon him from the shoulders of Mackinder, I had heard that he was feeling very deeply the unfortunate turn which events had taken. Before I could greet him and put my questions, however, he spotted me and called out.

"Hullo," he said. "So your Don Cossacks have run away after all, as I knew they would!"

That he should have stuck to his old opinion and prejudice against the Don Cossacks stung me to the quick. I had found them a fascinating people with their strange spirit – full of beauty, melancholy, patience and simplicity – and a tragic people, too, symbolised by the wild sadness of their music. And to my own knowledge, at least one-half of the remaining forces now retiring before the immense numerical superiority of the Reds were Don Cossacks, who had stuck it out far longer than the much vaunted and more ornamental horsemen of the Kuban.

They had gone beyond hope of returning to their own valley of the Don and had continued a losing fight in spite of the doubtful intrigues of some of their chiefs, through the whole country of the Kuban, from which the local Cossacks never made the slightest efforts to rally round Wrangel, Skouro and Ulegai. They had been constantly snubbed by higher authority, and mistrusted by Denikin, Keyes, and many holders of the highest positions in the White Army, yet on the last day in Novorossiisk some had even had to swim their horses out to the ships and clamber on as best they could, leaving their mounts to drown alongside. The water was full of the bloated bodies of horses.

I was so disappointed at Keyes's outburst I went straight back to my coach and went to bed. My head was burning, my joints shaking, and I felt rotten in body and rotten in heart. It was all over, I thought – one long list of failures, which became more complete and more irremediable the more I looked at it. My work had ended in failure, too, failure in ideals, failure in plan, failure in execution. And what would history say of the failure of the British Mission to South Russia and of the inefficiency of most of its members?

I found myself desperately wanting to go to the *Brauenfels* and say good-bye to the Smaguins before they sailed, and to point out how sorry I was for all the failure. I was even willing to risk meeting the eyes of my old friends, who might say, "See what your promised English help has brought us!" Then I realised that I was taking a disproportionate view. Something was wrong. I had dreamt it all. No, I hadn't because someone was asking me how I felt, and saying that they would take me to a hospital. Why to a hospital, I wondered. I'd had a headache before, and besides I was going to the Crimea with Wrangel after tea. I wanted some tea. Was tea ready? Where was Vassili, the cook?

No, it wasn't tea-time, they said. It was breakfast time and a ship was going soon. Several officers I didn't know came to say goodbye to me before I went in the motor-boat, then there was oblivion, and I woke up half-on, half-off a stretcher – being carried out of the coach. I must look round and wave to it, to say goodbye. I couldn't. I was bound to that stretcher, but there were no ropes.

And then – who is this giant, who is growing bigger and bigger, with a white head and a red band round it? It's the general, Holman, and everybody is standing still because of him. He has come to say goodbye too, before I go to the Crimea in a motor-boat. He will go in Elliott's aeroplane, and when we get to the Crimea we'll all go together to Poltava, and we'll capture the armoured train, and have breakfast with the Smaguins.

But he says he is not going to the Crimea, and holds out something for me. I suppose it to be medicine, but it is hard, and has a pin, and he is attaching it to my chest. Everybody says something nice and smiles, and he says "Well done" and

"Good luck", and something hurts inside me all over, not pain, something so much nicer than pain, but it hurts so much I have to pull the blanket over my head.

So I knew what spotted typhus felt like.

Though every coach we used was disinfected by burning chemicals inside it to kill the lice and though even the seats were removed and disinfected separately, in the last few days after Sossika I had had to use infected coaches, and I had been bitten by a louse. After escaping it all those months, to go down with the disease just when I wanted to be my fittest to get to the Crimea to carry on was hard luck. I was already delirious and when I came through the last of the crisis a week later in hospital in Constantinople my head was shaved; my eyes were bloodshot, the lashes gummed up; my lips were cracked and sore and my teeth were discoloured. In addition I could talk only in a whisper, I was quite deaf, half blind and had lost more than a stone in weight. But I *still* thought I'd had bad luck.

Now perhaps I think differently!

Many skilful writers on Russia have eulogised her with descriptions of her vastness, her whiteness, her simplicity, her cruelty. With these more gifted people I cannot compete. But I can still say that Russia drew me with her mystery, calls to me even now after all these years with her mystery. The spell which she cast upon me will never die.

We may not have succeeded in what we had gone to do, but we tried our hardest and, successful or not, a tribute is due to all those personnel, officers and civilians, Russian as well as British, who gave of their best for a cause which we at any rate considered a just one.

Without their loyal help I alone could have done nothing.

After Novorossiisk, Wrangel hoped that by fighting on in the Crimea, he would obtain better terms for an amnesty. But up to the retreat Great Britain had spent nearly £100,000,000 and France about £35,000,000 in their efforts to bolster the White Armies, but with the exception of what little equipment was evacuated to the Crimea, everything, tanks, guns, aeroplanes, hospitals, were lost when Novorossiisk was evacuated.

Wrangel was therefore disowned by the British, though the French gave recognition to his government. His outnumbered troops were finally defeated, however, in November, 1920. The men who were evacuated yet again with him – nearly 50,000 of them – split up and settled in China, the Balkans, the Baltic States, Germany, Bulgaria, France, Britain, the United States and South America. Their fall from power was awful. Generals swept streets, cleaned shoes and became doormen at restaurants run by princes and their wives. Only a few prospered. Most simply vanished.

Wrangel died in Brussels in 1928 after heroic efforts to better the lot of his men. He was buried in the Russian Church in Belgrade after a huge funeral attended by military and naval delegations from all over the world. Six of his old comrades came from as far away as South America and the Guard of Honour consisted of thirty Cossacks, all of whom wore the Cross of St. George for bravery under fire. The marshal of ceremonies was Wrangel's old comrade, Kutyepov, who soon afterwards disappeared in Paris and was believed to have been murdered. General Romanovski was murdered in Constantinople. Denikin died in the United States in 1947.

As for Williamson, what Holman had pinned on his chest was an immediate D.S.O. for his work and for the field gun action against the armoured train. On his return to England, he returned to duty with the British army after recovering from typhus. He went to India in 1922, married in 1926, and returned to England in 1928, becoming a lieutenant-colonel in 1935. On the outbreak of war in 1939 he was Commander, Royal Artillery, 50th Northumbrian Division, and became Commander of Corps Medium Artillery of the III Corps in France from 1939 to 1940, returning to England via Dunkirk. He was Artillery Commander for the Vth Corps from 1940 to 1942, when he was again mentioned in despatches, and Senior Military Liaison Officer of the East Civil Defence Region from 1942 to 1945. He retired in 1945 as a brigadier. He was too active, however, to settle down to doing nothing and he became Chief Executive Officer to the Board of Trade from 1946 to 1953, and was elected to the Chichester R.D.C. in 1960 and to the West Sussex County Council in 1961.

As for the others: during the final collapse, a paper, *Donskoy Vestnik*, was produced by Sidorin and his chief of staff, Keltchevski, its editor being the fat and smiling Count Du Chayla. Although the paper was an official one, articles trying to rouse the hostility of the Cossacks against the Volunteers and to excite them against the generals and high dignitaries and to secede from the rest of Russia were included in it. With the aid of Bogaievski, Wrangel – now Commander-in-Chief in place of Denikin – dismissed Sidorin and Keltchevski and summoned Du Chayla before a military tribunal. The inquiry revealed that Sidorin and Keltchevski were the ringleaders and that Du Chayla had played only a minor part. He attempted to commit suicide when arrested and severely wounded himself, and a military tribunal sentenced Sidorin and Keltchevski to hard labour, though Wrangel commuted the sentence to dismissal from the service. The tribunal decided that Du Chayla, as Williamson had suspected, was only a common adventurer and a minor accomplice and he was acquitted. He went abroad and continued his policy of hostility even after the army had left Russian soil.

Moussia and Alex Smaguin escaped to Paris where Alex

obtained a job with the Salvation Army and died there about 1930. Following his death Moussia disappeared and, despite all his efforts after his return from India – which have continued to this day – Williamson has never been able to discover what happened to her.

Svegintsgev, Holman's Russian liaison officer, ended up running an antique shop in Berkeley Street, London. The other interpreter who had accompanied Williamson and Holman on their first trip, Prince Obolenski, also got safely to England and in World War II, another Prince Obolenski was killed flying with the R.A.F. Holman retired soon after his return to England and died in the thirties. Lambkirk, the part-Russian officer, became a businessman and joined ARCOS, the trading company set up to work between Russia and Britain when diplomatic relations were established after the civil war. He died in 1925. Angus Campbell managed to get his interpreters to Scotland and set them up in homes on the family estate. He died in the fifties.

As for Bogaievski, after Novorossiisk, he reached Prinkipo and then Paris, where he died. His wife returned – like many other White Russians – to the Balkans and she was killed during a bombing raid in Belgrade in World War II. Kolchak, the Commander of the Eastern Armies and the man most concerned with the Czechs, whose defiance of the Soviets had brought about the whole idea of anti-Red armies, was finally betrayed by them. His train, retreating east, was stopped by them and in return for a promise of their own safety, they handed him over to the Bolsheviks. He was shot and his body pushed under the ice of the frozen River Ushakovka.

Svietlana Mouraviev married an Italian, and her sister Irene married a Dutchman. Williamson saw Irene once more after recovering from typhus, when he went to Florence, where he had heard she was living. Lack was killed in a car accident in the fifties, and Agaiev committed suicide in the Balkans in the twenties, as also did Tchebyshov in Paris.

Elliott, the pilot who flew Williamson in search of the gas shells, became Air Chief Marshal Sir William Elliott, and

Collishaw, the leader of 47 Squadron became an Air Vice Marshal. Both served in World War II, Collishaw commanding R.A.F. units at Alamein. Kaledin's widow died of influenza in 1920. The reputation of the terrifying Budenny, unfortunately did not stand up to the more disciplined troops of the Nazis in World War II. Still moustached but now with a well-developed taste for self-indulgence, he proved inept and was the commander of the 500,000 Russians lost or captured around Kiev in 1941. The vicious Mahkno, the leader of the Greens, managed to survive until 1922, in face of the Soviet Government's determination to liquidate him, then escaped to Poland with a beautiful Jewish girl whose family he had murdered and whom he had taken prisoner. He eventually married her.

There were still one or two left. When the Germans invaded Russia in 1941 and captured Novocherkassk, Pavlov, another of Williamson's friends and a constant adversary of the Communist regime, chose what he considered the lesser of two evils and organised Cossack regiments for the Germans. He was later killed in Poland. The regiments were ordered to Italy in 1944 and when the war ended in 1945 they surrendered to the British. Under agreements made between the Russians and the British, they were later handed over, despite violent protests, to the Russian authorities and in January, 1947, the Kremlin announced that several of the generals had been hanged. Among them were Krasnov and the redoubtable Skouro, the leader of the Wolves.

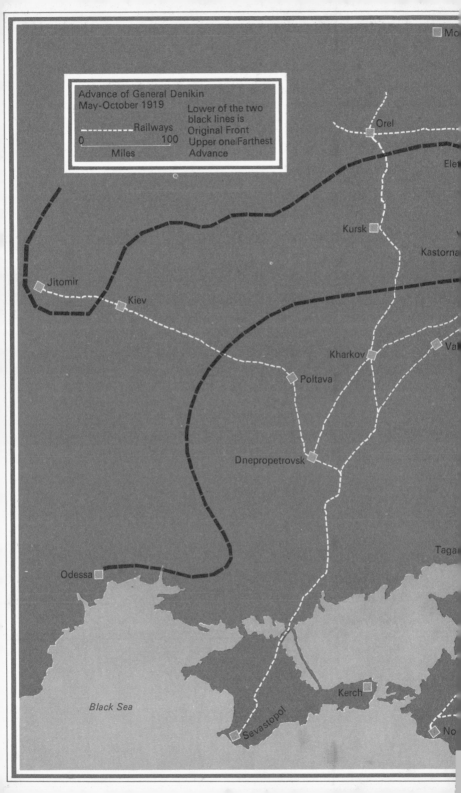

Advance of General Denikin
May–October 1919

Lower of the two
black lines is
Original Front
Upper one Farthest
Advance

--- Railways

0   100

Miles

Mo

Orel

Ele

Kursk

Kastorna

Jitomir

Kiev

Kharkov

Va

Poltava

Dnepropetrovsk

Tagan

Odessa

Kerch

Black Sea

Sevastopol

No